PEST CONTROL

TIME
LIFE ®
BOOKS ®

Other Publications:

AMERICAN COUNTRY

VOYAGE THROUGH THE UNIVERSE

THE THIRD REICH

THE TIME-LIFE GARDENER'S GUIDE

MYSTERIES OF THE UNKNOWN

TIME FRAME

FIX IT YOURSELF

FITNESS, HEALTH & NUTRITION

SUCCESSFUL PARENTING

HEALTHY HOME COOKING

UNDERSTANDING COMPUTERS

LIBRARY OF NATIONS

THE ENCHANTED WORLD

THE KODAK LIBRARY OF CREATIVE PHOTOGRAPHY

GREAT MEALS IN MINUTES

THE CIVIL WAR

PLANET EARTH

COLLECTOR'S LIBRARY OF THE CIVIL WAR

THE EPIC OF FLIGHT

THE GOOD COOK

WORLD WAR II

HOME REPAIR AND IMPROVEMENT

THE OLD WEST

PEST CONTROL

TIME-LIFE BOOKS
ALEXANDRIA, VIRGINIA

Fix It Yourself was produced by
ST. REMY PRESS

MANAGING EDITOR	Kenneth Winchester
MANAGING ART DIRECTOR	Pierre Léveillé

Staff for *Pest Control*

Series Editor	Brian Parsons
Series Assistant Editor	Kent J. Farrell
Editor	Heather L. Mills
Series Art Director	Diane Denoncourt
Art Director	Normand Boudreault
Research Editor	Jim McRae
Senior Designer	Julie Léger
Designers	Lousnak Abdalian, Robert Galarneau, Luc Germain
Contributing Writers	Patricia Ryffranck, Fran Slingerland, John Woolfrey
Contributing Illustrators	Gérard Mariscalchi, Jacques Proulx
Cover	Robert Monté
Index	Christine M. Jacobs
Administrator	Natalie Watanabe
Production Manager	Michelle Turbide
Coordinator	Dominique Gagné
Systems Coordinator	Jean-Luc Roy
Photographer	Robert Chartier

Time-Life Books Inc. is a wholly owned subsidiary of
THE TIME INC. BOOK COMPANY

President and Chief Executive Officer	Kelso F. Sutton
President, Time Inc. Books Direct	Christopher T. Linen

TIME-LIFE BOOKS INC.

EDITOR	George Constable
Director of Design	Louis Klein
Director of Editorial Resources	Phyllis K. Wise
Director of Photography and Research	John Conrad Weiser
PRESIDENT	John M. Fahey Jr.
Senior Vice Presidents	Robert M. DeSena, Paul R. Stewart, Curtis G. Viebranz, Joseph J. Ward
Vice Presidents	Stephen L. Bair, Bonita L. Boezeman, Mary P. Donohoe, Stephen L. Goldstein, Juanita T. James, Andrew P. Kaplan, Trevor Lunn, Susan J. Maruyama, Robert H. Smith
New Product Development	Trevor Lunn, Donia Ann Steele
Supervisor of Quality Control	James King
PUBLISHER	Joseph J. Ward

Editorial Operations

Production	Celia Beattie
Library	Louise D. Forstall
Correspondents	Elisabeth Kraemer-Singh (Bonn); Christina Lieberman (New York); Maria Vincenza Aloisi (Paris); Ann Natanson (Rome).

THE CONSULTANTS

Consulting editor **David L. Harrison** served as an editor for several Time-Life Books do-it-yourself series, including *Home Repair and Improvement, The Encyclopedia of Gardening* and *The Art of Sewing.*

Richard Day is a founder of the National Association of Home and Workshop Writers and has written magazine articles and books about home care and repair subjects for nearly a quarter of a century.

Dr. Chris Christensen has been an extension entomologist at the University of Kentucky since 1974, specializing in agricultural and urban entomology, and for 12 years also served as the Pesticide Training Coordinator for Kentucky. He lectures extensively and organizes pest control seminars throughout the U.S., and has written several papers and a handbook for technicians in the industry.

Dr. George W. Rambo runs a pest control consultation service in Herndon, Virginia, writes about pest control and gives lectures throughout the United States and in Europe. He worked for the National Pest Control Association for 14 years, and also worked as an entomologist in the Maryland Department of Agriculture, Office of Pesticide Regulation.

Gerald Wittenberg, President of the 35-year-old Montreal Pest Control Company since 1981, deals with residential, industrial and commercial pest control. The company stresses prevention in conjunction with the safe and limited use of pesticides, and is a member of the National, the Canadian and the Quebec Pest Control Associations.

Library of Congress Cataloging-in-Publication Data
Pest Control
      p. cm. – (Fix it yourself)
Includes index.
ISBN 0-8094-7404-2 (trade).
ISBN 0-8094-7405-0 (library).
1. Household pests–Control.
2. Garden pests–Control.
I. Time-Life Books. II. Series.
TX325. P452 1990
648'. 7–dc20   90-46307
                               CIP

For information about any Time-Life book, please write:
Reader Information
Time-Life Customer Service
P.O. Box C-32068
Richmond, Virginia
23261-2068

CONTENTS

HOW TO USE THIS BOOK

Pest Control is divided into three sections. The Emergency Guide on pages 8 to 13 provides information that can be indispensable, even lifesaving, in the event of a household emergency. Take the time to study this section *before* you need the important advice it contains.

The Repairs section—the heart of the book—is a comprehensive approach to troubleshooting pest control problems. Shown below are four sample pages from the prevention-focused chapter on pestproofing your house, with captions describing the various features of the book and how they work. For example, if the

troublespot is the basement or crawlspace, the Troubleshooting Guide on page 16 lists a number of procedures to follow; if, for instance, the floor is of soil, it will send you to page 19 for step-by-step directions on installing a vapor barrier. The remedy-focused chapters on indoor pests *(page 36)*, outdoor pests *(page 58)*, and lawn and garden pests *(page 74)* also include charts to help you identify and control specific types of pests.

Each job is rated by degree of difficulty and by the average time it will take for a do-it-yourselfer; this rating is only a suggestion. Before undertaking a job, read the instructions carefully.

Introductory text
Describes common pest control problems and troublespots, as well as basic pest control approaches for specific features or areas of the house.

Variations
Differences in approach to pest control are described throughout the book, depending on the specific feature or problem of the house.

Anatomy diagram
Locates and describes the various features and areas of the house subject to pest control problems.

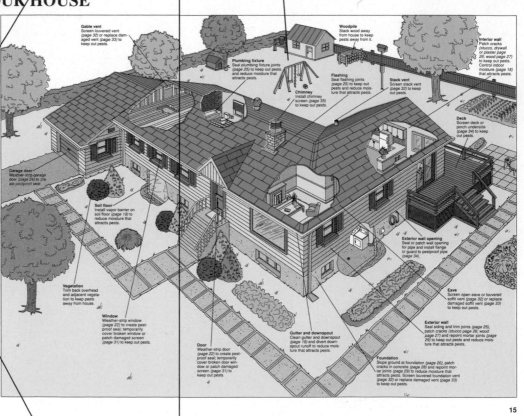

Tools and techniques
General information on tools and equipment is included in the chapter entitled Tools & Techniques *(page 112)*. When a specific tool or method is required for a pest control job, it is described within the step-by-step repair.

Cross-references
Direct you to important information elsewhere in the book, including instructions for working safely with pesticides, or with ladders or on the roof.

Then, be guided by your own confidence and the time available to you, as well as the tools and supplies on hand. For stubborn pests such as ticks or time-consuming control jobs such as weather-stripping windows, you may wish to call for professional help. You will still have saved yourself time and money by identifying the pest or the control job needed.

Most of the repairs in *Pest Control* can be made with basic tools and supplies; occasionally, you may need to buy a special product or rent specific equipment. For information on tools and equipment, refer to Tools & Techniques *(page 112)*.

Pest control can be simple and worry-free if you work logically and systematically, following all safety tips and precautions. Refer to the chapter entitled Working Safely *(page 98)* for specific safety information on using pesticides and working on ladders or on the roof. Always wear the safety gear recommended for a job, and ensure that children and pets are kept safe from harm well away from the work area. Concentrate on the job, exercising caution and patience; do not rush or attempt to take short cuts. Safely store or dispose of any leftover pesticide as soon as you have finished using it.

Troubleshooting Guide
To use this chart, locate the entry that most closely resembles your pest control trouble-spot or problem in column 1, then follow the recommended procedures in column 2.

Step-by-step procedures
Follow the numbered job sequence carefully. Depending on the result of each step, you may be directed to a later step or to another part of the book to complete the job.

Insets
Provide close-up views of specific steps and illustrate variations in techniques.

Degree of difficulty and time
Rate the complexity of each job and how much time it should take to perform for a homeowner with average do-it-yourself skills. If a specialized tool is required for a job, it is also indicated.

Name of repair
You will be referred by the Troubleshooting Guide to the first page of a specific job.

Lead-ins
Bold lead-ins summarize each step or highlight the key action pictured in the illustration.

EMERGENCY GUIDE

Preventing problems in pest control. Controlling pests in and around your home need not be dangerous; with good work habits and the right tools and equipment, an emergency is unlikely to arise. However, an accident involving a chemical pesticide or a bite from an insect or animal is always a possibility. Be prepared for any pest control emergency by studying the information included in this chapter—before you need it. The Troubleshooting Guide on page 9 puts procedures for pest control emergencies at your fingertips and refers you to pages 10 through 13 for more detailed instructions.

The list of safety tips at right covers basic guidelines for undertaking the pest control jobs presented in this book. Before starting any job, read the chapter entitled Working Safely *(page 98)*, then take the time to set up properly for the job, gathering together the tools, supplies and safety gear recommended. Consult Tools & Techniques *(page 112)* for information on the proper use of tools and equipment.

Follow strict safety precautions when using a chemical pesticide for a pest control job. Familiarize yourself with the procedure for cleaning up a chemical spill quickly and safely *(page 12)*. Know how to assist a victim of toxic chemical exposure, either to flush a chemical from the eye or the skin *(page 11)* or to treat a victim of toxic-vapor exposure or ingested poison *(page 12)*. Store a well-stocked first-aid kit in a convenient, accessible location; in the event of a medical emergency, you will want anyone to be able to find it quickly to administer first aid for minor injuries *(page 13)*. Store pesticides safely and install a smoke detector near the storage area. In the event of a pesticide fire, leave the house immediately and call the fire department from the home of a neighbor; inform firefighters of the nature of the fire so they can prepare themselves properly.

Avoid physical contact with an insect or animal pest during a pest control job. If you are allergic to insect stings, never attempt a pest control job involving a stinging insect; call a pest control professional. Consult a physician to get a prescription insect-sting allergy kit and have him instruct you in its use; keep the kit handy whenever you are outdoors. In the event of a bite or sting from a pest, know the proper procedure for handling the situation. You can assist the victim of a spider or insect bite or sting *(page 9)* or the victim of a snakebite, animal bite or tick bite *(page 10)*. If there are skunks in your area, keep a commercial skunk-odor neutralizer on hand; know how to use it to treat the victim of a skunk attack *(page 11)*.

If you are ever in doubt about your ability to handle a pest control emergency, do not hesitate to call for help. Post the telephone numbers for your local fire department, hospital emergency room, poison control center and animal control agency near the telephone; in most areas, dial 911 in the event of a life-threatening emergency. Also seek technical help when you need it; even in a situation that is not an emergency, a qualified pest control professional or county extension agent can answer questions about safe, effective pest control.

SAFETY TIPS

1. Before beginning any pest control job presented in this book, read the entire procedure; familiarize yourself with the safety information presented and always wear the safety gear recommended for the job.

2. To prevent an accident during a pest control job, keep children and pets away from the work area; set up barriers around the work area before starting the job and remove them only when it is safe for others to re-enter the area.

3. Carefully read the manufacturer's instructions on the label of any pesticide before purchasing, using or storing it. Never eat, drink or smoke when using a pesticide.

4. Do not use a pesticide on fruits or vegetables unless the label indicates it is safe, and then only as close to harvest time as the label indicates. Wash harvested fruits and vegetables thoroughly before cooking or eating them.

5. Buy and mix only enough of a pesticide for the job at hand. To store any leftover pesticide, place it in a tightly sealed, clearly labeled container and keep the container in a locked cabinet safely away from children.

6. Thoroughly clean any tools, equipment and safety gear used to apply a pesticide, then store them safely. Take a shower, then launder any pesticide-contaminated clothing separately from other clothing.

7. Bag empty pesticide containers and pesticide-soaked waste materials separately from other household refuse and keep it outdoors in a safe place until you can dispose of it. Call the local department of environmental protection or public health for advice about proper disposal procedures.

8. Avoid spider and insect bites and stings during a pest control job. Wear any hand, head and facial protection recommended for the job as well as long sleeves and long pants with snug-fitting cuffs. Avoid tick and flying insect bites by applying a repellent *(page 58)*.

9. Do not undertake a pest control job involving a stinging insect if you are allergic to insect stings; call a pest control professional. In the event of an allergic reaction to an insect sting, seek emergency help immediately; then, consult a physician to obtain an insect-sting allergy kit and a medical identification bracelet or card for the allergy.

10. To prevent heat exhaustion in hot, sunny weather, work only in the shade and avoid working outdoors at midday when the sun is hottest; wear a hat and light-colored clothing.

11. Follow basic safety rules for working on ladders *(page 98)*. Work with a helper or within earshot of someone else and only in good conditions—never when it is wet or windy.

12. Post the telephone numbers for your local emergency services near the telephone: the poison control center, the hospital emergency room, the fire department and your physician, as well as the animal control agency and the county extension service.

TROUBLESHOOTING GUIDE

PROBLEM	PROCEDURE
Spider or insect bite or sting	Treat spider or insect bite or sting (p. 9)
Snakebite	Treat snakebite (p. 10)
Animal bite	Treat animal bite (p. 10)
Tick bite	Treat tick bite (p. 10)
Skunk attack	Treat victim of skunk attack (p. 11)
Chemical splashed in eye	Flush chemical from eye (p. 11)
Chemical spilled on skin	Flush chemical from skin (p. 11)
Exposure to toxic chemical vapors suspected: headache, dizziness, faintness, fatigue or nausea	Treat exposure to toxic chemical vapors (p. 12)
Poison chemical ingested	Treat ingested-poison victim (p. 12)
Chemical spilled in work area	Clean up chemical spill (p. 12)
Chemical fire: flames or smoke from pesticide or other chemical	Evacuate house and call fire department from home of neighbor; inform fire department of type of chemical involved in fire
Cut	Treat cut (p. 13)
Splinter	Remove splinter (p. 13)
Sprain or strain	Treat sprain or strain (p. 13)
Fall from roof or ladder	Treat victim of fall (p. 13)

HANDLING BITES AND STINGS

Treating a spider or insect bite or sting. For a black widow or a brown recluse (fiddleback) spider bite or a scorpion sting, seek emergency help. For a bee sting, remove the stinger and sac immediately. **Caution:** Do not use tweezers; they can squeeze additional venom from the sac into the victim. Use a credit card to scrape the stinger and sac off the skin (left); if they are embedded, work them out using the tip of a needle sterilized over a flame or in rubbing alcohol. If the victim has a known allergy to the bite or sting, help him administer any medication required. Wash the skin with soap and water. To reduce any pain or swelling, apply an ice pack; to relieve any itching, apply hydrocortisone cream or calamine lotion and do not scratch the skin. Monitor the victim and seek emergency help for any sign of an allergic reaction: physical weakness or dizziness; labored breathing; an itchy rash or hives; swelling around the eyes, lips, tongue or throat; abdominal pain or nausea; a weak, irregular or rapid pulse; or, loss of consciousness. Consult a physician if the wound becomes infected or any pain or itching does not subside in 2 to 3 days.

HANDLING BITES AND STINGS (continued)

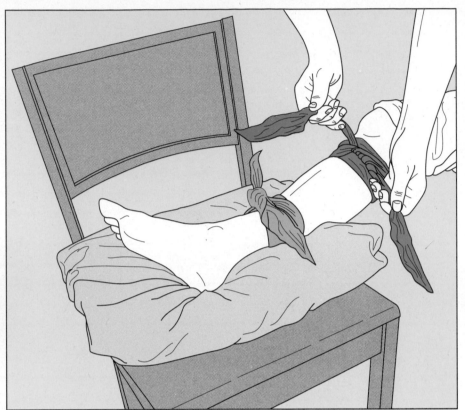

Treating a snakebite. Most snakes in the U.S. and Canada are not poisonous; the victim of a snakebite may experience no more than its initial pinch. A bite from a rattlesnake or a copperhead, water-moccasin or coral snake, however, can constitute a serious medical emergency if venom is injected; although a lethal amount of venom is seldom injected, treat any potentially poisonous snakebite as serious. Do not administer any medication to the victim. Call for emergency help, then have the victim rest comfortably, keeping the injury below the level of the heart, if possible. Remove any footwear, jewelry or clothing from the injured area. For a snakebite on a limb, limit the poisoning effects of any venom by restricting the flow of blood to and from the snakebite. Tie a cloth strip or belt around the limb 4 inches from each side of the snakebite *(left)*; tie it tight enough for a finger to fit under it and loosen it if any swelling occurs. Keep the victim calm until emergency help arrives.

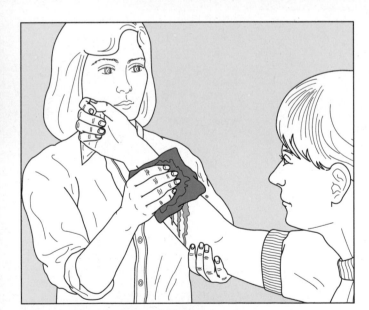

Treating an animal bite. To stop any bleeding, elevate the wound and apply direct pressure to it using a sterile gauze dressing *(above)*. If bleeding persists or the wound is deep or gaping, seek emergency help. Otherwise, gently clean the wound with soap and water. Apply a gauze dressing to the wound, then wrap the dressing with a gauze roller bandage and secure it with medical tape. Consult a physician to inspect the wound and administer any tetanus or rabies treatment. Report the incident to your local police or public health department.

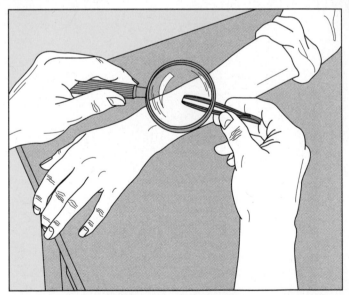

Treating a tick bite. Using a magnifying glass if necessary, inspect the skin and brush off any tick. If a tick is attached to the skin, use tweezers to pull it off *(above)*; avoid crushing the tick. Put the tick in a jar with a few drops of rubbing alcohol, then seal the jar. Wash the skin and your hands with soap and water, then apply an antiseptic ointment to the skin. Consult a physician to inspect the wound; bring the tick with you to find out whether it carries Lyme Disease or Rocky Mountain Spotted Fever. Check for and remove any ticks from a household pet *(page 36)*.

TREATING A VICTIM OF A SKUNK ATTACK

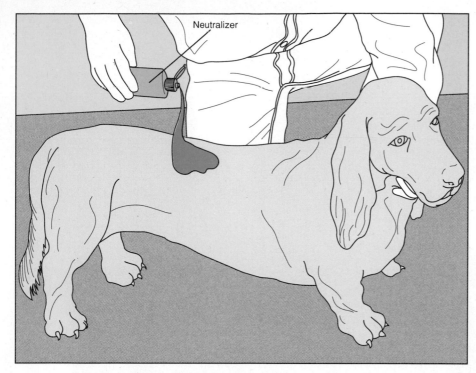

Neutralizing skunk spray. If the victim of a skunk attack is sprayed in the eye, flush the spray from the eye as you would a chemical *(step below, left)*, then seek emergency medical or veterinary help. To remove skunk spray from skin, clothing or pet fur, wear rubber gloves and use paper towels to blot up as much of the skunk spray as possible; do not wash the affected area or you risk spreading the skunk spray. To remove skunk spray odor, buy a commercial skunk-odor neutralizer from a veterinarian and follow the manufacturer's instructions to use it. To use the neutralizer shown, pour it onto the affected area of skin, clothing or pet fur *(left)*, then rub it in thoroughly; for a pet, ensure you apply the neutralizer on any affected area inside the ears, under the collar and at the tip of the tail. Let the neutralizer dry. If odor remains, repeat the treatment. Launder any affected clothing separately from other clothing.

PROVIDING FIRST AID FOR CHEMICAL EXPOSURE

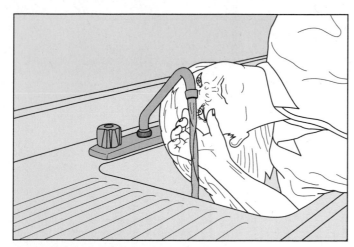

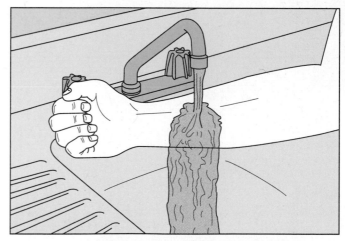

Flushing a chemical from the eye. Holding the eyelids of the injured eye apart, position it under a gentle flow of cool water from a faucet *(above)*; tilt the head to one side to prevent washing the chemical into the uninjured eye. Outdoors, flush the injured eye the same way using a flow of water from a garden hose. **Caution:** Remove any nozzle from the garden hose to prevent an eye injury from a strong jet of water. Flush the eye for 15 to 30 minutes, then cover both eyes with gauze dressings to prevent eye movement. Seek emergency help, taking the chemical container with you.

Flushing a chemical from the skin. Remove any clothing from the affected skin area and wipe or brush off the chemical immediately. If the chemical burns the skin, do not apply any ointment or medication on it; cover it lightly with a gauze dressing and seek medical help, taking the chemical container with you. Otherwise, flush the skin with a gentle flow of cold water from a faucet *(above)*. Wash the skin with soap and water, then pat it dry. Launder any affected clothing separately from other clothing. Consult a physician if any skin rash or irritation develops.

PROVIDING FIRST AID FOR CHEMICAL EXPOSURE (continued)

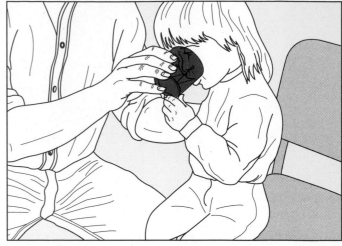

Treating exposure to chemical vapors. Exposure to toxic vapors can cause headache, dizziness, faintness, fatigue or nausea; at the first sign of any symptom, leave the work area immediately and get fresh air. Loosen any tight clothing around the waist, neck and chest; remove any clothing splashed by a chemical. If you feel faint, sit with your head between your knees *(above)*. Have someone ventilate the work area and close all chemical containers. If any symptom persists, seek medical attention.

Treating an ingested-poison victim. Remove any foreign substance from the victim's mouth. Immediately call a poison control center or hospital emergency room with information about the type and amount of poison ingested and the victim's age and weight. **Caution:** Do not give the victim any food or drink and do not induce vomiting unless advised to do so. If advised to induce vomiting, give the victim warm water *(above)* or syrup of ipecac. Seek emergency help, taking the chemical container with you.

CLEANING UP A CHEMICAL SPILL

Safely cleaning a spill. Immediately open windows and exterior doors, extinguish all sources of heat or flame and turn off equipment operating nearby. **Caution:** For a spill of more than 1 gallon of a product marked EXTREMELY FLAMMABLE or POISON, leave and call the fire department. Otherwise, clean up the spill quickly wearing rubber boots, heavy rubber gloves and safety goggles; if the spilled product is marked POISON, also wear a respirator. For a liquid spill, spread clay-based cat litter on it, then scoop up the material with a whisk broom and dustpan *(left)*. For a powder spill, spread damp sand or soil on it, then scoop up the material the same way. Wipe up any residue using a clean cloth dampened with water, then scrub the area using a solution of detergent and water *(inset)*. Place chemical-soaked waste materials in a metal container double-lined with heavy-duty plastic garbage bags. Call your local department of environmental protection or public health for recommended disposal procedures.

PROVIDING MINOR FIRST AID

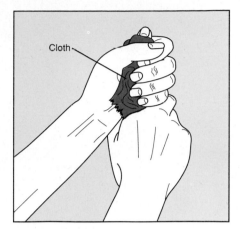

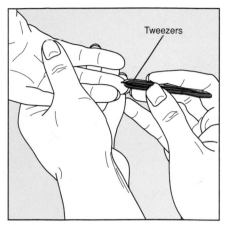

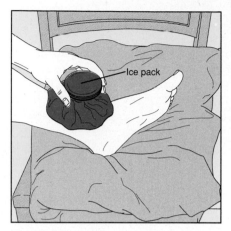

Treating a cut. A wound from a rusty or dirty object may require treatment for tetanus; consult a physician. To stop any bleeding, elevate the wound and apply direct pressure to it using a clean cloth *(above)*; if the cloth becomes blood-soaked, add another one over the first one. If the bleeding persists or the wound is deep or gaping, seek emergency help. Otherwise, clean the wound with soap and water, then bandage it. Consult a physician if the wound becomes infected.

Removing a splinter. Wash the skin around the splinter with soap and water. A metal splinter may require treatment for tetanus; consult a physician. Otherwise, sterilize a needle and tweezers in rubbing alcohol or over a flame. Ease out the splinter from under the skin using the needle, then pull the splinter out with the tweezers *(above)*. Wash the wound again with soap and water. Consult a physician if you cannot remove the splinter or if the wound becomes infected.

Treating a sprain or strain. Rest as much as possible until any pain or swelling subsides—usually several days. To relieve pain and swelling, administer cold treatments for 48 hours, then heat treatments. Lie or sit in a position that minimizes discomfort. For a cold treatment, apply an ice pack *(above)* for 15 to 20 minutes. For a heat treatment, apply a hot-water bottle or a heating pad for the same time interval. Consult a physician if any pain or swelling persists after 3 days.

TREATING A VICTIM OF A FALL

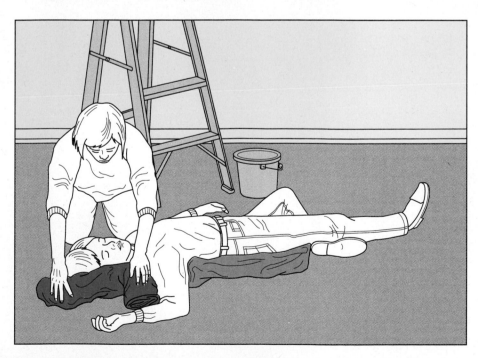

Treating a fall victim. A victim of a fall who has injured his back, neck or head may also have injured his spine. Signs of a spinal injury can include any of the following: pain in the back, neck or head; tingling or loss of feeling or movement in a limb; loss of bladder or bowel control; fluid or blood flowing from the ears or nose; loss of consciousness. Call for emergency help immediately. **Caution:** Do not move the victim if a spinal injury is suspected or he is in pain. Reassure the victim that emergency help is on the way, then immobilize his back, neck and head with blankets *(left)* or pillows. Keep the victim warm by covering him with a blanket and keep others away. Do not give the victim anything to eat or drink or apply a hot-water bottle or heating pad.

PESTPROOFING YOUR HOUSE

The most effective pest control strategy is a strategy of prevention. It is easier to inspect your home thoroughly and undertake the maintenance and minor repairs required to keep a pest out of the house than to eradicate a pest that has taken up residence. Refer to the illustration at right and the Troubleshooting Guide on pages 16 and 17 to identify points around your house that can provide access for an unwelcome insect, animal or bird; then, refer to the pages indicated to undertake the necessary pestproofing job.

Indoors, make the house as inhospitable as possible to pests by regularly cleaning household surfaces, especially hard-to-reach areas behind and under furniture and appliances. Take the steps necessary to control indoor moisture *(page 18)* that attracts pests and provides a comfortable feeding and breeding ground for them. Inspect floor, wall, ceiling and foundation surfaces for cracks and openings that allow pests to enter the house. Patch any crack in the stucco, plaster or drywall *(page 26)*, wood *(page 27)*, concrete *(page 28)* or mortar joints *(page 29)* of these surfaces and repair any wood rot *(page 28)* as soon as you notice it.

Pay particular attention to doors and windows; their open joints are natural entry points for insect and small-animal pests. Use a draft gauge to identify pest entry points at the joints of windows and doors *(page 21)*, then weather-strip a faulty window or door *(page 22)* or garage door *(page 24)* to create a pestproof seal around it. Cover a broken window pane and patch a damaged screen *(page 31)* to keep pests out. Inspect the trim joints around the exterior of a window or door and recaulk a joint *(page 25)* that is faulty.

Outdoors, ensure that the house walls, foundation, eaves and roofing materials are well sealed and in good repair, and keep the lawn and garden well tended. Identify the points through which a pest can enter the house, then pestproof them. Screen a louvered gable, soffit or foundation vent *(page 32)* or replace the vent if it is damaged *(page 33)* to keep out pests. Screen a deck or porch underside *(page 30)* against an animal pest, or screen a stack vent or open eave *(page 32)* or a chimney *(page 35)* against an animal or bird pest. Pestproof a wall opening for a pipe by sealing or patching the opening and pestproofing the pipe *(page 34)*. Reduce moisture around the foundation that can attract pests by cleaning gutters and downspouts *(page 19)* and diverting downspout runoff *(page 21)*; if necessary, slope the ground at the foundation *(page 20)* to keep water away from it.

Most pestproofing jobs are easily undertaken with only a few basic carpentry tools; the materials and supplies required are usually readily available at a building supply center. Refer to Tools & Techniques *(page 112)* for instructions on using tools properly. Before starting any job, read the chapter entitled Working Safely *(page 98)* for instructions on using safety gear and working safely on ladders or the roof. Familiarize yourself with the safety advice in the Emergency Guide *(page 8)*. If you doubt your ability to successfully complete a pestproofing job, do not hesitate to consult a building or pest control professional.

Gable vent
Screen louvered vent *(page 32)* or replace damaged vent *(page 33)* to keep out pests.

Garage door
Weather-strip garage door *(page 24)* to create pestproof seal.

Soil floor
Install vapor barrier on soil floor *(page 19)* to reduce moisture that attracts pests.

Vegetation
Trim back overhead and adjacent vegetation to keep pests away from house.

Window
Weather-strip window *(page 22)* to create pestproof seal; temporarily cover broken window or patch damaged screen *(page 31)* to keep out pests.

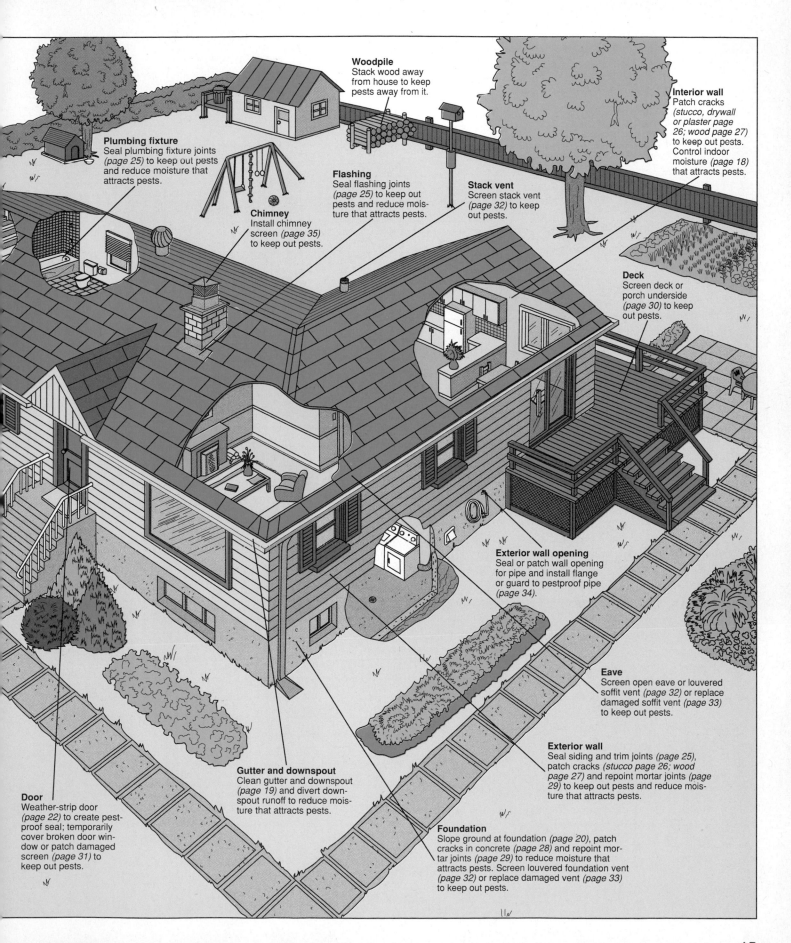

Woodpile
Stack wood away from house to keep pests away from it.

Interior wall
Patch cracks *(stucco, drywall or plaster page 26; wood page 27)* to keep out pests. Control indoor moisture *(page 18)* that attracts pests.

Plumbing fixture
Seal plumbing fixture joints *(page 25)* to keep out pests and reduce moisture that attracts pests.

Flashing
Seal flashing joints *(page 25)* to keep out pests and reduce moisture that attracts pests.

Stack vent
Screen stack vent *(page 32)* to keep out pests.

Chimney
Install chimney screen *(page 35)* to keep out pests.

Deck
Screen deck or porch underside *(page 30)* to keep out pests.

Exterior wall opening
Seal or patch wall opening for pipe and install flange or guard to pestproof pipe *(page 34)*.

Eave
Screen open eave or louvered soffit vent *(page 32)* or replace damaged soffit vent *(page 33)* to keep out pests.

Exterior wall
Seal siding and trim joints *(page 25)*, patch cracks *(stucco page 26; wood page 27)* and repoint mortar joints *(page 29)* to keep out pests and reduce moisture that attracts pests.

Door
Weather-strip door *(page 22)* to create pest-proof seal; temporarily cover broken door window or patch damaged screen *(page 31)* to keep out pests.

Gutter and downspout
Clean gutter and downspout *(page 19)* and divert downspout runoff to reduce moisture that attracts pests.

Foundation
Slope ground at foundation *(page 20)*, patch cracks in concrete *(page 28)* and repoint mortar joints *(page 29)* to reduce moisture that attracts pests. Screen louvered foundation vent *(page 32)* or replace damaged vent *(page 33)* to keep out pests.

15

TROUBLESHOOTING GUIDE

TROUBLESPOT	PROCEDURE
House interior	Control indoor moisture *(p. 18)*
	Clean surfaces regularly; keep surfaces tidy
	Seal and dispose of garbage regularly
	Inspect incoming household products and furnishings for pests
	Inspect pets for pests *(p. 36)*
Basement or crawlspace	Clean surfaces regularly; keep surfaces tidy
	Seal and dispose of garbage regularly
	Insulate cold-water pipes *(p. 18)* □◒
	Install vapor barrier on soil floor *(p. 19)* □◒
	Identify pest entry points at windows and doors *(p. 21)*; weather-strip faulty window or door *(p. 22)* □◒
	Seal joints *(p. 25)* □○
	Seal or patch wall opening for pipe and install flange or guard to pestproof pipe *(p. 34)* ▣◒
	Patch cracks *(stucco, drywall or plaster p. 26; wood p. 27; concrete p. 28)* □○
	Repoint mortar joints *(p. 29)* ▣◒
	Patch rotted wood *(p. 28)* □○
	Ensure basement floor drain has grate
Interior wall	Patch cracks *(stucco, drywall or plaster p. 26; wood p. 27; concrete p. 28)* □○
	Seal joints *(p. 25)* □○
	Patch rotted wood *(p. 28)* □○
Bathroom	Clean surfaces regularly; keep surfaces tidy
	Control indoor moisture *(p. 18)*
	Insulate cold-water pipes *(p. 18)* □◒
	Repair leaking plumbing pipes and fixtures
	Ensure drains are clean
	Seal joints *(p. 25)* □○
	Identify pest entry points at window *(p. 21)*; weather-strip faulty window *(p. 22)* □◒
	Seal or patch wall opening for pipe and install flange or guard to pestproof pipe *(p. 34)* ▣◒
	Ensure adequate ventilation
Kitchen	Clean surfaces regularly; clean spills and dirty dishes immediately; keep surfaces tidy
	Seal and dispose of garbage regularly
	Store food in refrigerator or in tightly-sealed containers
	Control indoor moisture *(p. 18)*
	Insulate cold-water pipes *(p. 18)* □◒
	Repair leaking plumbing pipes and fixtures
	Ensure drains are clean
	Seal joints *(p. 25)* □○
	Identify pest entry points at windows and doors *(p. 21)*; weather-strip faulty window or door *(p. 22)* □◒
	Seal or patch wall opening for pipe and install flange or guard to pestproof pipe *(p. 34)* ▣◒
	Ensure adequate ventilation

DEGREE OF DIFFICULTY: □ **Easy** ▣ **Moderate** ■ **Complex**
ESTIMATED TIME: ○ **Less than 1 hour** ◒ **1 to 3 hours** ● **Over 3 hours**

TROUBLESPOT	PROCEDURE
Attic	Clean surfaces regularly; keep surfaces tidy
	Screen louvered gable or soffit vent *(p. 32)* □○; replace damaged gable or soffit vent *(p. 33)* □◗
	Ensure adequate ventilation
	Seal joints *(p. 25)* □○
	Patch rotted wood *(p. 28)* □○
Window	Identify pest entry points at window *(p. 21)*; weather-strip faulty window *(p. 22)* □◗
	Temporarily cover broken window *(p. 31)* □○; have window replaced as soon as possible
	Patch damaged screen *(p. 31)* □○
Door	Identify pest entry points at door *(p. 21)*; weather-strip faulty door *(p. 22)* □◗
	Temporarily cover broken window of door *(p. 31)* □○; have window replaced as soon as possible
	Patch damaged screen of door *(p. 31)* □○
Garage door	Identify pest entry points at door *(p. 21)*; weather-strip faulty garage door *(p. 24)* □◗
Exterior wall	Control outdoor pests *(p. 58)* that may enter house
	Clean and refinish exterior wall surfaces regularly
	Trim back overhead and adjacent vegetation
	Seal joints *(p. 25)* □○
	Seal or patch wall opening for pipe and install flange or guard to pestproof pipe *(p. 34)* ◨◗
	Patch cracks *(stucco p. 26; wood p. 27; concrete p. 28)* □○
	Repoint mortar joints *(p. 29)* ◨◗
	Patch rotted wood *(p. 28)* □○
	Screen open underside of deck or porch *(p. 30)* ◨●
	Store firewood and lumber away from wall
	Store garbage tightly sealed and away from wall on raised stand *(p. 58)*
Foundation	Control outdoor pests *(p. 58)* that may enter house
	Divert downspout runoff *(p. 21)* □○
	Slope ground at foundation *(p. 20)* □●
	Trim back adjacent vegetation
	Seal joints *(p. 25)* □○
	Seal or patch wall opening for pipe and install flange or guard to pestproof pipe *(p. 34)* ◨◗
	Patch cracks *(stucco p. 26; wood p. 27; concrete p. 28)* □○
	Repoint mortar joints *(p. 29)* ◨◗
	Patch rotted wood *(p. 28)* □○
	Screen louvered foundation vent *(p. 32)* □○; replace damaged foundation vent *(p. 33)* □◗
	Screen open underside of deck or porch *(p. 30)* ◨●
Roof	Control outdoor pests *(p. 58)* that may enter house
	Inspect and repair roofing materials regularly
	Seal flashing joints *(p. 25)* □○
	Clean gutters and downspouts *(p. 19)* □◗
	Screen stack vent *(p. 32)* □◗
	Screen louvered gable or soffit vent *(p. 32)* □○; replace damaged gable or soffit vent *(p. 33)* □◗
	Screen open eave *(p. 32)* ◨●
	Install chimney screen *(p. 35)* ◨◗

DEGREE OF DIFFICULTY: □ **Easy** ◨ **Moderate** ■ **Complex**
ESTIMATED TIME: ○ **Less than 1 hour** ◗ **1 to 3 hours** ● **Over 3 hours**

CONTROLLING INDOOR MOISTURE

Controlling humidity in the house. Many pests, especially insect types, are attracted to a humid indoor environment in which they can nest and feed easily and comfortably. Indeed, the areas inside the house that are most vulnerable to pest infestations are those in which moisture levels are highest—the kitchen, bathroom, laundry room, attic and basement or crawlspace. Inspect the house thoroughly for signs of a humidity problem: mustiness; mold or mildew; blistered or peeling paint; rusted metal; rotted wood; frosted or wet windows; and damp spots or water marks on walls, floors or ceilings. Then, refer to the guidelines below to help you control an indoor moisture and humidity problem, making your home a less hospitable environment for a pest:

- Ensure that the humidistat of any humidifier is set to shut off the humidifier before condensation forms on the windows. If necessary, install a dehumidifier, especially in the basement.

- Ensure that the house is well-ventilated and that each vent to the outdoors is undamaged and unobstructed; if necessary, have vents installed, especially in the basement, crawlspace or attic.

- Install a vapor barrier on any soil floor in the basement or crawlspace *(page 19)*.

- Insulate cold-water pipes *(step below)* and the cold-air ducts of any air-conditioning system.

- To reduce indoor humidity, ensure that the bathroom, laundry room, kitchen range and clothes dryer are vented to the outdoors; avoid hanging clothes indoors to dry.

- To reduce indoor humidity in a cold-winter area, ensure that the house is adequately insulated and that vapor barriers are installed properly at the appropriate locations; keep the house well heated.

- To eliminate cold-weather condensation on windows of single-pane glass, consider installing storm windows or replacing the windows with windows of double- or triple-pane glass.

- To prevent water from leaking into the house through damaged roofing or siding, inspect the roofing and siding regularly; have any damage repaired as soon as you notice it.

- Prevent water from pooling at and leaking through the foundation by servicing the gutters and downspouts *(page 19)*, diverting downspout runoff *(page 21)* and sloping the ground at the foundation *(page 20)*.

- Repair any leaking plumbing pipe or fixture, or any leaking appliance. Empty any refrigerator drain pan regularly.

- To reduce indoor humidity, avoid leaving water in pet bowls or in houseplant saucers; reduce the number of houseplants.

- To minimize indoor moisture, avoid curing firewood in the house; cure it outdoors well away from any foundation wall.

INSULATING COLD-WATER PIPES

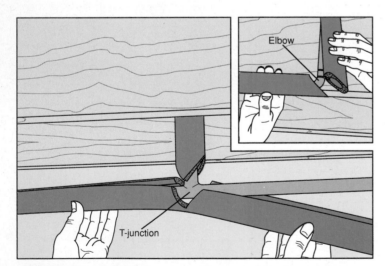

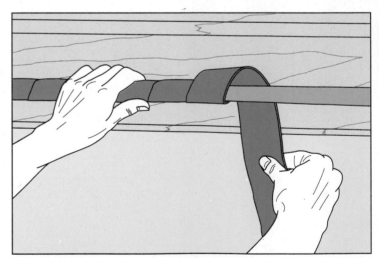

Installing insulation sleeves. Buy pre-slit foam insulation sleeves to fit the pipe at a building supply center. Starting at one end of the pipe, separate a sleeve along its slit and fit it around the pipe with its slit facing up; if necessary, cut it to length with a utility knife. Work to the other end of the pipe the same way, butting adjacent sleeves together. At a T-junction, notch one sleeve to fit around the junction and taper another sleeve to fit the notch, then install the sleeves *(above)*. At an elbow, cut a sleeve for each side of it at a 45° angle, then fit the sleeves around the pipe with the cut ends butted together *(inset)*. Use duct tape to seal the slits and joints of the sleeves.

Installing insulation tape. Buy adhesive-backed, aluminum-coated foam insulation tape at a building supply center. Use a cloth moistened with a solution of mild detergent and water to clean dirt and particles off the pipe, then dry it thoroughly. Starting at one end of the pipe, unwind a lead of tape and press it firmly at a 45° angle onto the pipe. Wrap the tape snugly around the pipe and work to the other end of it, applying the tape in a continuous strip and overlapping the edges slightly *(above)*; unwind and rewrap any tape that buckles or gapes. Wrap the tape around T-junctions, elbows and other fittings as snugly as possible the same way.

INSTALLING A VAPOR BARRIER

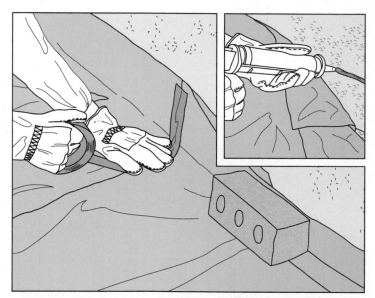

1 Installing polyethylene. Buy 6-mil polyethylene sheeting to cover the floor at a building supply center; if the floor is heavily trafficked, plan to install a double layer of sheeting. Wear soft-soled shoes; in a crawlspace, also a safety helmet. Level the soil of the floor using a spade and a garden rake. Use a utility knife to cut sections of sheeting long enough to lap 6 inches up the walls; trim any section to fit at an obstruction such as a post footing. Lay the sheeting one section at a time on the floor, lapping it up the walls *(above)*, then weight down the ends with bricks. Continue the same way, overlapping adjacent sections of sheeting by 12 inches.

2 Adhering the polyethylene. Use duct tape to seal the seams between overlapping sections of sheeting *(above)* and the edges of the sheeting at obstructions. To adhere the sheeting to the walls, use a caulking gun loaded with construction-grade adhesive. Starting at one end of a wall, fold back the sheeting. Holding the gun at a 45° angle to the wall, squeeze the trigger to eject a bead of adhesive along it *(inset)*. Smooth the sheeting up the wall and onto the adhesive. Continue the same way to the other end of the wall, then along each other wall. If necessary, install a second layer of sheeting *(step 1)*. Lay plywood on the sheeting for walkways.

SERVICING GUTTERS AND DOWNSPOUTS

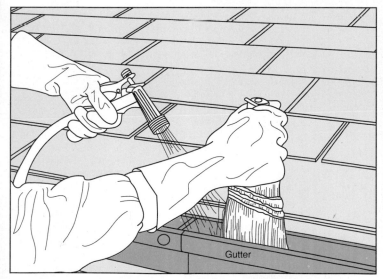

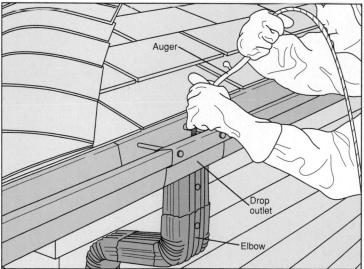

Cleaning out a gutter and downspout. Set up an extension ladder *(page 98)* on firm, level ground, ensuring that it is long enough for you to work without standing higher than three rungs from the top of it. Wearing rubber gloves, handpick and bag any leaves or other debris along the roof edge as well as from any leaf guard, open gutter and leaf strainer; reach down into an open drop outlet to pull out as much debris as possible. To flush the gutter and downspout, remove any leaf guard and leaf strainer, then use a garden hose to wash away dirt and grit, brushing it toward a downspout with a whisk broom *(above, left)*;

aim the hose into the drop outlet to flush it through the elbow and out the bottom of the downspout. If the downspout is not cleared by flushing it, unclog it using a trap-and-drain auger (plumber's snake). Push the auger coil into the drop outlet as far as possible, then lock the handle and slowly turn it clockwise *(above, right)*. When the handle moves easily, stop turning to feed in more coil and continue until the downspout is unclogged; if necessary, also work from the bottom of it. If water leaks or continues to drain poorly out of the gutter or downspout, have it repaired. Otherwise, reinstall any leaf guard or leaf strainer you removed.

SLOPING THE GROUND AT THE FOUNDATION

Outer stake

Line level

1 **Measuring the slope.** To ensure proper drainage away from a foundation wall, the ground should slope away from it by 1/2 to 1 inch every foot for a distance up to 6 feet from the wall; for any minimum distance required between the top of the wall and ground level, consult your municipal authorities. To measure the slope, drive a stake into the ground at the wall and 6 feet out from it. Using a line level, tie a string to the stakes level with the ground at the wall. Measure the distance between the string and the ground at the outer stake; if it is 3 inches or more, the slope is adequate. Otherwise, move the string on the outer stake 3 to 6 inches above the ground. Using the line level, move the string on the stake at the wall until it is level; its distance from the top of the wall must meet any local requirement for ground level. To set up a reference line for building up the slope, tie a string to the stake at the wall around the first string and to the outer stake at the ground (left).

Reference line

2 **Building up the slope.** Remove any sod or vegetation adjacent to the foundation wall within 6 feet of it, then install additional stakes and reference lines at intervals along it as you did to measure the slope (step 1). If you are raising the ground along the wall above the bottom of any basement window, have a window well installed. Buy enough topsoil at a garden center to raise the ground level to the height of the reference lines. Using a spade, dig into and break up the exposed soil adjacent to the wall. To build up the slope, use the spade to spread the topsoil on the area adjacent to the wall (left), mixing it with the existing soil; then, push soil toward the wall, banking it up to the level of the reference lines. Use the back of the spade to tamp the soil firmly, packing it level along the wall and sloping it evenly away from the wall. Use the back of a garden rake to smooth the soil surface. Remove the stakes and reference lines, then put back any sod or vegetation you removed.

DIVERTING DOWNSPOUT RUNOFF

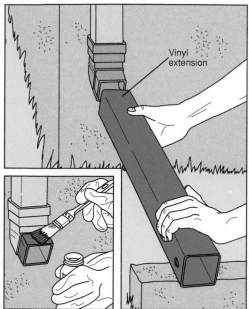

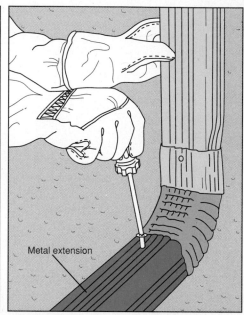

Splashblock

Vinyl extension

Metal extension

Diverting runoff at ground level. To prevent downspout runoff from pooling against a foundation wall, divert it away from the wall using a splashblock or an elbow extension. Buy a splashblock at least 18 inches long at a building supply center; to install it, position it on the ground directly below the downspout *(above, left)*. For an elbow extension, use a section of downspout about 3 feet long, ensuring that it matches the existing downspout; also use any connector, fastener or adhesive recommended by the manufacturer for installing it. For the vinyl downspout shown, wear rubber gloves to brush PVC solvent cement onto the outside end of the elbow *(inset)* and an inside end of the extension; then, push the cemented end of the extension onto the elbow *(above, center)*, supporting the other end of it on a block, if necessary. For the metal downspout shown, push the wider end of the extension snugly over the outside end of the elbow; then, drill a hole through the overlapped ends using a cordless drill fitted with a high-speed bit and drive a sheet metal screw into the hole *(above, right)*.

IDENTIFYING PEST ENTRY POINTS AT WINDOWS AND DOORS

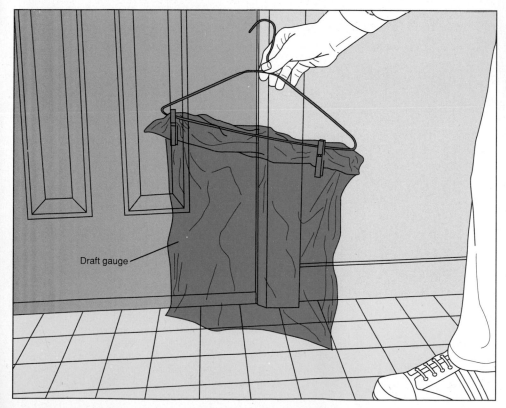

Draft gauge

Using a draft gauge. To permit a window sash or door to open and close, the joints between it and the frame are never permanently sealed. Consequently, these movable window and door joints may become entry points for insect and small-animal pests, especially if age and house settlement have caused the joints to widen. To determine whether the movable joints of your home's windows and doors are possible entry points for pests, wait for a windy day and use a draft gauge to check for inrushing air. To make a draft gauge, hang a piece of lightweight plastic film such as kitchen wrap on a wire coat hanger and secure it to the hanger with clothespins. To check each movable joint of a window or door, hold the draft gauge still near it *(left)*. If the plastic of the draft gauge flutters due to inrushing air, weather-strip the window or door *(page 22)* to seal the movable joints against pests.

PREPARING TO WEATHER-STRIP

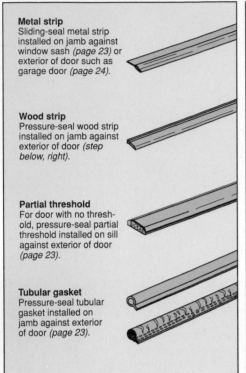

Metal strip
Sliding-seal metal strip installed on jamb against window sash *(page 23)* or exterior of door such as garage door *(page 24)*.

Wood strip
Pressure-seal wood strip installed on jamb against exterior of door *(step below, right)*.

Partial threshold
For door with no threshold, pressure-seal partial threshold installed on sill against exterior of door *(page 23)*.

Tubular gasket
Pressure-seal tubular gasket installed on jamb against exterior of door *(page 23)*.

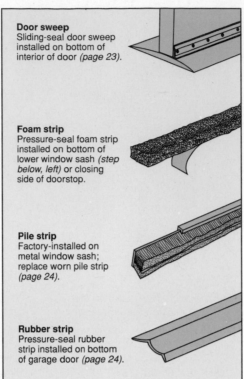

Door sweep
Sliding-seal door sweep installed on bottom of interior of door *(page 23)*.

Foam strip
Pressure-seal foam strip installed on bottom of lower window sash *(step below, left)* or closing side of doorstop.

Pile strip
Factory-installed on metal window sash; replace worn pile strip *(page 24)*.

Rubber strip
Pressure-seal rubber strip installed on bottom of garage door *(page 24)*.

Choosing weather stripping. Weather-strip the movable joints of a window, exterior door or garage door to create a pestproof seal. Use the chart at left to identify a type of weather stripping appropriate for the window or door, then refer to the page indicated to install it. In general, choose a pressure-seal type for a joint between two surfaces that close against each other, such as the joint between a door and a doorstop, or the joint between the bottom of a lower window sash or garage door and a sill. Choose a sliding-seal type for a joint between two surfaces that meet at a 90° angle—for example, the joint between the side or top of a door or window sash and a jamb, or the joint between a door and a threshold or sill. Buy weather stripping and any fasteners recommended for it at a building supply center, then follow the manufacturer's instructions to prepare the surface on which you plan to install it.

WEATHER-STRIPPING DOORS AND WINDOWS

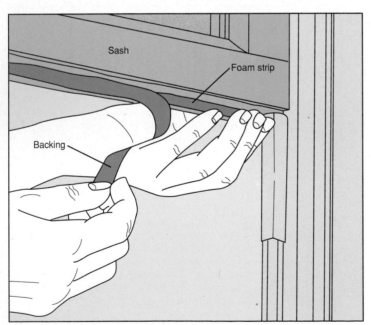

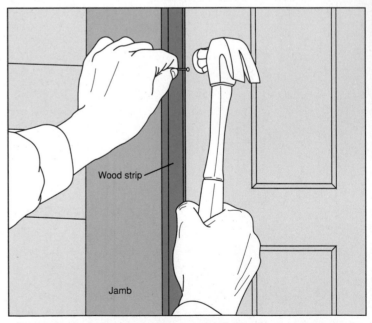

Installing foam-strip weather stripping. Install a foam strip *(step above)* on the bottom of a lower window sash or the closing side of a doorstop to create a pestproof seal. To install a foam strip on the bottom of a lower window sash, as shown, use scissors to cut a piece of foam strip equal in length to the sash. Peel the backing off one side of the piece and press it into place along the bottom of the sash. Then, peel the backing off the other side of the piece, smoothing it along the sash *(above)*. For a lasting grip, secure the piece with staples.

Installing wood-strip weather stripping. Install a wood strip *(step above)* on each door jamb against the exterior side of a door to create a pestproof seal. To install a wood strip on a jamb, use a backsaw and miter box to cut a piece of wood strip equal in length to the jamb; if an end of the piece will butt against the end of another piece on an adjacent jamb, cut it at a 45° angle. Working outside with the door closed, position the piece on the jamb with its foam edge pressed tightly against the door. Drive a nail every 6 inches along the piece *(above)* to secure it to the jamb.

WEATHER-STRIPPING DOORS AND WINDOWS (continued)

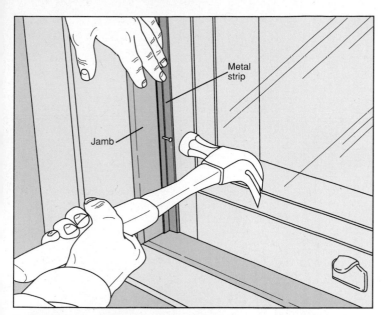

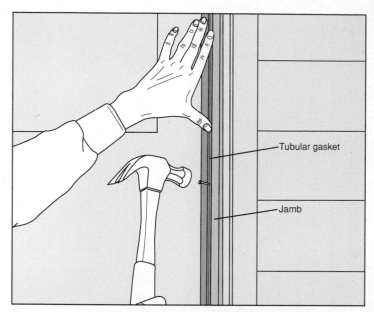

Installing metal-strip weather stripping. Install a metal strip *(page 22)* on each jamb against a window sash or the exterior side of a door to create a pestproof seal. For a window, as shown, use a hacksaw to cut a piece of metal strip equal in length to the window sash. Working inside with the sash closed, position the piece with its rigid edge on the jamb and its flexible edge bent and pressed tightly against the sash. Drive a nail into every dimple along the rigid edge *(above)* to secure the piece to the jamb.

Installing tubular-gasket weather stripping. Install a tubular gasket *(page 22)* on each jamb against the exterior side of a door to create a pestproof seal. Use scissors to cut a piece of tubular gasket equal in length to the jamb; if an end of the piece will butt against the end of another piece on an adjacent jamb, cut it at a 45° angle. Working outside with the door closed, position the piece with its flat edge on the jamb and its tubular edge pressed tightly against the door. Drive a nail every 6 inches along the flat edge *(above)* to secure the piece to the jamb.

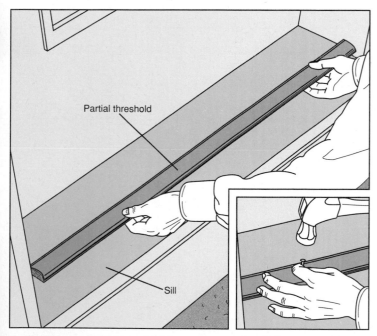

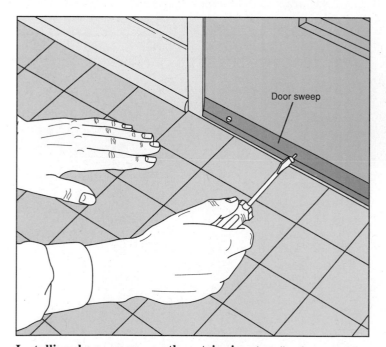

Installing partial-threshold weather stripping. For a door with no threshold, install a partial threshold *(page 22)* on the sill against the exterior side of it to create a pestproof seal. Cut a piece of partial threshold equal in length to the sill; for the type shown, take the metal cover off the foam-edged wood insert and cut each piece separately, then reassemble the pieces. Working outside with the door closed, position the piece on the sill *(above)* with its foam edge pressed tightly against the door. Drive a nail every 6 inches along the piece *(inset)* to secure it to the sill.

Installing door-sweep weather stripping. Install a door sweep *(page 22)* on the bottom of the interior side of a door to cover the gap beween it and the threshold, creating a pestproof seal. Cut a piece of door sweep equal in length to the door, leaving a screw hole near each end of it. Working inside with the door closed, position the piece against the bottom of the door with its flexible edge bent tightly against the floor, then use a pencil to mark the screw holes. Use a drill to bore a pilot hole for a screw at each mark, then reposition the piece and screw it to the door *(above)*.

WEATHER-STRIPPING DOORS AND WINDOWS (continued)

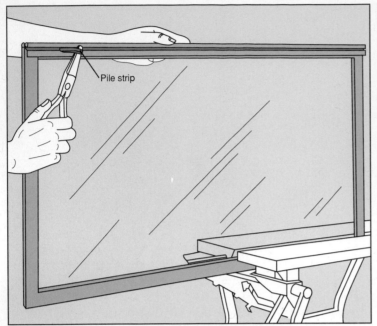

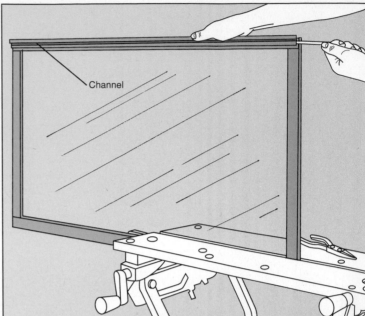

Replacing pile-strip weather stripping. If a metal window sash has worn pile-strip weather stripping *(page 22)*, replace the pile strip to ensure a pestproof seal. Remove the sash from the window, then use a screwdriver to loosen any metal tabs securing the ends of the pile strip. Use long-nose pliers to grasp one end of the pile strip and pull it out of the weather-stripping channel *(above, left)*. Take the pile strip to a window supplier to buy an exact replacement strip; if recommended by the supplier, also buy a splining tool to install it. Use an old toothbrush to clean the weather-stripping channel, then cut a piece of pile strip equal in length to the weather-stripping channel. To install the pile strip using a splining tool, lay it in position along the weather-stripping channel, then roll the splining tool along it to snap it into the channel. Otherwise, install the pile strip by feeding it into the weather-stripping channel *(above, right)*. Tighten any metal tabs to secure the ends of the pile strip, then reinstall the sash in the window.

WEATHER-STRIPPING A GARAGE DOOR

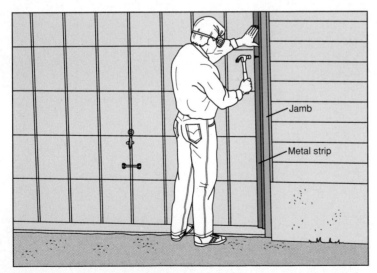

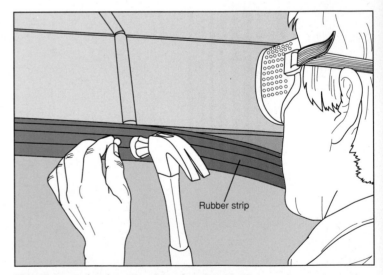

Weather-stripping the door sides and top. Install a metal strip *(page 22)* on each jamb against the exterior side of a garage door to create a pestproof seal. Use a hacksaw to cut a piece of metal strip equal in length to the jamb; if an end of the piece will butt against the end of another piece on an adjacent jamb, cut it at a 45° angle. Working outside with the door closed, position the piece with its rigid edge on the jamb and its flexible edge bent tightly against the door. Drive a nail into every dimple along the rigid edge *(above)* to secure the piece to the jamb.

Weather-stripping the door bottom. Install a rubber strip *(page 22)* on the bottom of a garage door to create a pestproof seal. Use scissors to cut a piece of rubber strip equal in length to the garage door. Open the garage door partway; if necessary, follow the manufacturer's instructions to deactivate any automatic door opener. Position the piece with its flat midsection centered against the bottom of the door and its wide flap oriented toward the door exterior. Drive a nail every 2 inches along the flat midsection *(above)* to secure the piece to the bottom of the door.

SEALING JOINTS

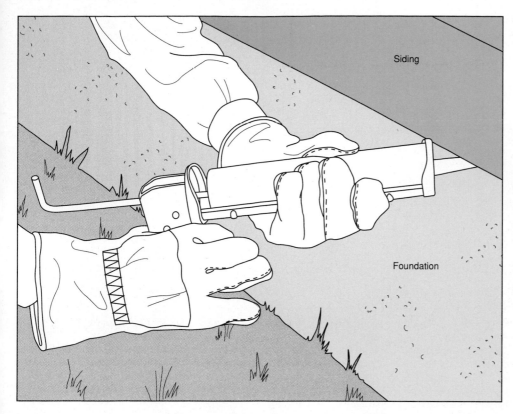

Caulking exterior siding joints. Inspect the sealed joints between sections of siding, between the siding and the foundation, and between the siding and any door or window trim, then reseal any faulty joint to prevent the entry of pests and moisture. For a joint between the siding and a foundation wall, as shown, use a putty knife to scrape out any old caulk. If the joint is deeper than 1/2 inch, buy a foam backing rod to fill it to within 1/4 inch of the surface at a building supply center; or, to rodent-proof the joint, buy enough steel wool to fill it the same way. To fill the joint, work along it to push the backing rod or steel wool firmly into place. Wearing work gloves, load a caulking gun with an exterior-grade caulk recommended for the joint. Starting at one end of the joint, hold the gun at a 45° angle to eject a continuous bead of caulk along it *(left)*. Wearing a rubber glove, run a wet finger along the caulk, pressing it into the joint.

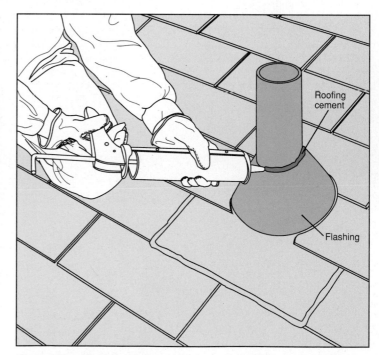

Caulking plumbing joints. Inspect the sealed joints at the edges of plumbing fixtures, then reseal any faulty joint to prevent the entry of pests and moisture. For a joint between a bathtub and a wall, as shown, use a putty knife to scrape out old caulk. Fill the bathtub with water, then tape each edge of the joint with masking tape. Load a caulking gun with a caulk recommended for the joint. Starting at one end of the joint, hold the gun at a 45° angle to eject a continuous bead of caulk along it *(above)*. Wearing a rubber glove, run a wet finger along the caulk, pressing it into the joint. Remove the masking tape. Let the caulk set for 24 hours before draining the bathtub.

Cementing flashing joints. Working safely on the roof *(page 98)*, inspect the sealed joints between flashing sections and between the flashing and the roofing material, then reseal any faulty joint to prevent the entry of pests and moisture. For a joint between the flashing and a stack vent, as shown, use a putty knife to scrape out old sealant. Wearing work gloves, load a caulking gun with roofing cement. Starting at a point along the joint, hold the gun at a 45° angle to eject a continuous bead of cement along it *(above)*. Wearing a rubber glove, run a wet finger along the cement, pressing it into the joint.

PATCHING A CRACK (STUCCO)

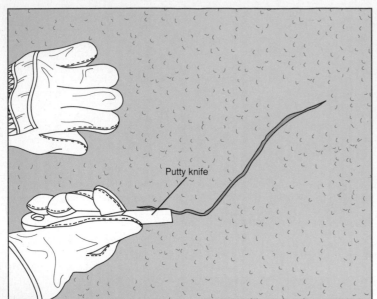

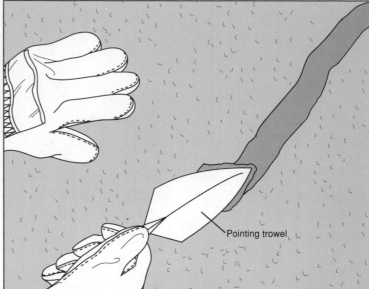

Patching a hairline or open crack. To prepare a hairline crack for patching, use a putty knife to clean out dirt and particles and deepen the crack slightly *(above, left)*. To prepare an open crack for patching, use a cold chisel and a ball-peen hammer; wearing work gloves and safety goggles, widen it to 1/4 inch and deepen it to 1/2 inch, undercutting the edges if possible or cutting them straight. Use a stiff fiber brush to clean debris out of the crack. Soak the crack with water, using the fine spray of a garden hose or brushing on water with a large paintbrush. Buy a premixed stucco patching compound at a building supply center. Wearing work gloves, prepare a sufficient quantity of the patching compound for the job, mixing it to a thick consistency. Starting at one end of the crack, use a pointing trowel to press the compound into the crack, smoothing it flush with the surface *(above, right)*. To replicate the texture in the surface, use an old paintbrush, a rectangular trowel or a sponge. Let the patching compound cure. If necessary, paint the patch to match the surrounding surface, first applying a primer recommended by the paint manufacturer.

PATCHING A CRACK (DRYWALL OR PLASTER)

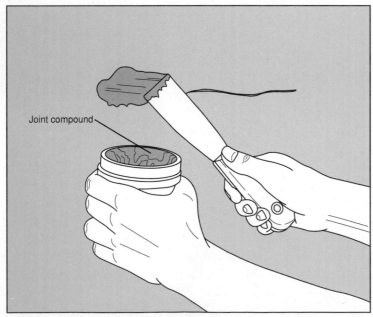

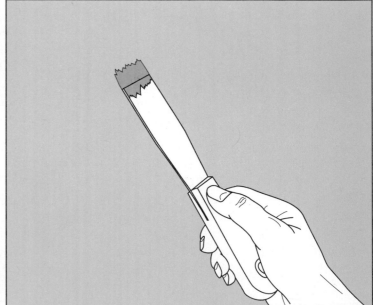

Patching a hairline crack or small hole. To fill a hairline crack or small hole, use pre-mixed joint compound. Using coarse sandpaper on a sanding block, roughen the surface around the damage, then wipe or brush off the dust. Moisten the surface with water from a spray bottle. To fill a hairline crack, use a putty knife to press the compound into the crack, smoothing it flush with the sturface *(above, left)*. To fill a small hole, press in the compound with a finger, then use a putty knife to smooth it flush with the surface *(above, right)*. Let the joint compound dry. Using medium sandpaper, lightly sand the surface, then wipe or brush off the dust. Paint the patch to match the surrounding surface, first applying a primer recommended by the paint manufacturer.

PATCHING A CRACK (DRYWALL OR PLASTER) (continued)

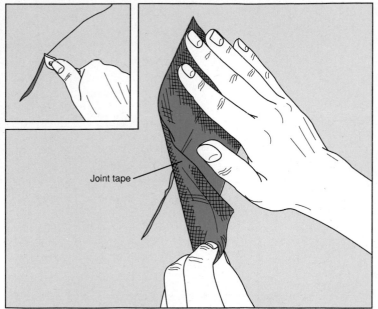
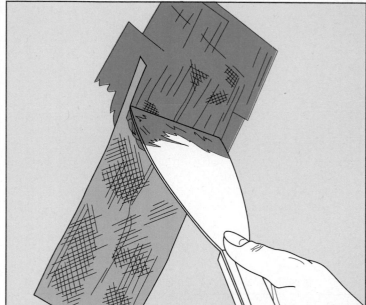

Joint tape

Patching an open crack. To fill an open crack, use fiber-mesh joint tape and pre-mixed joint compound. Open the edges of the crack by lightly drawing the tip of a can opener along it *(inset)*. Brush away loose particles with a soft-bristled brush. Moisten the surface with water from a spray bottle. Cut a length of tape slightly longer than the crack and press it over the crack *(above, left)*; if the crack is crooked or branched, apply several short lengths of tape without overlapping the ends. To fill the taped crack, use a putty knife to spread a thin layer of joint com- pound over the tape *(above, right)*, pushing it through the mesh. Let the compound dry. Spread a second, wider layer of compound over the first in one long stroke, then smooth the edges of the patch level with the sur- rounding surface. Let the compound dry. Using medium sandpaper on a sanding block, lightly sand the surface, then wipe or brush off the dust. Paint the patch to match the surrounding surface, first applying a primer recommended by the paint manufacturer.

PATCHING A CRACK (WOOD)

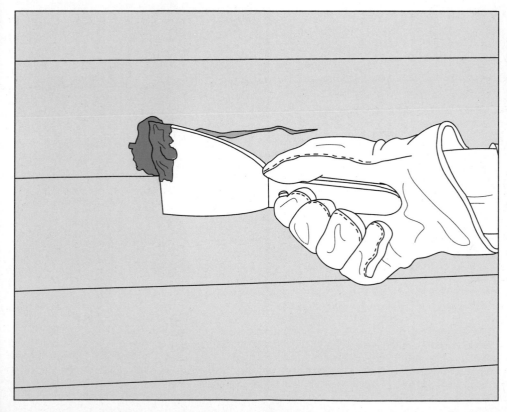

Patching a small hole or crack. To patch a small hole or crack, use pre-mixed wood patching compound; for exterior wood, use an exterior-grade wood patching compound. Pre- pare the patching compound following the man- ufacturer's instructions. To fill the crack or hole, load the tip of a putty knife with compound and smooth it over the damage *(left)*, overfilling the crack or hole slightly to allow for shrinkage. Let the compound dry; if the patch shrinks and dries below the surface level, fill it again. Use medium sandpaper on a sanding block to sand the patch flush with the surrounding surface, then wipe or brush off the dust. If necessary, paint or finish the patch to match the surrounding surface, first applying a primer or sealer recommended by the paint or finish manufacturer.

PATCHING ROT (WOOD)

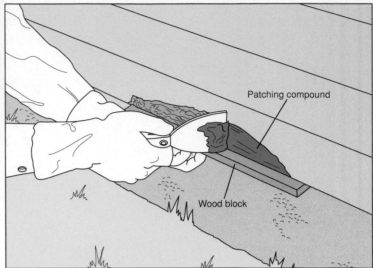

Patching compound

Wood block

Patching minor rot damage. To test for wood rot, poke the wood using an awl, pressing it in as deeply as possible. If the wood is soft and gives way, crumbling instead of splintering, it is weakened by rot. If the damage to the wood is extensive, call a building professional. To patch minor rot, wear work gloves and safety goggles to remove all the soft, damaged wood down to firm, healthy wood, digging out the damage with a paint scraper *(above, left)*, putty knife or wood chisel. Buy epoxy patching compound at a building supply center and prepare it following the manufacturer's instructions. Use a putty knife to pack patching compound into the damage, overfilling it slightly. Then, scrape off the excess patching compound, leveling the patch with the surrounding surface; if necessary, position a wood block along the edge of the surface as a guide *(above, right)*. To replicate any texture in the surface, rake the wet compound with the tip of the putty knife blade. Allow the patching compound to cure. Using medium sandpaper on a sanding block, lightly sand the surface, then wipe it clean. Paint or finish the patch to match the surrounding surface, first applying a primer or sealer recommended by the paint or finish manufacturer.

PATCHING A CRACK (CONCRETE)

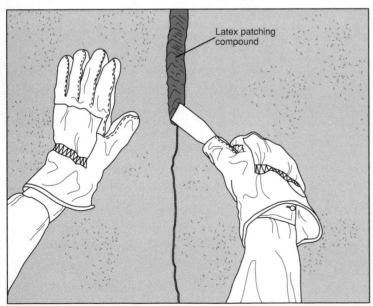

Latex patching compound

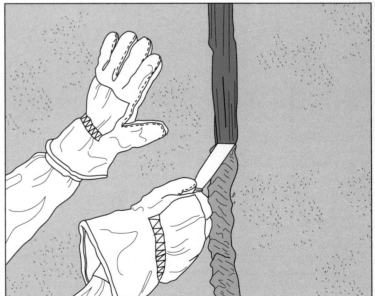

Patching a hairline crack. To prepare the crack for patching, use a stiff fiber brush to clean out dirt and particles. Buy a latex concrete patching compound at a building supply center; if recommended by the manufacturer, also a bonding agent. Follow the manufacturer's instructions to apply any bonding agent to the crack. Wearing work gloves, prepare a sufficient quantity of the patching compound for the job, mixing it to a thin consistency that can be worked to a featheredge. Starting at one end of the crack, use a putty knife to patch a section of it at a time with the patching compound. Draw the putty knife across the crack, using the tip of the blade to press in the patching compound; overfill the crack slightly. Continue the same way along the crack *(above, left)* to the other end of it. Then, draw the putty knife along the patch *(above, right)* to scrape off excess patching compound and smooth it flush with the surface. Allow the patching compound to cure for the time specified by the manufacturer; mist it with water when it lightens at the edges and keep plastic taped over it until it cures. If the patch cracks, suspect a structural problem and consult a building professional.

PATCHING A CRACK (CONCRETE) (continued)

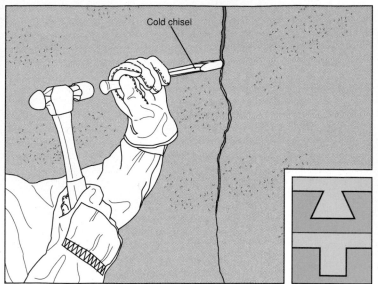

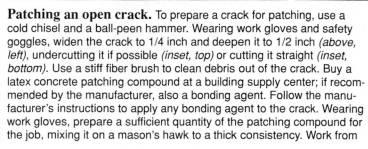

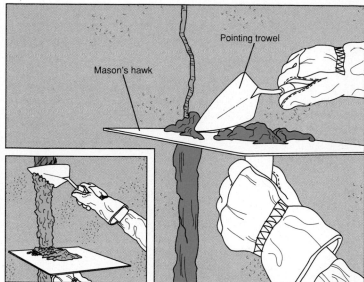

Patching an open crack. To prepare a crack for patching, use a cold chisel and a ball-peen hammer. Wearing work gloves and safety goggles, widen the crack to 1/4 inch and deepen it to 1/2 inch *(above, left)*, undercutting it if possible *(inset, top)* or cutting it straight *(inset, bottom)*. Use a stiff fiber brush to clean debris out of the crack. Buy a latex concrete patching compound at a building supply center; if recommended by the manufacturer, also a bonding agent. Follow the manufacturer's instructions to apply any bonding agent to the crack. Wearing work gloves, prepare a sufficient quantity of the patching compound for the job, mixing it on a mason's hawk to a thick consistency. Work from the bottom to the top of the crack to patch a section of it at a time. Holding the mason's hawk below the section, pack in the patching compound, pressing it in with a pointing trowel *(above, right)*; overfill the crack slightly. Working from the top to the bottom of the patch, draw the edge of the trowel along it, scraping off excess patching compound *(inset)*. Then, draw the back of the trowel along the patch to smooth it flush with the surrounding surface. Allow the patching compound to cure for the time specified; mist it with water when it lightens at the edges and keep plastic taped over it until it cures. If the patch cracks, suspect a structural problem and consult a building professional.

REPOINTING MORTAR JOINTS

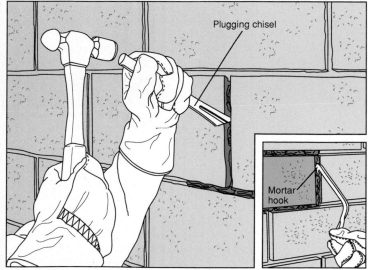

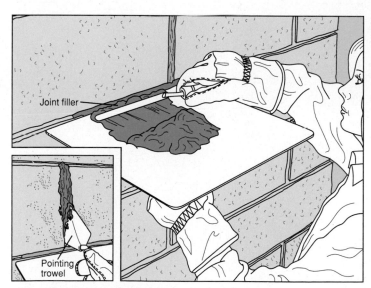

1 Cutting back and cleaning the joint. Wearing work gloves and safety goggles, use a plugging chisel or cold chisel and a ball-peen hammer to cut back the joint to a depth of 1/2 to 3/4 inch *(above)*—far enough to break up the damaged surface mortar and reach the solid mortar behind it. Use a mortar hook to rake large pieces of broken mortar out of the cut-back joint *(inset)*, then use a stiff fiber brush to clean dust and small mortar particles out of it. Soak the joint and the adjacent blocks or bricks with water, using the fine spray of a garden hose or brushing on water with a large paintbrush.

2 Repointing the joint. Mix a batch of mortar *(page 112)* on a mason's hawk. To repoint more than one joint, first repoint any vertical joint, then any horizontal joint. For a vertical joint, hold the mason's hawk below it and use a pointing trowel to pack in mortar *(inset)*, overfilling it slightly. Draw the edge of the trowel along the joint to scrape off excess mortar. For a horizontal joint, hold the mason's hawk below it and use a joint filler to slice off and pack in mortar *(above)*, overfilling it slightly. Draw the edge of the joint filler along the joint to scrape off excess mortar.

REPOINTING MORTAR JOINTS (continued)

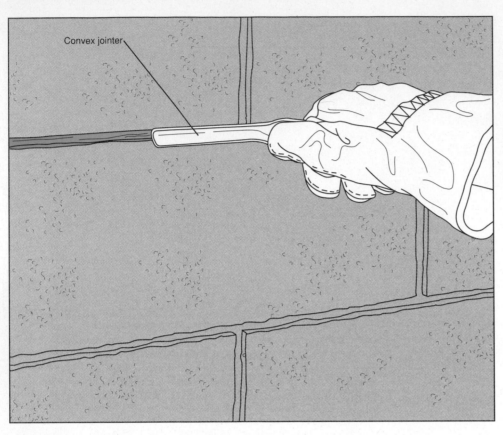

Convex jointer

3 **Striking the joint.** Allow the mortar to set until it is just hard enough to hold a thumbprint—usually about 30 minutes. To strike a repointed joint, examine the other joints to determine the jointing tool to use. For a concave joint, use a convex jointer or the back of an old spoon. For a V-shaped joint, use a V-shaped jointer or the tip of a pointing trowel. For a flush joint, use the edge of a pointing trowel. To strike more than one joint, first strike any vertical joint, then strike any horizontal joint. To strike a concave joint, as shown, wet a convex jointer with clean water, then use firm, steady pressure to draw it along the joint *(left)*. Use the edge of a pointing trowel to scrape off excess mortar forced out of the joint by the pressure of the jointer. Allow the mortar to set for 24 hours, then use a stiff fiber brush to scrub any mortar residue off the adjacent blocks or bricks. Allow the mortar to cure, keeping it damp for at least 3 days; mist the surface occasionally with the fine spray of water from a garden hose.

PESTPROOFING A DECK OR PORCH UNDERSIDE

Enclosing a deck or porch underside. To keep pests out of an open area under a deck or porch, enclose it with hardware cloth and wooden lattice. Buy 1/4-inch mesh hardware cloth and panels of pressure-treated wooden lattice at a building supply center. Enclose the underside one section at a time between each pair of adjacent posts; if the posts are not of wood, first fasten a wooden furring strip to them. To enclose a section, measure its length and height. Wearing work gloves and safety goggles, use tin snips to cut a piece of hardware cloth to fit; use a saw to cut a piece of lattice to size. To install the hardware cloth, hold it taut in position and use a staple gun to staple it every 4 inches to the posts or furring strips. To install the lattice, hold it in position against the hardware cloth and nail it every 6 inches to the posts *(left)* or furring strips with weather-resistant nails. To provide access to the underside, enclose one section with an access panel; staple the hardware cloth to the back of the lattice, then screw the lattice to the posts *(inset)* or furring strips with weather-resistant screws.

PESTPROOFING A BROKEN WINDOW PANE

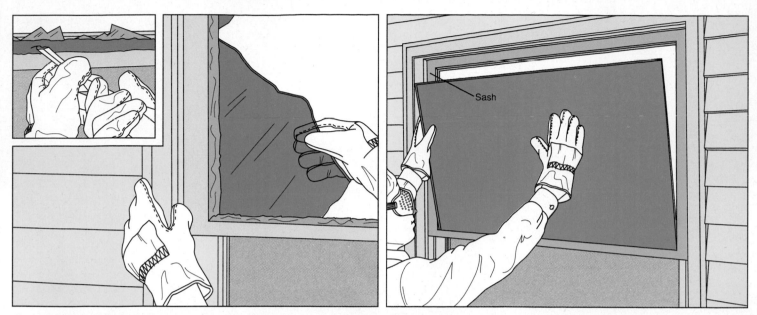

Covering a broken window. Temporarily cover a broken pane to keep pests out until it can be replaced. Wearing work gloves and safety goggles, work from the top to the bottom of the pane to carefully remove any shards of glass, pulling each shard straight out of the sash *(above, left)*. For a stubborn shard, wiggle it gently to pull it out; if necessary, use an old chisel to gently scrape away any glazing compound holding the shard *(inset)*, then pull it out. Place the broken glass in a cardboard box for disposal. Measure the opening of the sash and cut a piece of heavy cardboard to fit. Position the cardboard in the opening *(above, right)* then tape each edge of it securely to the sash with masking tape. Have the pane replaced as soon as possible.

PESTPROOFING A DAMAGED WINDOW SCREEN

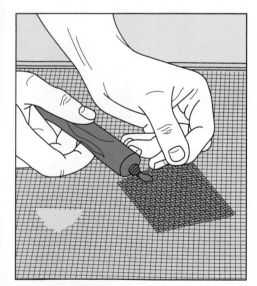

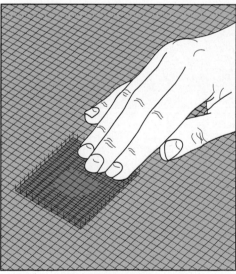

Patching a fiberglass screen. To patch a tiny hole, smooth together the broken ends of the fibers, then apply a drop of silicone-rubber adhesive to bond them. To patch a larger hole, buy a piece of matching screen at a building supply center and cut a patch to cover it. Apply a thin coat of silicone-rubber adhesive along each edge of the patch *(above)*, then press it into position. Dab off excess adhesive using a clean cloth.

Patching a metal screen. To patch a tiny hole, straighten and smooth together the broken ends of the wires, then apply a drop of waterproof glue to bond them; dab off excess glue using a clean cloth. To patch a larger hole, remove the screen and use scissors to trim the edges of the hole. Buy a piece of matching screen at a building supply center and cut a patch 2 inches longer and wider than the hole. Pull out the first few wires along each edge of the patch, then neatly bend the exposed wire ends at a 90° angle to the surface. Lay the patch over the hole *(above, left)* and push the bent wire ends through the mesh. Turn the screen over and press down the bent wire ends onto the mesh *(above, right)* to secure the patch. Then, reinstall the screen.

PESTPROOFING AN AIR VENT

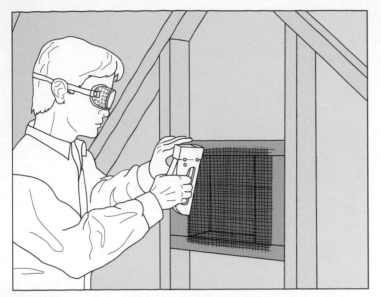

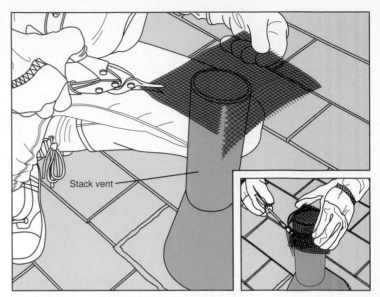

Installing a screen on a louvered vent. If a louvered air vent in a gable, soffit or foundation wall has no insect screen, install a screen on the back of it to keep out pests. Work indoors to measure the wood frame around the vent; if there is no frame, make one by fastening a wood piece to the surface along each edge of the vent. Buy a piece of 18-by-16 mesh insect screen at a building supply center, then wear work gloves and cut it to fit the frame. Holding the screen taut in position over the back of the vent, use a staple gun to staple it *(above)* every 4 inches to the frame.

Installing a screen on a stack vent. Install a screen on a stack vent to keep out pests; check that a screen is permitted by the local plumbing code. Buy 1/4-inch mesh hardware cloth at a building supply center. Working safely on the roof *(page 98)*, wear work gloves and use tin snips to cut a piece of hardware cloth to fit over the stack vent opening. Lay the piece over the opening and notch its corners *(above)*, then fold it down over the vent. Secure the piece to the vent with a stainless steel hose clamp, using a screwdriver to tighten it *(inset)*. Remove the screen in winter to prevent ice and snow blockage.

PESTPROOFING AN OPEN EAVE

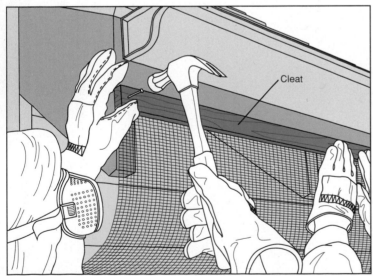

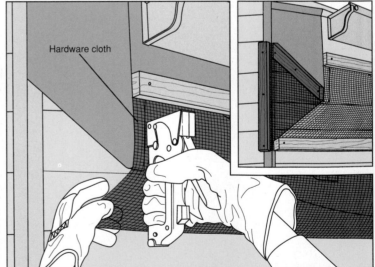

Installing a screen on an open eave. To keep pests out of an open eave, work safely on a ladder *(page 98)* with a helper on another ladder to install a screen on it. For an eave with exposed rafter ends, as shown, measure the distance from the top to the bottom of a rafter end, then to the house wall at a 45° angle to it; then, measure the length of the eave. Buy 1/4-inch mesh hardware cloth to cover the area at a building supply center. Wearing work gloves and safety goggles, use tin snips to cut sections of hardware cloth to extend from the top of the rafter ends to the house wall; cut adjacent sections to overlap 2 inches on a rafter end. To fasten each section, cut two 1-by-2 cleats equal in length to the section width. Working one section at a time, position the top of it against the tops of the rafter ends; place a cleat across it and nail the cleat to the rafter ends *(above, left)*, then pull the section taut and staple it to the rafter ends *(above, right)*. To secure the bottom of the section, pull it taut against the house wall, then place a cleat across it and nail the cleat to the wall. Continue the same way along the eave to the other end. For the triangular opening at each end of the eave, cut a section of hardware cloth to fit, fastening the sides of it with cleats and tying the bottom of it to the adjacent section with mechanic's wire *(inset)*.

REPLACING AN AIR VENT

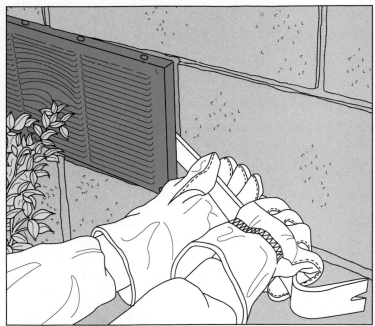

Replacing a foundation vent. Replace a damaged foundation vent to keep pests out of a basement or crawlspace. Working outdoors, use a putty knife to scrape any sealant off the edges of the vent; or, if necessary, wear safety goggles and work gloves to chip any mortar off the edges of the vent using a cold chisel and a ball-peen hammer. Insert a pry bar into the joint between the vent and the wall, then work along the joint to pry the vent out of the wall *(above, left)*; if you cannot pry out the vent, work indoors to remove any mortar or screws holding the back of it, then work outdoors again to pry it out. Buy a vent to fit the wall open-

ing at a building supply center; choose a louvered type with an insect screen. Working outdoors, load a caulking gun with an exterior-grade caulk and apply a bead of it along each flange of the vent. Then, fit the vent into the wall opening *(above, right)*, setting it flush with the surface. To seal the joint between the vent and the wall, apply a continuous bead of caulk along it; then, wear a rubber glove and run a wet finger along the caulk to press it into the joint. If necessary, work indoors to screw the back of the vent to the sides of the wall opening.

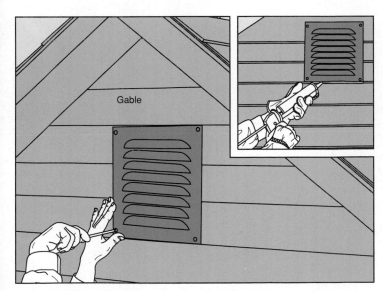

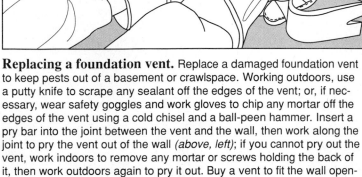

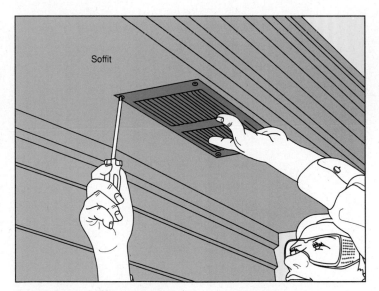

Replacing a gable vent. Replace a damaged gable vent to keep pests out of an attic. Working safely on a ladder *(page 98)* outdoors, use a putty knife to scrape any sealant off the edges of the vent. Then, unscrew the vent *(above)* and lift it out. Buy a vent to fit the gable opening at a building supply center; choose a louvered type with an insect screen. Load a caulking gun with an exterior-grade caulk and apply a bead of it along each flange of the vent. Fit the vent in the opening and drive in the screws. To seal the joint between the vent and the gable, apply a continuous bead of caulk along it *(inset)*; then, wear a rubber glove and run a wet finger along the caulk to press it into the joint.

Replacing a soffit vent. Replace a damaged soffit vent to keep pests out of an attic. Working safely on a ladder *(page 98)* outdoors, use a putty knife to scrape any sealant off the edges of the vent. Then, unscrew the vent *(above)* and lift it out. Buy a vent to fit the soffit opening at a building supply center; choose a louvered type with an insect screen. Load a caulking gun with an exterior-grade caulk and apply a bead of it along each flange of the vent. Fit the vent in the opening and drive in the screws. To seal the joint between the vent and the soffit, apply a continuous bead of caulk along it; then, wear a rubber glove and run a wet finger along the caulk to press it into the joint.

PESTPROOFING A WALL OPENING FOR A PIPE

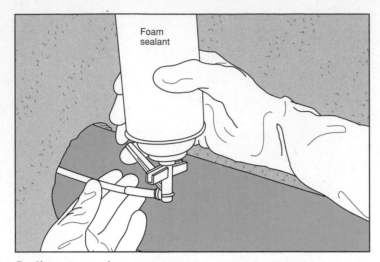

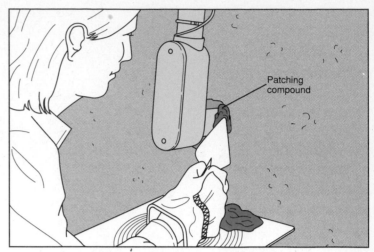

Sealing an opening. To keep pests out of a wall opening for a pipe, patch an opening in concrete or masonry *(step right)* or seal the opening. Seal an opening up to 1/4 inch in width with caulk *(page 25)*. To seal a wide opening for a dryer vent pipe, as shown, buy foam sealant at a building supply center. Working indoors, use a putty knife to scrape any old sealant out of the opening, then follow the manufacturer's instructions to apply the foam sealant. Wearing rubber gloves and safety goggles, hold the container upside down and fit the dispenser tube into the opening, then depress the trigger *(above)*, filling the opening to the level recommended. Let the sealant cure. If necessary, work outdoors to seal the opening exterior the same way.

Patching an opening. To keep pests out of a wall opening for a pipe, seal the opening *(step left)* or patch an opening in concrete or masonry. To patch an opening for a supply pipe, as shown, buy a latex concrete patching compound at a building supply center. Working outdoors, use a stiff fiber brush to clean debris out of the opening, then follow the manufacturer's instructions to use the patching compound. Wearing work gloves, pack the patching compound into the opening with a pointing trowel *(above)*; overfill the opening slightly, then scrape off excess patching compound and smooth the patch flush with the surrounding surface. Let the patching compound cure. If necessary, work indoors to seal the opening interior the same way.

PESTPROOFING A PIPE

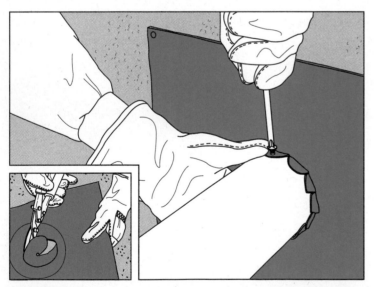

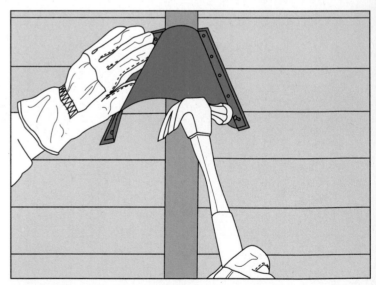

Installing a flange. To pestproof the wall opening for a pipe, install a flange on the pipe. For a dryer vent pipe, as shown, buy 24-gauge sheet metal for a flange at a building supply center. Mark a circle equal to the pipe diameter at the center of the metal, then mark a circle 2 inches smaller than the pipe diameter concentric to the first circle. Wearing work gloves and safety goggles, use tin snips to cut out the smaller circle *(inset)*; then, cut V-shaped notches between the edge of the smaller circle and the marked outline of the larger circle to form tabs. Bend up the tabs with pliers, then fit the flange on the pipe. Fasten the flange at each corner to the wall, then fasten each tab to the pipe with a sheet metal screw *(above)*.

Installing a guard. To pestproof an exterior vertical pipe against climbing pests, install a guard on the pipe; buy 24-gauge sheet metal for a guard at a building supply center. To make the guard, wear work gloves and safety goggles; use tin snips to cut the metal, then bend it by hand to form a semicircular cone with a neck that fits snugly around the pipe and flanges that sit flush against the wall, as shown. Punch holes for fasteners along each flange, then fit the guard over the pipe against the wall. To fasten the guard to siding, drive a nail through each hole in the flanges *(above)*; to fasten the guard to concrete or masonry, use screw anchors and weather-resistant screws.

PESTPROOFING A CHIMNEY

Installing a screen in an open flue. Screen a chimney to keep out pests. If the chimney has a rain cap, install screening in it *(step below)*. If the chimney has an open flue, work safely on the roof *(page 98)* to measure the flue opening. Buy a chimney screen to fit the chimney at a building supply center; the type shown fits onto the outside edges of the flue with clips holding it against the inside edges. Wearing work gloves, stand on the high side of the chimney and fit the chimney screen onto it at an angle, fitting two adjacent clips into the flue *(above, left)*. Lowering the chimney screen into position slowly, press the other clips inward to fit them into the flue, then push the chimney screen straight down into place *(above, right)*. Have the chimney screen cleaned along with the chimney once each year.

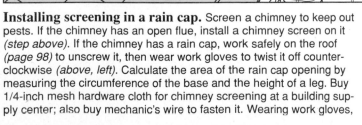

Installing screening in a rain cap. Screen a chimney to keep out pests. If the chimney has an open flue, install a chimney screen on it *(step above)*. If the chimney has a rain cap, work safely on the roof *(page 98)* to unscrew it, then wear work gloves to twist it off counterclockwise *(above, left)*. Calculate the area of the rain cap opening by measuring the circumference of the base and the height of a leg. Buy 1/4-inch mesh hardware cloth for chimney screening at a building supply center; also buy mechanic's wire to fasten it. Wearing work gloves, cut the hardware cloth to size with tin snips *(inset)*, allowing for an overlap in its length of about 2 inches. Roll up the hardware cloth and fit it into the rain cap, letting it unfurl tightly against the inside of the base. Cut strips of wire about 5 inches long and tie the hardware cloth to the top and bottom of the legs of the rain cap, twisting the ends together with pliers *(above, right)*. Twist the rain cap clockwise onto the chimney and put back any screws. Have the chimney screening cleaned along with the chimney once a year; replace the screening when it becomes brittle.

INDOOR PESTS

Your indoor living area is where you relax in comfort, surrounded by the possessions you treasure, but it is also vulnerable to pests that can mar the beauty of its surfaces, damage its furnishings and make life outright loathsome. Ants, grain beetles, flour moths and cockroaches may infest the kitchen. Clothes moths and carpet beetles may eat holes in cherished fabrics. Bedbugs, fleas and ticks may drive a pet or family member to distraction. Bats in the attic and mice or rats in the basement may make these areas unusable.

A typical indoor living area with its pest troublespots is shown at right. Fortunately, discouraging pests from taking up residence inside your home is not difficult. Keep household surfaces clean and in good repair. Store food tightly sealed or in the refrigerator. Keep trash cans tightly sealed on a stand away from the house. Launder or dry-clean bedding, clothing, upholstery and draperies regularly. Inspect pets for pests such as fleas and ticks that they may carry indoors. Control indoor humidity.

If careful maintenance does not eliminate a troublesome indoor pest problem, use the Troubleshooting Guide *(page 38)* to help choose an appropriate pest control method, then refer to the pages indicated to undertake the pest control job. To identify an unknown pest, consult the chart on page 39 for descriptions of common indoor pests and their typical locations; if you cannot identify a pest, consult your local county extension agent or a pest control professional for help. In general, first try controlling a pest using the least harsh, most environmentally safe method—for example, a bait station or trap, if one is available. If a bait station or trap is not available for a pest or does not control it, consult the chart on page 41 to choose a pesticide.

When buying a pesticide, choose the least harmful product available that is recommended for indoor use on the pest. Carefully follow the manufacturer's instructions to mix and apply a pesticide, and use only as much as necessary until the pest is eradicated. Before using a pesticide on a household surface, a pet or a houseplant, test it on a small, inconspicuous spot; if it damages a surface or causes an adverse reaction in a pet or a houseplant, choose another pesticide. Do not overuse a pesticide and risk contaminating indoor air, food and water or harming family members, pets and houseplants; if necessary, consult a pest control professional.

While many indoor pest control jobs require only the use of easy-to-use aerosol sprays and traps, some call for more specialized tools and materials that are readily available at a pest control or garden center. Refer to Tools & Techniques *(page 112)* for instructions on choosing, setting up and using application tools. Before starting any pest control job, read the chapter entitled Working Safely *(page 98)* for instructions on choosing the appropriate safety gear, preparing the work area, and mixing and disposing of pesticides. Familiarize yourself with the safety advice in the Emergency Guide *(page 8)*. If you doubt your ability to complete a job, do not hesitate to consult a pest control professional.

Attic
Undisturbed darkness and excess heat or dampness may attract silverfish or spiders and animals such as bats or mice. Structural wood may attract carpenter ants or powderpost beetles. Pestproof attic and roof *(page 14)*.

Bathroom
Dampness may attract cockroaches, flies, silverfish or spiders and animals such as mice. Thoroughly clean surfaces regularly. Pestproof bathroom *(page 14)*.

Pet
Pet active outdoors may carry fleas or ticks indoors from lawn. Check pet regularly for fleas and ticks.

Bedroom
Bedding may be infested by pests such as bedbugs. Carpeting, upholstery and draperies may be infested by pet-borne pests such as fleas or ticks and fabric pests such as clothes moths or carpet beetles. Launder or dry-clean bedding and clean surfaces regularly. Pestproof interior walls and windows *(page 14)*.

Clothes closet
Clothing may be infested by fabric pests such as clothes moths or carpet beetles. Regularly clean surfaces and check clothes for damage.

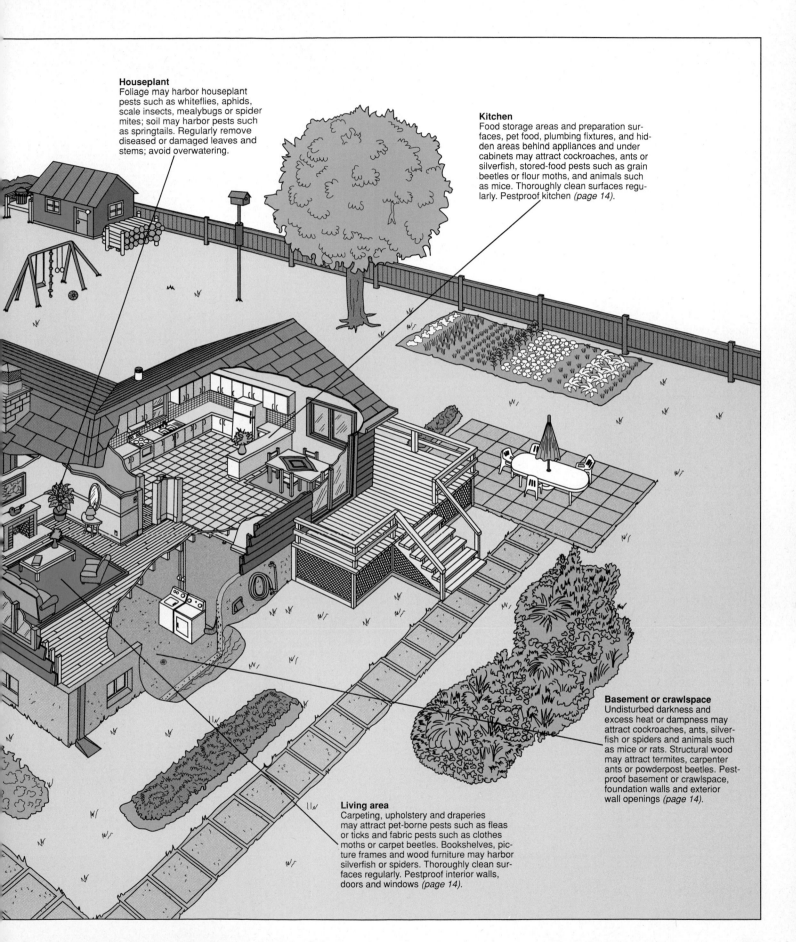

Houseplant
Foliage may harbor houseplant pests such as whiteflies, aphids, scale insects, mealybugs or spider mites; soil may harbor pests such as springtails. Regularly remove diseased or damaged leaves and stems; avoid overwatering.

Kitchen
Food storage areas and preparation surfaces, pet food, plumbing fixtures, and hidden areas behind appliances and under cabinets may attract cockroaches, ants or silverfish, stored-food pests such as grain beetles or flour moths, and animals such as mice. Thoroughly clean surfaces regularly. Pestproof kitchen *(page 14).*

Basement or crawlspace
Undisturbed darkness and excess heat or dampness may attract cockroaches, ants, silverfish or spiders and animals such as mice or rats. Structural wood may attract termites, carpenter ants or powderpost beetles. Pestproof basement or crawlspace, foundation walls and exterior wall openings *(page 14).*

Living area
Carpeting, upholstery and draperies may attract pet-borne pests such as fleas or ticks and fabric pests such as clothes moths or carpet beetles. Bookshelves, picture frames and wood furniture may harbor silverfish or spiders. Thoroughly clean surfaces regularly. Pestproof interior walls, doors and windows *(page 14).*

TROUBLESHOOTING GUIDE

PROBLEM	PROCEDURE
Cockroaches	Keep area clean; seal or refrigerate food and seal garbage, pestproof house *(p. 14)*
	Control cockroaches using bait stations, pesticide *(p. 42)* ▣◖ or fogger *(p. 55)* ▣◖
	Treat outdoor house perimeter *(p. 56)* ▣◖
	Consult a pest control professional
Ants	Keep area clean; seal or refrigerate food and seal garbage, pestproof house *(p. 14)*
	Control ants using bait stations or pesticide; outdoors, using boiling water or pesticide *(p. 43)* ☐◖
	Consult a pest control professional
Stored-food pests: grain beetles or weevils or flour moths	Keep area clean; avoid using shelf paper
	Control stored-food pests using pesticide *(p. 44)* ☐◖
Flies: houseflies, vinegar flies or cluster flies	Keep area clean; seal or refrigerate food and seal garbage, pestproof house *(p. 14)*
	Control flies using jar traps, pest strips, pesticide *(p. 44)* ▣◖ or fogger *(p. 55)* ▣◖
	Treat outdoor house perimeter *(p. 56)* ▣◖
Fabric pests: clothes moths or carpet beetles	Keep area clean; launder or dry-clean fabric items regularly, pestproof house *(p. 14)*
	Control fabric pests *(p. 46)* ☐○
	Consult a pest control professional
Bedbugs	Keep area and bed clean; launder or dry-clean bedding regularly
	Control bedbugs by treating infested bedroom *(p. 46)* ▣◖
	Consult a pest control professional
Silverfish or firebrats	Keep area clean, pestproof house *(p. 14)*
	Control silverfish and firebrats using jar traps, bait stations, pesticide *(p. 47)* ▣◖ or fogger *(p. 55)* ▣◖
	Treat outdoor house perimeter *(p. 56)* ▣◖
	Consult a pest control professional
Spiders	Keep area clean, pestproof house *(p. 14)*
	Control spiders *(p. 48)* ▣○
	Treat outdoor house perimeter *(p. 56)* ▣◖
Fleas or ticks	Keep area and pets clean; keep lawn trimmed and clear of debris
	Control fleas or ticks on pets *(p. 49)* ▣●
	Control fleas and ticks indoors using pesticide *(p. 50)* ▣● or fogger *(p. 55)* ▣●; outdoors using pesticide *(p. 51)* ▣●
	Consult a pest control professional
Houseplant pests: whiteflies, mealybugs, scale insects, aphids, red spider mites or springtails	Control houseplant foliage pests *(p. 51)* ☐◖
	Control houseplant soil pests *(p. 52)* ☐◖
Wood damage due to suspected wood pests: termites, carpenter ants or powderpost beetles	Identify insect damage to wood *(p. 53)*
	Consult a pest control and a building professional
Mice or rats	Keep area clean; seal or refrigerate food and seal garbage, pestproof house *(p. 14)*
	Control mice and rats using trap or poison-bait pesticide *(p. 54)* ▣○
	Consult a pest control professional
Bats	Do not capture bats; seal off area from other indoor areas, pestproof house *(p. 14)*
	Control bats by evicting them *(p. 55)* ▣○
	Consult a pest control professional
Skunks, raccoons, opossums, squirrels or snakes	Consult a pest control professional

DEGREE OF DIFFICULTY: ☐ Easy ▣ Moderate ■ Complex
ESTIMATED TIME: ○ Less than 1 hour ◖ 1 to 3 hours ● Over 3 hours

IDENTIFYING AN INDOOR PEST

PEST	CHARACTERISTICS	LOCATIONS
Cockroach	**German cockroach:** Winged, crawling insect 1/2 to 5/8 inch long *(shown)*. Light brown with two dark-brown or black streaks on back of head and long, whip-like antennae.	Nocturnal insect active in warm, moist indoor areas such as kitchen or bathroom. May crawl indoors or be carried indoors on boxes or bags. Feeds on almost any material and may contaminate food.
	American cockroach: Flying or crawling insect 1 1/2 to 2 inches long shaped like German cockroach. Red- to dark-brown with yellow band on back of head and long, whip-like antennae.	Nocturnal insect active in warm, damp areas such as outdoors near sewer or septic tank and indoors near appliance, water pipe or drain, especially in basement or crawlspace. May contaminate food.
	Brown-banded cockroach: Winged, crawling insect 1/2 to 5/8 inch long shaped like German cockroach. Dark brown with light brown stripes across body, red- or light-brown wings and long, whip-like antennae.	Nocturnal insect active in warm, dry indoor areas above floor level such as in furniture and behind pictures or clocks. May contaminate food.
	Oriental cockroach: Crawling insect 1 to 1 1/2 inches long shaped like German cockroach; also known as waterbug or palmetto bug. Dark brown to black with long, whip-like antennae; only male has wings. Slower moving than other types and emits foul odor.	Nocturnal insect active in cool, damp areas such as outdoors near sewer or septic tank and indoors near water pipe or drain, especially in basement or crawlspace; may nest in moisture-producing appliance. May contaminate food.
Ant	Crawling insect 1/16 to 1/4 inch long. Segmented body varies in color from yellow to black. Legged thorax and large, distinct head featuring elbowed antennae, large eyes and chewing mouthparts. May transmit disease.	Forms colonies outdoors in soil and rotting wood, especially in protected areas under stones, concrete or asphalt and in wall or floor voids. Adults feed on wide range of human foods, moving indoors to nest and feed when outdoor supplies low. May contaminate food.
Stored-food pest	**Beetle:** Flour beetle *(shown, top)* one of many species of beetles and weevils that infest stored food products. Adult 1/16 to 3/16 inch long ranges in color from red-brown to black; larva up to 1/4 inch long ranges in color from white to brown.	Feeds on stored food products such as flour, spices, cereal, dried fruits, nuts, candy, dry pet food and chocolate. Carried indoors in infested food products, then migrates to other stored products, leaving holes in packages and larvae and larval skins in infested food; some types leave foul odor in food.
	Moth: Angoumois grain moth *(shown, bottom)* one of many species of four-winged flour moths that infest stored food products. Adult with wingspan of 1/4 to 3/4 inch may be purple, gray, copper or cream; larva up to 1/2 inch long may be white or cream.	Feeds on stored food products such as whole grains, nuts, flour, dry pet food, dried beans and chocolate. Usually flies indoors and active in evening or in dim light, laying eggs in or near stored food products and leaving silken larval threads in infested food.
Fly	**Housefly:** Two-winged, flying insect 3/16 to 5/16 inch long *(shown, top)*. Light gray with four dark stripes on thorax and head with large, red, compound eyes ringed by gold stripe. May contaminate food.	Usually lays eggs outdoors in moist, fermenting, organic matter such as animal manure, grass clippings and garbage. Adults may fly indoors, lighting on surfaces and feeding on various materials from excrement to food waste.
	Vinegar fly: Minute flying insect up to 1/16 inch long *(shown, bottom)*; also known as fruit fly. Tan-colored with pointed, white-speckled wings held tent-like over body when at rest.	Active around decaying organic matter such as overripe or rotting fruit or vegetable and organic debris in drain, sewer or trash can. Lays eggs in organic debris on which larvae feed.
	Cluster fly: Two-winged, flying insect slightly larger than housefly. Dark gray with fine golden hair on thorax and irregular, pale gray markings on abdomen.	May fly indoors in cool weather; active in colonies that cluster in dark, quiet locations in cupboards, attics and wall voids. In warm weather, commonly seen flying sluggishly at windows.
Fabric pest	**Moth:** Clothes moth *(shown, top)* one of species of moths that infests household fabrics. Adult with wingspan of 1/2 inch may be tan, yellow or brown; larvae up to 1/2 inch long typically white with black head.	Lays eggs between fibers of household fabrics and in dust-filled crevices around house. Larvae feed on fibers of clothes, carpets, upholstery, draperies and linens; prefer to feed on animal fibers such as fur and wool, but also feed on soiled synthetic fibers.
	Beetle: Carpet beetle *(shown, bottom)* one of species of beetles that infests household fabrics. Adult up to 3/16 inch long ranges in color from black to mottled yellow and brown; larvae 1/4 to 1/2 inch long usually brown and bristly-haired.	Lays eggs between fibers of household fabrics. Larvae feed on fibers of clothes, carpets, upholstery, draperies and linens; prefer to feed on animal fibers such as fur, wool, silk, feathers, horn and tortoise shell, but also feed on plant fibers such as cotton and jute or soiled synthetic fibers.

IDENTIFYING AN INDOOR PEST (continued)

PEST	CHARACTERISTICS	LOCATIONS
Bedbug	Flat, oval-shaped, red-brown insect 3/16 inch long; enlarges and may change color when feeding on blood of victim. Bite leaves red, swollen, itchy patch on skin and may cause allergic reaction in some victims.	Nocturnal; may hide in mattress or in nearby wood cracks during day. Also found behind baseboards and pictures as well as in furniture.
Silverfish	Crawling, carrot-shaped insect 1/2 inch long; firebrat relative similar. Ranges in color from white to silver-gray, mottled gray and brown with two long antennae and three posterior, tail-like appendages.	Active in cool, damp areas such as near water pipe in basement or crawlspace; firebrat active in warm, moist areas near appliance, furnace or hot water pipe. Feeds on starches such as bookbinding and wallpaper glue, fabric, paper and grain.
Spider	Eight-legged, crawling pest up to 3/4 inch long ranging in color from gray to brown; two-part body with mottled abdomen. Bite poisonous to insect prey; may cause allergic reaction in human victim, but usually harmless. Brown Recluse Spider or Black Widow Spider *(page 62)* may be dangerous.	Usually crawls indoors from outdoors. Active in dark, damp areas, spinning web in hidden locations and corners, especially in basement or crawlspace. Presence of large numbers indicates presence of insects on which they can feed.
Flea	Wingless, narrow-bodied, black or brown insect 1/8 inch long. Well-developed hind legs permit vertical jump of 4 or more inches. Bite produces itchy, red swelling on pet or human victim; may transmit disease.	Found outdoors cocooned; usually carried indoors after lighting on host pet. Lays eggs on pet that may be spread indoors when pet scratches. Larvae feed on organic matter such as dried blood, feces, hair and lint.
Tick	Adult 1/8 to 3/16 inch long and red-brown in color. Back of some types has white markings; Lone Star Tick has silver spot. Larva 1/32 inch long. Enlarges and may change color when feeding on blood of victim; may transmit Lyme Disease or Rocky Mountain Spotted Fever.	Found outdoors in long grass; usually carried indoors after attaching to face, ear, neck, shoulder or toe of pet. Lays eggs indoors in cracks and crevices, often above floor level. Larvae seek out skin of pets and humans for feeding.
Houseplant pest	**Whitefly:** Moth-like, flying insect 1/20 inch long *(shown)*; white in color. Sucks sap from leaves of houseplant and secretes sticky "honeydew;" causes speckled or mottled leaves.	Adults active in colonies on underside of houseplant leaves; hover around leaves and rise in cloud if leaves disturbed. Larvae appear as green scale on underside of leaves.
	Mealybug: Waxy, oval-shaped insect 1/6 to 1/4 inch long; white in color. Sucks sap from leaves of houseplant and secretes sticky "honeydew;" stunts plant growth and causes leaves to wither and yellow.	Appear in colonies on underside of houseplant leaves and on inner stems or twigs; some types burrow into soil and infest roots. Some types lay eggs in cottony sacs; other types produce live young.
	Scale insect: Scaly, oval-shaped insect 1/8 to 1/4 inch long; may be white, red, brown or black. Sucks sap from leaves of houseplant and secretes sticky "honeydew;" stunts plant growth and causes leaves to curl and wrinkle.	Adults immobile and appear as clusters of cottony or glossy lumps or bumps on houseplant leaves and stems.
	Aphid: Winged, waxy or wooly insect 1/8 inch long; may be green, red, brown, purple, yellow or black. Sucks sap from leaves of houseplant and secretes sticky "honeydew;" stunts plant growth and causes leaves to yellow.	Adults active in rapidly growing colonies on houseplant leaves, stems and buds. Some types lay eggs; other types produce live young.
	Red spider mite: Eight-legged, red-brown mite 1/60 inch long; most common of several species of mites that infest houseplants. Sucks sap from leaves of houseplant; stunts plant growth and causes leaves to yellow or brown.	Active in hot, dry conditions and multiplies rapidly, often leaving fine, dusty webbing on underside of houseplant leaves. Can be detected using magnifying glass.
	Springtail: Globular insect 1/8 inch long; may be white, gray or blue. Feeds and lays eggs on decaying organic matter such as fallen leaves and soil at base of houseplant; may also feed on young leaves.	Active in soil at base of houseplant and in water of saucer under houseplant. May be seen crawling on or jumping off soil when disturbed.

CHOOSING A PEST CONTROL PRODUCT

PEST	PESTICIDE OR BAIT
Cockroach (includes American, brown-banded, German and Oriental types)	Kill directly using aerosol pesticide containing cyfluthrin. Treat infested area using bait station containing avermectin, chlorpyrifos, hydramethylnon, propoxur, sulfluramid or tetramethrin; using pesticide dust containing bendiocarb, boric acid or silica gel; using liquid pesticide containing cyfluthrin, cypermethrin, diazinon, fenoxycarb, fenvalerate, hydroprene, permethrin, propoxur or pyrethrins; or, using fogger containing pyrethrins. Treat outdoor house perimeter using pesticide containing carbaryl, chlorpyrifos, diazinon, malathion or propoxur.
Ant	Kill directly using pesticide containing boric acid, cyfluthrin, cypermethrin, diatomaceous earth, fenvalerate, permethrin or pyrethrins. Treat infested area using bait station containing hydramethylnon, methoprene or sulfluramid; or, using pesticide containing boric acid, cyfluthrin, cypermethrin, diatomaceous earth, fenvalerate, permethrin or pyrethrins. Treat outdoor house perimeter or destroy nest using pesticide containing acephate, bendiocarb, carbaryl, chlorpyrifos, cypermethrin, diazinon, fenvalerate, malathion, permethrin or propoxur.
Stored-food pest (includes flour beetle and grain moth)	Kill directly using aerosol pesticide containing pyrethrins. Treat infested area using pesticide containing allethrin, bendiocarb, chlorpyrifos, diazinon, fenvalerate, malathion, propoxur or pyrethrins.
Fly (includes housefly, vinegar fly and cluster fly)	Kill directly using pesticide containing pyrethrins, resmethrin or tetramethrin. Treat infested area using pesticide containing pyrethrins, resmethrin or tetramethrin; using pest strip containing dichlorvos; or, using fogger containing pyrethrins. Treat outdoor house perimeter using pesticide containing chlorpyrifos, diazinon or malathion.
Fabric pest (includes clothes moth and carpet beetle)	Kill directly using aerosol pesticide containing pyrethrins. Treat infested area using pesticide containing bendiocarb, chlorpyrifos, diazinon, malathion, permethrin, propoxur or pyrethrins; for infested item, use non-staining type recommended for it.
Bedbug	Treat infested area using pesticide dust containing boric acid, diatomaceous earth or silica gel; or, using liquid pesticide containing bioallethrin, malathion or pyrethrins; for infested bed frame or box spring, use type recommended for it.
Silverfish or firebrat	Kill directly using pesticide containing cyfluthrin, pyrethrins or tetramethrin. Treat infested area using bait station containing chlorpyrifos, hydramethylnon or propoxur; using pesticide dust containing bendiocarb, boric acid or silica gel; using liquid pesticide containing cyfluthrin, cypermethrin, diazinon, fenoxycarb, fenvalerate, hydroprene, permethrin, propoxur or pyrethrins; or, using fogger containing pyrethrins. Treat outdoor house perimeter using pesticide containing carbaryl, chlorpyrifos, diazinon, malathion or propoxur.
Spider	Kill directly using aerosol pesticide containing pyrethrins. Treat outdoor house perimeter using pesticide containing bendiocarb, chlorpyrifos, diazinon, fenvalerate, malathion, propetamphos or propoxur.
Flea	Treat infested pet using pesticidal shampoo, dip, spray or powder containing, carbaryl, d-limonene, pyrethrins or resmethrin. Treat infested area using pesticide containing, fenoxycarb, methoprene or pyrethrins; or, using fogger containing pyrethrins; for pet bedding, use pesticide containing carbaryl, malathion, methoprene or pyrethrins. Treat outdoor house perimeter using pesticide containing bendiocarb, carbaryl, chlorpyrifos, diatomaceous earth, diazinon, malathion, propoxur or pyrethrins with silica aerogel.
Tick	Treat infested pet using pesticidal shampoo, dip, spray or powder containing, carbaryl, d-limonene, pyrethrins or resmethrin. Treat infested area using pesticide containing chlorpyrifos, cyfluthrin, cypermethrin, diazinon, fenvalerate, malathion, permethrin, propoxur or pyrethrins; or, using fogger containing pyrethrins. Treat outdoor house perimeter using pesticide containing carbaryl, chlorpyrifos, diazinon, malathion or propoxur.
Houseplant pest (includes whitefly, mealybug, scale insect, aphid, spider mite and springtail)	Treat mildly infested leaves and stems using insecticidal soap concentrate containing potassium salts of fatty acids, following manufacturer's instructions to mix it; or, using mixture of 2 1/2 ounces of non-detergent household soap per gallon of water. Treat heavily infested leaves and stems using pesticide containing malathion, pyrethrins or resmethrin. Treat infested soil using pesticide or pesticide stick containing disulfoton.
Mouse	To bait live trap or snap trap, use lure such as nutmeat, chocolate, dried fruit, bacon, marshmallow or peanut butter. To poison-bait, use pesticide containing brodifacoum, bromadiolone, chlorophacinone, cholecalciferol or diphacinone.
Rat	To bait snap trap, use lure such as hot dog, bacon, nutmeat, marshmallow or peanut butter. To poison-bait, use pesticide containing brodifacoum, bromadiolone, bromethalin, chlorophacinone, cholecalciferol or diphacinone.

Choosing a pesticide or bait. To choose a type of pest control product appropriate for a pest, use the chart above for examples of the active ingredient required; a range of products is usually available at a pest control center, garden center or home center. Carefully check the label of a pest control product to ensure that it is recommended for indoor use on the pest you are trying to control and the surfaces to which you are applying it. Always start by choosing the least toxic pesticide available, changing to a more toxic pesticide only if necessary. When choosing a form of pesticide—aerosol, liquid, wettable powder or dust—ensure that you have on hand and know how to set up and use any application tool needed *(page 116)*. Prepare to work safely with the pesticide *(page 98)*, following the manufacturer's instructions to mix it, prepare the work area and choose the safety gear necessary for the job. After a pest control job, safely store or dispose of any leftover pesticide.

CONTROLLING COCKROACHES

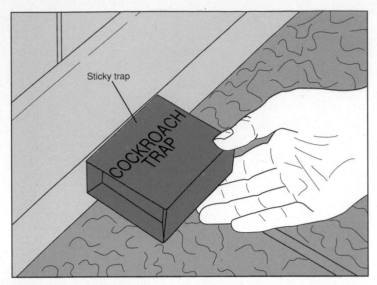

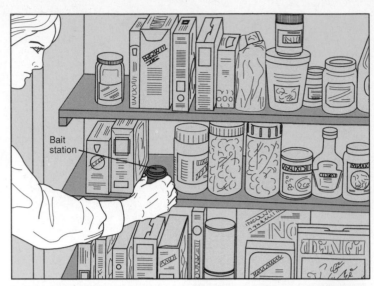

Identifying infested areas. To identify cockroach-infested areas, buy sticky traps at a home center and follow the manufacturer's instructions to use them. The type shown is a cardboard sheet that folds into a box with a sticky interior. Place traps where cockroaches are sighted or may be active—for example, in the kitchen, bathroom and basement, under and behind appliances, furniture and plumbing fixtures, near garbage cans, on counters, in cabinets and closets, and at wall edges *(above)*. Check the traps daily and treat an infested area using bait stations *(step right)* or a pesticide *(steps below)*.

Using bait stations. To control cockroaches in an infested area, buy bait stations *(page 41)* and follow the manufacturer's instructions to use them. To set up a bait station of the type shown, peel off its removable cover. Place the bait stations at the desired locations, positioning them at the intervals specified along the perimeter of the infested area—under and behind appliances, furniture and plumbing fixtures, near garbage cans, on counters, in cabinets *(above)* and closets, and at wall edges. Replace the bait stations as recommended.

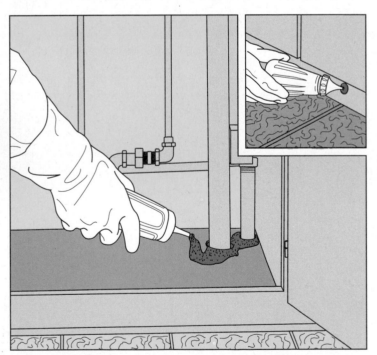

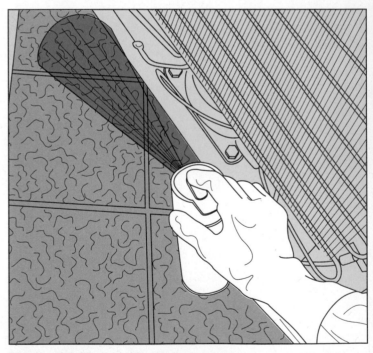

Using a pesticide dust. To control cockroaches in a dry infested area other than a countertop or food storage area, choose a pesticide dust *(page 41)*; if necessary, also an application tool *(page 116)*. Prepare to work safely with the pesticide *(page 98)*, then follow the manufacturer's instructions to apply it along the perimeter of the infested area—under and behind appliances, furniture and plumbing fixtures, near garbage cans, in cabinets and closets, and at wall edges. For the product shown, squeeze a light coating on the surface *(above)* and into any crack. For a heavy infestation, also gain access to any hidden area *(page 56)* such as the void under a cabinet to treat it *(inset)*.

Using a liquid pesticide. To control cockroaches in an infested area, choose a liquid pesticide *(page 41)*; if necessary, also an application tool *(page 116)*. Prepare to work safely with the pesticide *(page 98)*, then follow the manufacturer's instructions to apply it along the perimeter of the infested area—under and behind appliances, furniture and plumbing fixtures, near garbage cans, in cabinets and closets, and at wall edges. For the aerosol product shown, hold the container 12 inches from the surface and spray a light coating on it and into any crack. For a heavy infestation, also gain access to any hidden area *(page 56)* to treat it *(above)*.

CONTROLLING ANTS

Bait
station

Using bait stations. To control ants in an infested area, observe them to identify their entry points. Treat the entry points of the infested area using a pesticide *(step below, left)* or bait stations. Buy bait stations *(page 41)* and follow the manufacturer's instructions to use them. To set up a bait station of the type shown, use an awl to punch out the knockout holes in the side of it. Place the bait stations at the desired locations, positioning them at the intervals specified at the entry points of the infested area—along baseboards, door thresholds *(left)* and window sills, near garbage cans, on counters, and in cabinets and closets. Replace the bait stations as recommended. Locate and treat any nest outdoors *(step below, right)*.

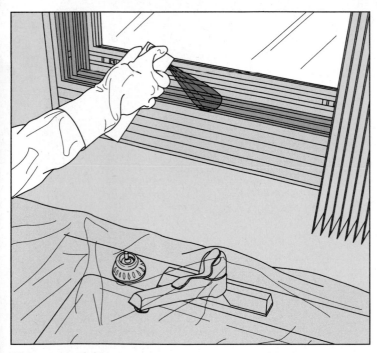

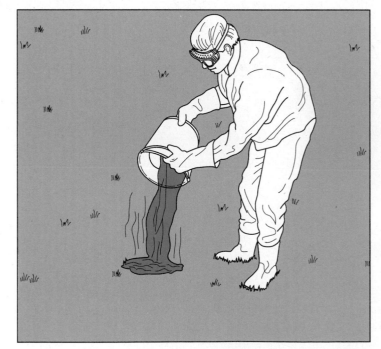

Using a pesticide. To control ants in an infested area, observe them to identify their entry points. Treat the entry points of the infested area using bait stations *(step above)* or a pesticide. Choose a pesticide *(page 41)*; if necessary, also an application tool *(page 116)*. Prepare to work safely with the pesticide *(page 98)*, then follow the manufacturer's instructions to apply it. For the aerosol product shown, spray it at the entry points of the infested area—along baseboards, door thresholds and window sills *(above)*, near garbage cans, in cabinets and closets, and at wall edges. Locate and treat any nest outdoors *(step right)*.

Treating an outdoor nest. Before resorting to a pesticide, try using boiling water to destroy the nest of the ants. Work on a warm, dry morning. Wearing safety goggles, rubber gloves and rubber boots, fill a metal bucket with 1 gallon of boiling water, then carefully pour it on the nest *(above)*. Watch the nest for several days; if it remains active, repeat the treatment daily until it is no longer active. If you cannot control the ants using boiling water, choose a pesticide *(page 41)*; if necessary, also an application tool *(page 116)*. Prepare to work safely with the pesticide *(page 98)*, then follow the manufacturer's instructions to apply it.

CONTROLLING STORED-FOOD PESTS

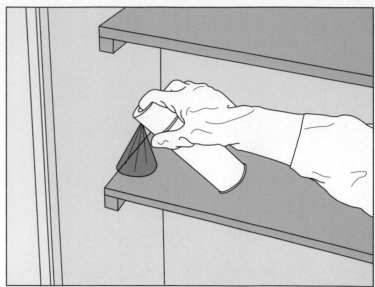

Using a pesticide. Inspect the stored foods in each storage area. Seal any infested product in a heavy-duty plastic garbage bag and dispose of it in an outdoor trash can. Transfer uninfested loose, boxed or bagged products into tightly sealed containers. Empty each storage area and vacuum it thoroughly, then vacuum the entire room, paying close attention to cracks and crevices where food particles may accumulate. Wash the surfaces of each storage area thoroughly using hot, soapy water *(above, left)*. Watch each storage area for several days; if pests remain active in a storage area, treat it using a pesticide. Choose a pesticide *(page 41)*; if necessary, also an application tool *(page 116)*. Prepare to work safely with the pesticide *(page 98)*, following the manufacturer's instructions to apply it. For the aerosol product shown, hold the container in turn near each surface and spray a light coating on it *(above, right)* and into any crack. For a heavy infestation, also gain access to any hidden area *(page 56)* to treat it. Check stored foods periodically for reinfestation.

CONTROLLING FLIES

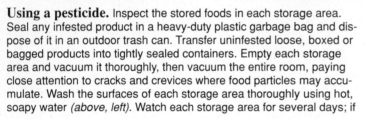
Flyswatter

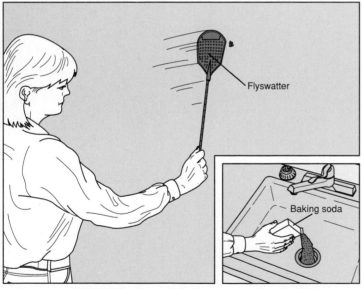
Baking soda

Jar trap

Preventing infestations. Use preventive measures to avoid a fly infestation. Store food in sealed containers or in the refrigerator. Seal indoor trash cans tightly and empty them regularly. Wash and dry food preparation surfaces after each use. Scrub each house drain clean once a week, then pour 1/2 cup of baking soda *(inset)* and 1/2 cup of white vinegar down it. Plug the drain and let any fizzing stop, then unplug it and pour boiling water down it. Swat any fly on a surface using a plastic mesh flyswatter *(above)*, then wash the surface and the flyswatter with hot, soapy water. If necessary, control flies using jar traps *(step right)*, pest strips or a pesticide *(page 45)*.

Using a jar trap. To control flies in an area, set up homemade jar traps. For vinegar flies, pour 1/2 inch of wine into a long-necked bottle. For other flies, pour 1/2 inch of a mixture of 1 part molasses, 3 parts water and a little brewer's yeast into a wide-mouthed jar; fit an open-bottom paper cone into the mouth of the jar and tape it in place above the mixture. Place the jar traps at desired locations close to where the flies are commonly seen—in a sunny spot on a window sill *(above)*, for example. Check each jar trap daily; pour water into it to drown any trapped flies, then dispose of the contents. Set up new jar traps as necessary using the same procedure.

CONTROLLING FLIES (continued)

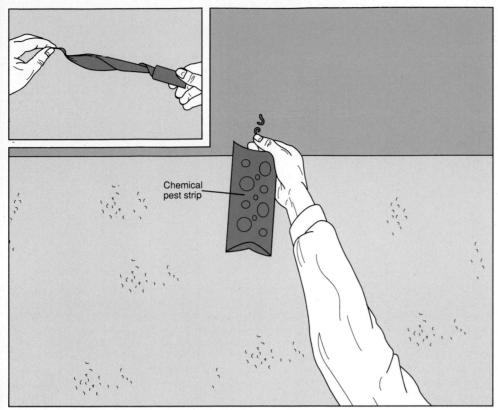

Chemical pest strip

Using pest strips. To control flies in an area, use pest strips. For a living area, choose flypaper pest strips; for a storage area, basement, garage or attic, choose chemical pest strips *(page 41)*. Follow the manufacturer's instructions to set up the pest strips, hanging them from the ceiling of the area away from any food—if possible, near a window or door. For the flypaper pest strip shown, unravel it *(inset)*, then tape or tack it to the ceiling at the desired location. Replace flypaper pest strips when they fill with flies, wearing rubber gloves to dispose of them in an outdoor trash can. For the chemical pest strip shown, slide it into the holder, then hang the holder from a hook installed at the desired location *(left)*. Replace chemical pest strips as recommended by the manufacturer—usually every 3 months.

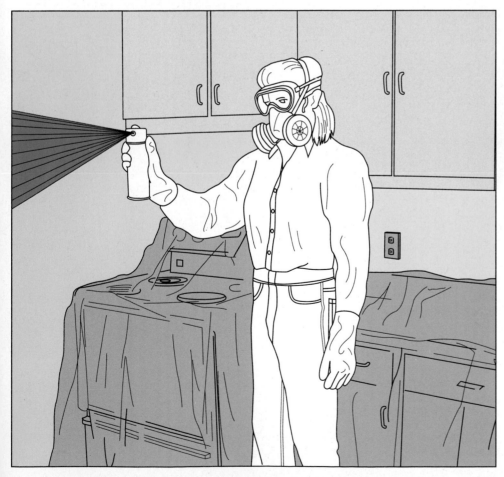

Using a liquid pesticide. To control a heavy infestation of flies in an area, choose a liquid pesticide *(page 41)*; if necessary, also an application tool *(page 116)*. Prepare to work safely with the pesticide *(page 98)*, then follow the manufacturer's instructions to thoroughly mist the air of the infested area with it. Close the doors and windows of the area, then work from one end to the other end of it. For the aerosol product shown, hold the container away from you and use a steady side-to-side motion to mist the air with short bursts of spray *(left)*. Leave the area and close the door behind you. Allow the pesticide to act for the time specified—usually 1 hour. Then, open the windows and doors of the area to ventilate it for 1 hour. Sweep or vacuum up dead or stunned flies and dispose of them in an outdoor trash can.

CONTROLLING FABRIC PESTS

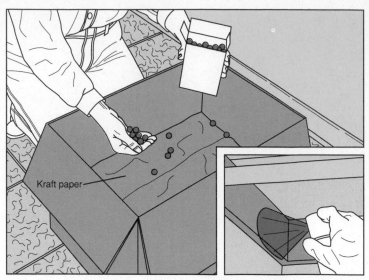

Treating carpeting, upholstery and draperies. For pest-infested carpeting, upholstery or draperies, move the item outdoors into direct sunlight. Let the item air for 6 to 8 hours and thoroughly clean the area in which it was located. Have the item professionally treated or treat it yourself using a pesticide. Choose a pesticide *(page 41)*; if necessary, also an application tool *(page 116)*. Prepare to work safely with the pesticide *(page 98)*, following the manufacturer's instructions to apply it on infested surfaces of the item. For the aerosol product shown, hold the container 6 to 12 inches from the item to spray it *(above)*; with carpeting, also spray the floor under it.

Treating clothing. For pest-infested clothing, throughly clean it and the area in which it is located. Choose a pesticide *(page 41)*; if necessary, also an application tool *(page 116)*. Prepare to work safely with the pesticide *(page 98)*, following the manufacturer's instructions to apply it on all surfaces of the area. For the aerosol product shown, hold the container 12 inches from the surface to spray it *(inset)* and into any cracks. Keep stored clothing in sealed boxes, garment bags, or airtight chests or trunks. Put clothes into a box in layers, separating each layer with sheets of kraft paper, a few mothballs *(above)* and then more sheets of kraft paper.

CONTROLLING BEDBUGS

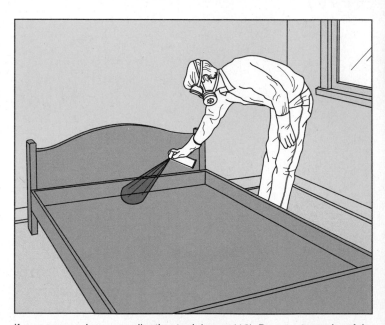

Treating an infested bedroom. For an infested bedroom, launder or dry-clean the bedclothes. Stand the mattress upright outdoors on a plastic sheet in direct sunlight *(above, left)* and let it air for 6 to 8 hours, then vacuum it thoroughly. Vacuum the bedroom thoroughly from floor to ceiling, paying close attention to door and window frames, electrical fixtures, and cracks or crevices in the walls, baseboards and floor near the bed; immediately dispose of the used vacuum cleaner bag in an outdoor trash can. To treat the bedroom, choose a pesticide *(page 41)*;

if necessary, also an application tool *(page 116)*. Prepare to work safely with the pesticide *(page 98)*, following the manufacturer's instructions to apply it—on the bed frame and box spring, the door and window frames, the electrical fixtures, and cracks or crevices in the walls, baseboards and floor near the bed. For the aerosol product shown, hold the container in turn near each surface to spray a light coating on it *(above, right)* and into any crack.

CONTROLLING SILVERFISH AND FIREBRATS

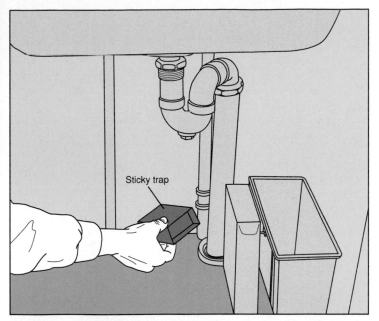

Identifying infested areas. To identify infested areas, buy sticky traps at a home center and follow the manufacturer's instructions to use them. The type shown is a cardboard sheet that folds into a box with a sticky interior. Place traps where silverfish or firebrats are sighted or may be active—for example, in the kitchen, bathroom and basement, under and behind appliances, furniture and plumbing fixtures *(above)*, near garbage cans, on counters, in cabinets and closets, and at wall edges. Check the traps daily and treat an infested area using jar traps *(step right)*, bait stations or a pesticide *(steps below)*.

Using jar traps. To control silverfish or firebrats in an infested area, set up homemade jar traps. For a jar trap, place 1 teaspoon of flour into a wide-mouthed jar, then wrap masking tape around the outside of it. Place the jar traps every few feet along the perimeter of the infested area—under and behind appliances, furniture *(above)* and plumbing fixtures, on counters, in cabinets and closets, and at wall edges. Check each jar trap daily; pour hot, soapy water into it to drown any trapped silverfish or firebrats, then dispose of the contents. Set up new jar traps as necessary using the same procedure.

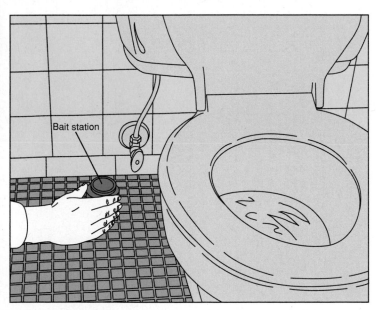

Using bait stations. To control silverfish or firebrats in an infested area, buy bait stations *(page 41)* and follow the manufacturer's instructions to use them. To set up a bait station of the type shown, peel off its removable cover. Place the bait stations at the desired locations, positioning them at the intervals specified along the perimeter of the infested area—under and behind appliances, furniture and plumbing fixtures *(above)*, in cabinets and closets, and at wall edges. Replace the bait stations as recommended.

Using a pesticide dust. To control silverfish or firebrats in a dry infested area away from food, choose a pesticide dust *(page 41)*; if necessary, also an application tool *(page 116)*. Prepare to work safely with the pesticide *(page 98)*, then follow the manufacturer's instructions to apply it along the perimeter of the infested area—under and behind appliances, furniture and plumbing fixtures, in cabinets and closets, and at wall edges. For the product shown, squeeze a light coating on the surface *(above)* and into any crack. For a heavy infestation, also gain access to any hidden area *(page 56)* such as the void behind a shoe molding to treat it *(inset)*.

CONTROLLING SILVERFISH AND FIREBRATS (continued)

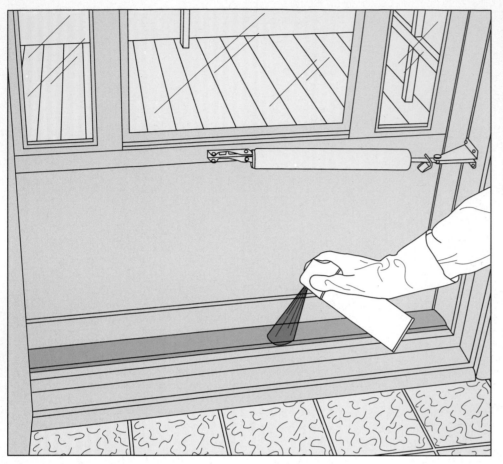

Using a liquid pesticide. To control silverfish or firebrats in an infested area, choose a liquid pesticide *(page 41)*; if necessary, also an application tool *(page 116)*. Prepare to work safely with the pesticide *(page 98)*, then follow the manufacturer's instructions to apply it along the perimeter of the infested area—under and behind appliances, furniture and plumbing fixtures, in cabinets and closets, and at wall edges. For the aerosol product shown, hold the container 12 inches from the surface and spray a light coating on it *(left)* and into any crack. For a heavy infestation, also gain access to any hidden area *(page 56)* to treat it.

CONTROLLING SPIDERS

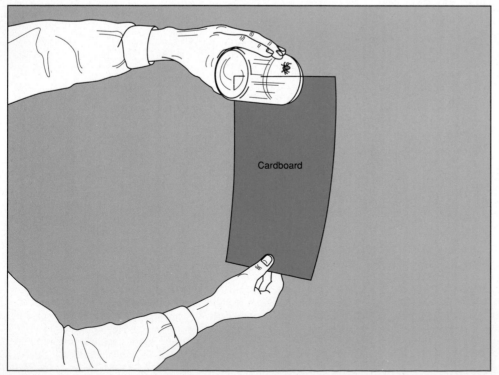

Cardboard

Removing spiders. Check the indoors to identify spider-infested areas. To control spiders in an area, sweep or vacuum it thoroughly to remove any spiders and webs—under and behind appliances, furniture, wall hangings, draperies and plumbing fixtures, in cabinets and closets, and at wall edges. To remove an occasional spider, trap it when it is at rest on a smooth surface. Place a wide-mouthed jar against the surface over the spider, then slide a thin piece of cardboard along the surface and behind the mouth of the jar to seal it *(left)*. Holding the cardboard against the mouth of the jar, carry the trapped spider outdoors to free it. Control a heavy infestation of spiders using a liquid pesticide as you would for an infestation of flies *(page 46)*.

CONTROLLING PET FLEAS AND TICKS (LIGHT INFESTATION)

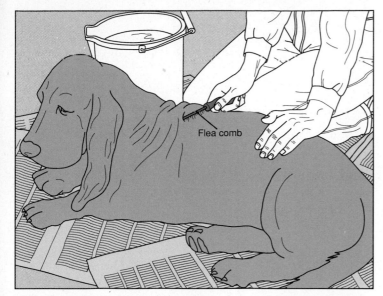

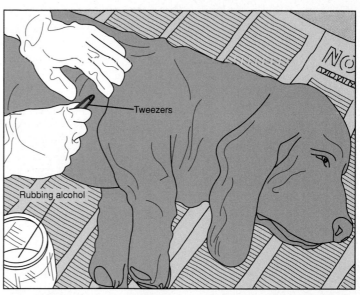

Combing out fleas. To control a light infestation of fleas, comb the fleas out of the pet's fur daily using the finest-toothed flea comb possible. Lay the pet on newspaper and have on hand a bucket of soapy water. Starting at the pet's head, insert the flea comb into the fur with its teeth touching the skin, then draw it toward the tail *(above)*. Remove the flea comb to flick caught fleas into the soapy water. Continue the same way until the pet is thoroughly combed, then wash the flea comb using soap and water.

Hand-picking ticks. To control a light infestation of ticks, hand-pick the ticks off the pet using flat-tipped tweezers. Wearing rubber gloves, lay the pet on newspaper and have on hand a jar of rubbing alcohol. Working from the pet's head to the tail, separate the fur to find ticks on the skin, especially at the head, neck, shoulders and paws. If a tick is near the eye, ear or genitals, consult a veterinarian. Otherwise, pull off the tick without crushing it *(above)*, then drop it into the rubbing alcohol. Apply antiseptic to the bite; for any infection, consult a veterinarian.

CONTROLLING PET FLEAS AND TICKS (HEAVY INFESTATION)

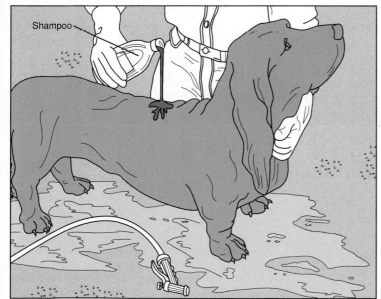

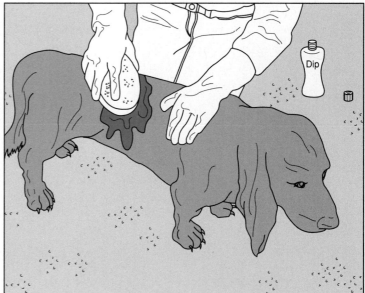

1 Using a shampoo or dip. For a heavy infestation of fleas or ticks, use a pesticidal shampoo or dip on the pet once a week; every 2 or 3 days between shampoos or dips, use a powder or spray *(step 2)*. Start treating any infested area indoors *(page 50)* or outdoors *(page 51)* the same day as the first pet treatment. Buy a pesticidal shampoo or dip for fleas or ticks *(page 41)* and work outdoors on a concrete or asphalt surface to apply it. For the shampoo product shown, wear rubber gloves to soak the pet with water from a garden hose. Working from the pet's head to the tail, pour shampoo onto the fur *(above, left)*, avoiding the eyes and nose. Rub the shampoo into the pet's fur and skin by hand, then let it sit for the time specified. Rinse the pet with water and comb the fur to remove dead fleas or ticks. For the dip product shown, follow the manufacturer's instructions to dilute it with water. Working from the pet's head to the tail, use a sponge to apply the dip to the fur *(above, right)*, avoiding the eyes and nose. Rub the dip into the pet's fur and skin by hand, then allow it to dry for the time specified. Comb the pet's fur to remove fleas or ticks.

CONTROLLING PET FLEAS AND TICKS (HEAVY INFESTATION) (continued)

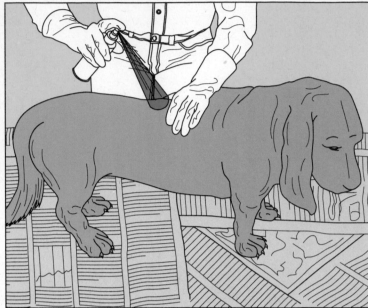

2 **Using a powder or spray.** Every 2 or 3 days between shampoos or dips *(step 1)*, use a pesticidal powder or spray on the pet. Buy a pesticidal powder or spray for fleas or ticks *(page 41)* and work outdoors on a concrete or asphalt surface to apply it. For the powder product shown, wear rubber gloves to work from the pet's head to the tail and down to the paws. Sprinkle a light coating of powder onto the pet's fur *(above, left)*, then rub it into the fur and skin by hand; avoid the eyes and nose. Allow the powder to sit for the time specified, then comb the pet's fur thoroughly to remove dead fleas or ticks. For the spray product shown, work from the pet's head to the tail and down to the paws, carefully avoiding the eyes, nose, genitals and any wound. Hold the container 6 inches from the pet and spray the fur *(above, right)* until it is damp, lifting it slightly to ensure that the spray reaches the skin. Allow the spray to dry for the time specified, then comb the pet's fur thoroughly to remove fleas or ticks.

CONTROLLING FLEAS AND TICKS INDOORS

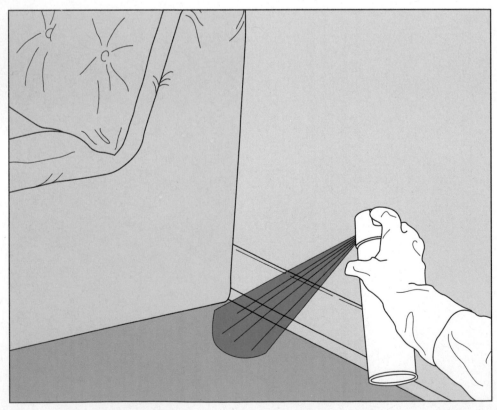

Using a pesticide indoors. To control fleas or ticks indoors, treat any area in which the pests have been sighted or may be active—for example, an area used by an infested pet. Vacuum the area thoroughly, especially any cracks in the floors, walls and baseboards. Also vacuum the carpeting and the upholstery in the area; have a heavily infested item professionally cleaned. Wash any pet bedding in hot, soapy water or heat it in a hot dryer for 10 minutes; discard any heavily infested item. Then, choose a pesticide *(page 41)*; if necessary, also an application tool *(page 116)*. Prepare to work safely with the pesticide *(page 98)*, then follow the manufacturer's instructions to apply it on vulnerable surfaces in the area—cracks and crevices in floors, walls and baseboards, carpeting, and upholstery. For the aerosol product shown, hold the container 3 feet from the surface and spray it *(left)* until it is damp. For a heavy infestation, gain access to any hidden area *(page 56)* to treat it. Let the surfaces dry, then vacuum the area again and discard the used vacuum cleaner bag in an outdoor trash can. Repeat the treatment following the manufacturer's instructions.

CONTROLLING FLEAS AND TICKS OUTDOORS

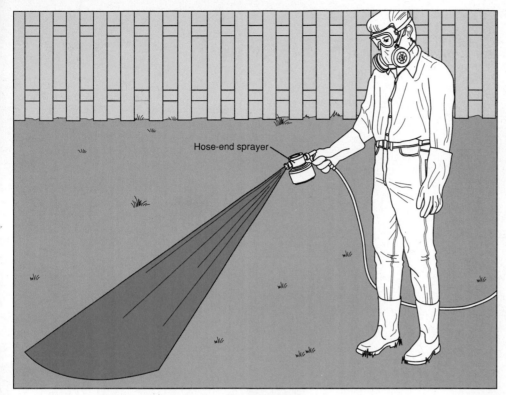

Hose-end sprayer

Using a pesticide outdoors. Prevent a pet from picking up fleas or ticks outdoors and carrying them indoors by using a pesticide to treat the lawn. Mow the lawn and trim its edges, then rake it thoroughly. Choose a pesticide *(page 41)* and an application tool *(page 116)*, then prepare to work safely with the pesticide *(page 98)*. To use a hose-end sprayer, as shown, work section by section from one end to the other end of the lawn. Walking backwards, use a steady side-to-side motion to thoroughly coat each section with pesticide *(left)*. After treating the lawn, keep off it for the time specified—usually 24 hours. To maximize the effectiveness of the treatment, mow and rake the lawn regularly. If necessary, repeat the treatment following the manufacturer's instructions; if you are dusting using diatomaceous earth, repeat the treatment every 10 days during the growing season.

CONTROLLING HOUSEPLANT FOLIAGE PESTS

Cotton swab

1 Handpicking insects. Move an infested plant away from healthy plants, then inspect it thoroughly using a magnifying glass. Remove infested leaves and stems that are damaged and dispose of them in an outdoor trash can. For a heavy infestation, use a pesticide *(step 3)*. Otherwise, handpick the insects, then use an insecticidal soap *(step 2)*. To handpick the insects, prepare a jar of a mixture of 1 teaspoon of mild detergent and 1/2 cup of rubbing alcohol per quart of water. Use your fingers or a pair of tweezers to pull off insects and drop them into the mixture; for an adhered insect, dislodge it by dabbing a little of the mixture on it using a cotton swab *(above)*.

2 Using an insecticidal soap. Buy an insecticidal soap *(page 41)* and follow the manufacturer's instructions to dilute it with water. For a plant with smooth, sturdy foliage, apply the soap solution using a soft, clean cloth. For a plant with delicate or fuzzy foliage, apply the soap solution using a spray bottle. For a plant with thick, dense foliage, immerse the foliage for 2 minutes into a sink filled with the soap solution. Pack crumpled newspaper into the pot of the plant to keep the soil from falling out, then hold the newspaper in place and invert the pot to immerse the foliage *(above)*. Let the foliage dry before exposing it to sunlight.

CONTROLLING HOUSEPLANT FOLIAGE PESTS (continued)

3 **Using a pesticide.** Choose a pesticide *(page 41)*; if necessary, also an application tool *(page 116)*. Prepare to work safely with the pesticide *(page 98)*, then follow the manufacturer's instructions to apply it. Test the pesticide first on a small section of foliage and wait 48 hours; if it is damaged, try another pesticide. To apply the spray product shown, wear rubber gloves and work from the top to the bottom of the plant. Holding the nozzle 8 to 10 inches away from the plant, spray a thorough coating of the pesticide on it *(left)*, including the underside of the leaves; avoid spraying any buds or flowers. Let the pesticide act for the time specified, keeping children and pets away from the plant. If necessary, repeat the treatment following the manufacturer's instructions.

CONTROLLING HOUSEPLANT SOIL PESTS

1 **Flushing out insects.** Move an infested plant away from healthy plants. To control insects in the soil of a plant, first try flushing them out. Fill a sink or basin with enough water to cover the pot of the plant, then immerse the pot in the water *(left)* and allow it to stand overnight; the insects should float to the surface of the water. Remove the pot and drain the sink or basin. To prevent a reinfestation, place the plant in a warm, dry location on its own saucer; avoid overwatering it by allowing the soil to dry completely between waterings. If insects remain in the soil of the plant, try flushing them out again; or, use a pesticide *(step 2)* or pesticide sticks *(step 3)*.

CONTROLLING HOUSEPLANT SOIL PESTS (continued)

Pesticide stick

2 **Using a pesticide.** Choose a pesticide *(page 41)*; if necessary, also an application tool *(page 116)*. Prepare to work safely with the pesticide *(page 98)*, then follow the manufacturer's instructions to apply it. For the pesticide product shown, set the pot of the plant in a basin or on a saucer and slowly drench the soil with it *(above)*. Let the pesticide act for the time specified, keeping children and pets away from the plant. If necessary, repeat the treatment following the manufacturer's recommendations—usually once a week until the infestation is controlled.

3 **Using pesticide sticks.** Buy pesticide sticks *(page 41)* and follow the manufacturer's instructions to use them; for the type of sticks shown, three are needed for a 6-inch pot. Wearing rubber gloves, push the sticks into the soil at intervals along the edge of the pot *(above)* until they are completely covered. Water the plant thoroughly, then let the sticks act for the time specified; keep children and pets away from the plant. If necessary, replace the sticks following the manufacturer's recommendations until the infestation is controlled.

IDENTIFYING WOOD INSECT DAMAGE

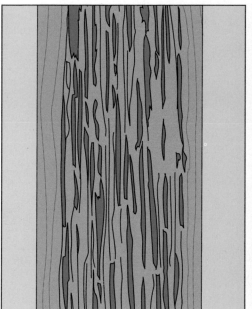

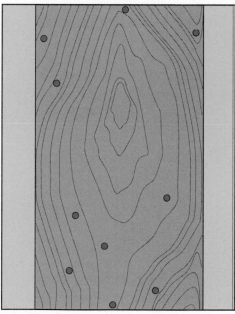

Controlling wood-eating insects. Inspect the structural wood of the house periodically for signs of insect damage. Termites burrow into and eat wood along the grain, creating dark bulges and blisters filled with tunnel-like galleries and leaving behind discarded wings and seed-like fecal pellets; subterranean termites build mud-like tubes from their underground nest up a foundation wall *(above, left)* to find wood. Carpenter ants burrowing for nests form channels in wood *(above, center)*, especially damp wood in the basement and at doors and windows; they leave piles of chewed wood resembling sawdust. Powderpost beetles bore into wood and lay eggs; the larvae feed on the wood and exit the wood as adults, leaving small round holes *(above, right)* and piles of chewed wood resembling powder. If you see termite, carpenter ant or powderpost beetle damage in any structural wood of the house, consult a pest control professional as soon as possible; also consult a building professional about repairs needed to the wood.

CONTROLLING MICE AND RATS

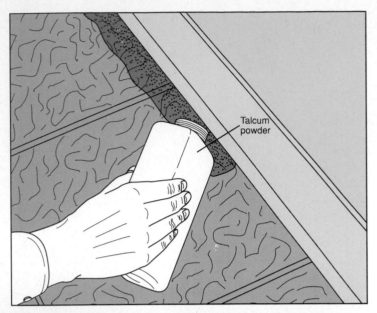

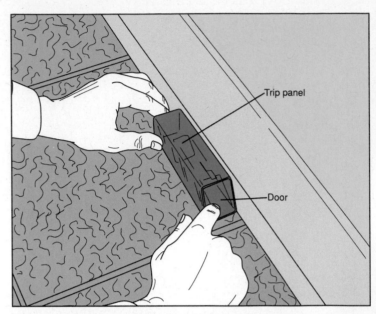

Identifying infested areas. Identify runways used by mice or rats by sprinkling talcum powder where they are sighted or may be active—for example, in the kitchen, bathroom, basement and attic, under and behind appliances, furniture and plumbing fixtures, near garbage cans, on counters, in cabinets and closets, and at wall edges *(above)*. Check the talcum powder daily for tracks that indicate a runway used by mice or rats; also look for droppings or marks on walls left by them. Treat an infested area using a snap trap or poison-bait pesticide *(steps below)*; for mice, first try using a live trap *(step right)*.

Using a live trap for mice. Set up a live trap every 10 feet along a runway used by mice. Buy live traps at a pest control center, then choose a bait *(page 41)*. To set up the type of live trap shown, push down and lock the door in the trip panel, then position the bait beyond the trip panel and place the trap at the desired location *(above)*. To handle a trapped mouse, wear work gloves, carrying the trap outdoors to release the mouse in an uninhabited area or to submerge the trap in water and drown the mouse. Dispose of a used trap and any carcass in a heavy-duty plastic garbage bag in an outdoor trash can.

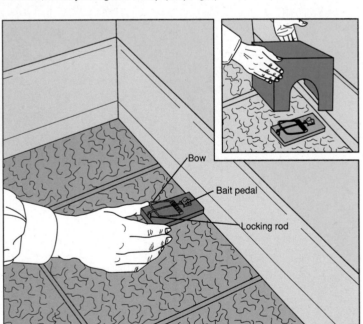

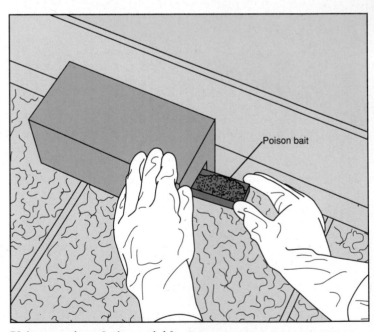

Using a snap trap. Set up a snap trap every 10 feet along a runway used by mice or rats. Buy snap traps at a pest control center, then choose a bait *(page 41)*. To set up the type of snap trap shown, position the bait on the bait pedal, then draw back the bow and secure the locking rod over it. Holding the trap carefully by the outer edges of the unbaited end, place it at the desired location—perpendicular to a wall with the baited end against it *(above)*. To keep children and pets away from the set trap, cover it using a cardboard box with a hole cut in each end *(inset)*. Dispose of a used trap and carcass in a heavy-duty plastic garbage bag in an outdoor trash can.

Using a poison-bait pesticide. Set up a poison-bait station every 10 feet along a runway used by mice or rats. Choose a poison-bait pesticide *(page 41)* and prepare to work safely with it *(page 98)*, then follow the manufacturer's instructions to use it. For the product shown, wear rubber gloves to sprinkle it into a shallow, cardboard container such as a matchbox, then place the container at the desired location and cover it using a cardboard box with a hole cut in each end *(above)*. Keep children and pets away from the poison-bait pesticide. Dispose of used poison-bait pesticide and any carcass in a heavy-duty plastic garbage bag in an outdoor trash can.

CONTROLLING BATS

Duct tape

Evicting bats. Before evicting bats from an area such as the attic, ensure that any young bats can fly; if necessary, consult your local county extension service or animal control agency for advice. To evict bats, make the area as inhospitable as possible by increasing its ventilation and lighting it continuously. Then, observe the bats at dusk for several days to identify the openings through which they enter and exit—usually marked with droppings or body-oil smudges. Pestproof all but the most heavily-used opening *(page 14)*, then install a one-way net over it to permit the bats to exit but not re-enter. Buy a piece of bird netting at a garden center and fit it over the opening, using duct tape to secure three sides of it *(left)* and leaving one side as an exit. After the bats leave, remove the net and pestproof the opening. To remove any bat droppings, wear a respirator to scrape them up and dispose of them in a heavy-duty plastic garbage bag in an outdoor trash can. Wash the area thoroughly using hot, soapy water.

FOGGING AN INFESTED AREA

Fogger

Using a fogger. Treat a pest-infested area using a pesticide fogger. Choose a pesticide fogger recommended for use on the pests *(page 41)* and prepare to work safely with it *(page 98)*, then follow the manufacturer's instructions to apply it. To prepare the area for fogging, remove food, plants and pets; cover any fish tank. If specified by the manufacturer, cover any electronic equipment and deactivate any smoke detector. Open drawers, cupboards and closets. Close the windows and doors of the area. To use the fogger shown, set it in the center of the area on a pile of newspapers on a surface covered with a plastic sheet. With the nozzle of the fogger aimed away from you, activate the fogger by removing the protective tab and locking down the activator button *(left)*. Leave the area and close the door behind you. Allow the fogger to act for the time specified, then open the windows and doors to ventilate the area for 1 hour. Sweep up dead or stunned pests and dispose of them in an outdoor trash can.

CREATING A PEST BARRIER OUTDOORS

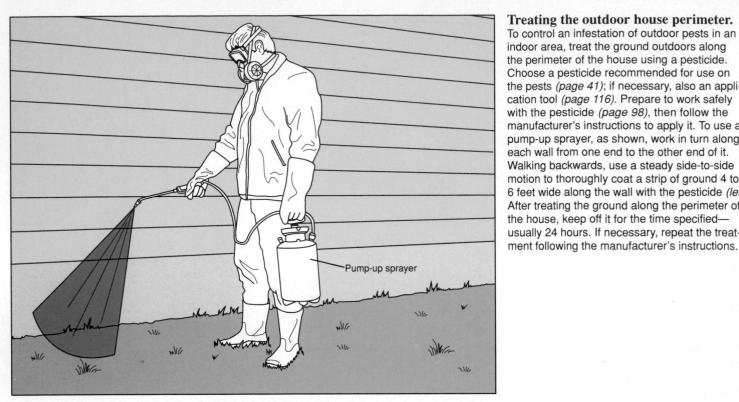

Treating the outdoor house perimeter.
To control an infestation of outdoor pests in an indoor area, treat the ground outdoors along the perimeter of the house using a pesticide. Choose a pesticide recommended for use on the pests *(page 41)*; if necessary, also an application tool *(page 116)*. Prepare to work safely with the pesticide *(page 98)*, then follow the manufacturer's instructions to apply it. To use a pump-up sprayer, as shown, work in turn along each wall from one end to the other end of it. Walking backwards, use a steady side-to-side motion to thoroughly coat a strip of ground 4 to 6 feet wide along the wall with the pesticide *(left)*. After treating the ground along the perimeter of the house, keep off it for the time specified—usually 24 hours. If necessary, repeat the treatment following the manufacturer's instructions.

Pump-up sprayer

GAINING ACCESS TO HIDDEN AREAS

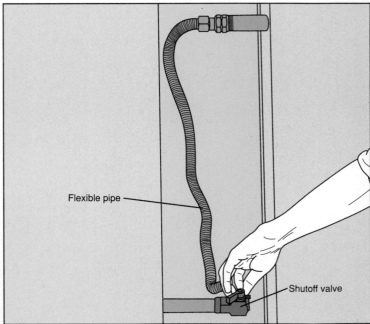

Flexible pipe

Shutoff valve

Gaining access behind an appliance. To treat an area behind an appliance, move the appliance just enough for you to reach comfortably behind it; if necessary, work with a helper. To move an electrical appliance, unplug it, then grasp it firmly and pull it out from the wall *(above, left)*. For an appliance such as a gas range with a supply line of only rigid pipe, have a professional move it or try gaining access behind it by removing the storage or broiler drawer. For a gas appliance with a supply line of rigid pipe connected to flexible pipe, shut off the gas supply by turning the handle of the shutoff valve perpendicular to the rigid pipe *(above, right)*, then grasp the appliance firmly and pull it out from the wall. Vacuum the area behind the appliance and wash the exposed surfaces of the wall, floor and appliance. After treating the area, push the appliance back into place. Plug in an electrical appliance; for a gas appliance, restore the gas supply by turning the handle of the shutoff valve parallel to the rigid pipe, then relight each pilot.

GAINING ACCESS TO HIDDEN AREAS (continued)

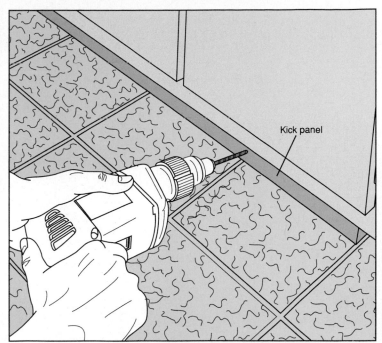

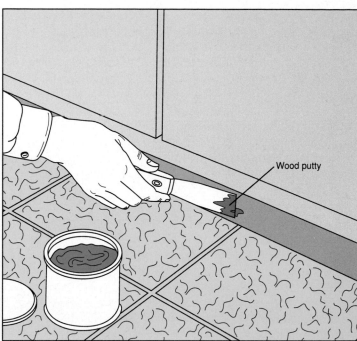

Gaining access under a cabinet. To treat the void area under a typical kitchen or bathroom cabinet, inspect the kick panel covering it. If there are no holes in the kick panel through which the void area behind it can be treated, wear safety goggles and use an electric drill to bore holes large enough for the nozzle of the application tool you plan to use every 6 inches along it *(above, left)*. After treating the void area behind the kick panel, seal the holes with wood putty. Using a flexible putty knife, work the wood putty into each hole, overfilling it slightly; then, scrape off the excess *(above, right)*. Let the wood putty dry, then smooth it using fine sandpaper and brush away sanding particles. Touch up the finish of the surface, first applying any sealer or primer recommended by the finish manufacturer.

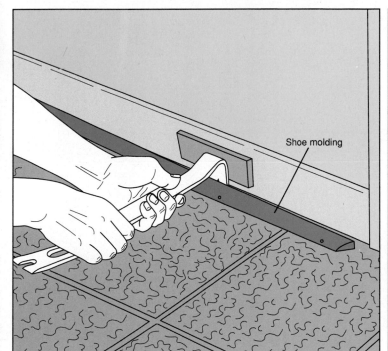

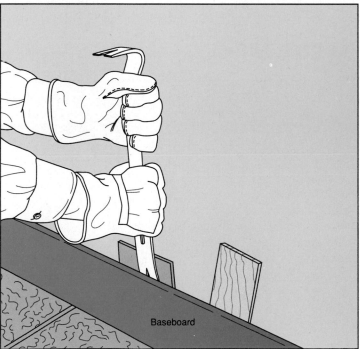

Gaining access behind a shoe molding or baseboard. To treat the void area behind a shoe molding or baseboard, remove them. To remove a shoe molding, run a utility knife along the joint between it and the baseboard to break any paint bond. Work the blade of a wide putty knife behind the shoe molding as far down as possible at one end of it and gently pry it out enough to fit in the end of a pry bar. Protecting the baseboard with a wood block, work the pry bar along the shoe molding, pulling it out slightly at each nail *(above, left)* and gradually widening the gap between it and the baseboard until it is removed. To remove a baseboard, follow the same procedure, inserting wood shims between it and the wall as you work the pry bar along it *(above, right)*. After treating the void area behind a shoe molding or baseboard, reinstall the pieces you removed; if they are damaged, replace them.

OUTDOOR PESTS

Your outdoor living area beautifies your home and provides a comfortable site for family recreation and relaxation, but it is also vulnerable to pests that can destroy its beauty and make life miserable for anyone who ventures outdoors. While some pests such as honey bees and spiders are actually beneficial insects that should only be controlled if there is a serious infestation, other pests require immediate control. Fire ants, wasps, ticks and chiggers may nest in the lawn, damaging it as well as creating bite and sting hazards for anyone working or playing on it. Birds and squirrels may nest and feed around walls and eaves, leaving unsightly droppings and creating unwanted noise. Skunks, raccoons and opossums may raid garbage cans and gardens.

A typical outdoor living area with its pest troublespots is shown at right. Fortunately, discouraging pests from taking up residence on your property is rarely difficult. You can destroy insect breeding, feeding and harborage areas by keeping the lawn, trees, hedges, shrubs and gardens healthy, well-trimmed and clear of debris. Store trash cans tightly sealed on a stand away from the house. Pile wood tidily off the ground. Recreation areas, in particular, should be kept scrupulously clean.

If careful maintenance does not eliminate a troublesome outdoor pest problem, use the Troubleshooting Guide *(page 60)* to help choose an appropriate pest control method, then refer to the pages indicated to undertake the pest control job. To identify an unknown pest, consult the chart on page 61 for descriptions of common outdoor pests and their typical locations; if you cannot identify a pest, consult your local county extension agent or a pest control professional for help. In general, first try controlling a pest using the least harsh, most environmentally safe method—for example, a repellent or a trap, if one is available. If a repellent or a trap is not available for a pest or does not control it, consult the chart on page 63 to choose a pesticide.

When buying a pesticide, choose the least harmful product available that is recommended for outdoor use on the pest. To use a pesticide, carefully follow the manufacturer's instructions to mix and apply it, and only use as much as necessary to achieve the desired level of pest control. Since complete eradication of an outdoor pest is virtually impossible, do not overuse a pesticide and risk damaging beneficial insects, animals and plants; if necessary, consult a pest control professional.

While many outdoor pest control jobs require only the use of easy-to-use aerosol sprays and traps, some call for more specialized tools and materials that are readily available at a pest control or garden center. Refer to Tools & Techniques *(page 112)* for instructions on choosing, setting up and using application tools. Before starting any outdoor pest control job, read the chapter entitled Working Safely *(page 98)* for instructions on choosing the appropriate safety gear, preparing the work area, and mixing and disposing of pesticides. Familiarize yourself with the safety advice in the Emergency Guide *(page 8)*. If you doubt your ability to complete a job, do not hesitate to consult a pest control professional.

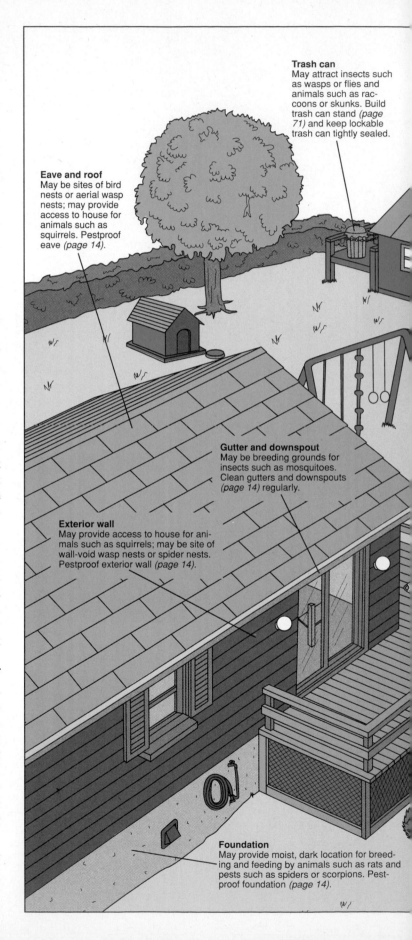

Trash can
May attract insects such as wasps or flies and animals such as raccoons or skunks. Build trash can stand *(page 71)* and keep lockable trash can tightly sealed.

Eave and roof
May be sites of bird nests or aerial wasp nests; may provide access to house for animals such as squirrels. Pestproof eave *(page 14)*.

Gutter and downspout
May be breeding grounds for insects such as mosquitoes. Clean gutters and downspouts *(page 14)* regularly.

Exterior wall
May provide access to house for animals such as squirrels; may be site of wall-void wasp nests or spider nests. Pestproof exterior wall *(page 14)*.

Foundation
May provide moist, dark location for breeding and feeding by animals such as rats and pests such as spiders or scorpions. Pestproof foundation *(page 14)*.

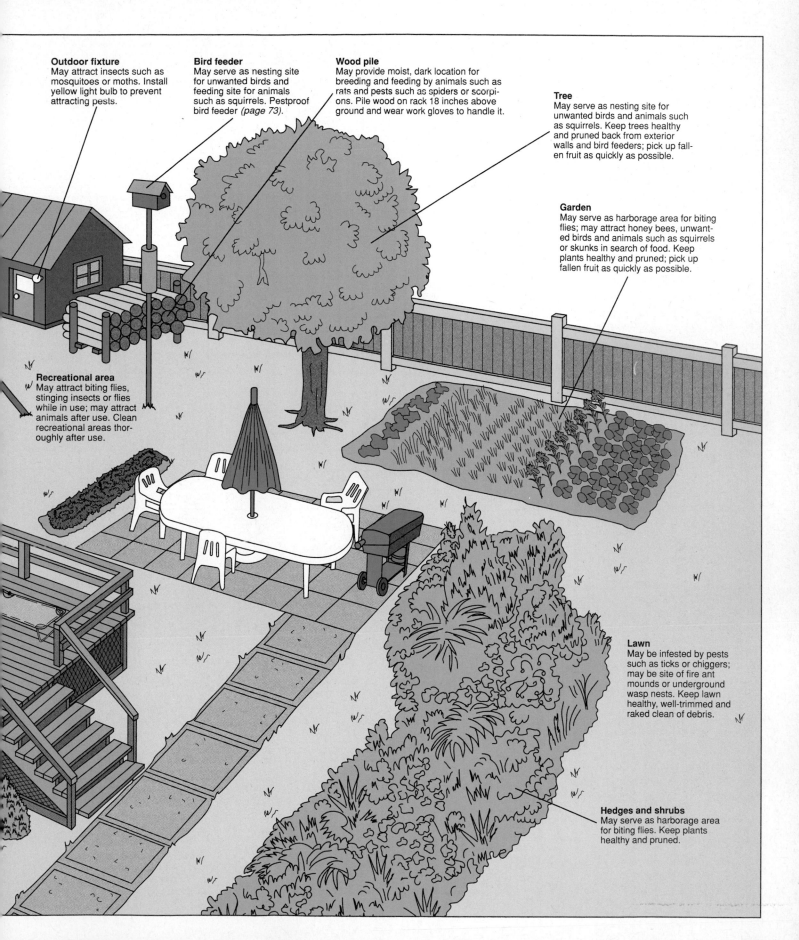

Outdoor fixture
May attract insects such as mosquitoes or moths. Install yellow light bulb to prevent attracting pests.

Bird feeder
May serve as nesting site for unwanted birds and feeding site for animals such as squirrels. Pestproof bird feeder *(page 73).*

Wood pile
May provide moist, dark location for breeding and feeding by animals such as rats and pests such as spiders or scorpions. Pile wood on rack 18 inches above ground and wear work gloves to handle it.

Tree
May serve as nesting site for unwanted birds and animals such as squirrels. Keep trees healthy and pruned back from exterior walls and bird feeders; pick up fallen fruit as quickly as possible.

Garden
May serve as harborage area for biting flies; may attract honey bees, unwanted birds and animals such as squirrels or skunks in search of food. Keep plants healthy and pruned; pick up fallen fruit as quickly as possible.

Recreational area
May attract biting flies, stinging insects or flies while in use; may attract animals after use. Clean recreational areas thoroughly after use.

Lawn
May be infested by pests such as ticks or chiggers; may be site of fire ant mounds or underground wasp nests. Keep lawn healthy, well-trimmed and raked clean of debris.

Hedges and shrubs
May serve as harborage area for biting flies. Keep plants healthy and pruned.

TROUBLESHOOTING GUIDE

PROBLEM	PROCEDURE
Biting flies: mosquitoes, blackflies or sandflies	Keep area free of standing water
	Pestproof house *(p. 14)*
	Control biting flies using repellent, smoke coil or pesticide *(p. 64)* ▱◖
Wasps: paper wasps, hornets or yellow jackets	Keep area clean; seal garbage
	Pestproof house *(p. 14)*
	Control wasps using outdoor trap or pesticide *(p. 65)* ▱○
	Consult a pest control professional
Honey bees	Prevent stings as you would for wasps *(p. 65)*
	Consult a pest control professional to control swarm or remove hive
Houseflies or blowflies	Keep area clean; seal garbage
	Control flies using outdoor trap *(p. 66)* ▱◖ or pesticide as you would for biting flies *(p. 64)* ▱◖
Common ants	Keep area clean
	Pestproof house *(p. 14)*
	Control common ants using pesticide as you would for biting flies *(p. 64)* ▱◖
Fire ants	Control fire ants using boiling water or pesticide *(p. 67)* ▱○
	Consult a pest control professional
Ticks or chiggers	Keep lawn trimmed and clear of debris
	Control ticks on pets *(p. 36)*
	Control ticks and chiggers using repellent or pesticide *(p. 68)* ▱◖
	Consult a pest control professional
Spiders	Keep area clean and free of firewood, lumber and debris
	Pestproof house *(p. 14)*
	Control spiders by removing webs or using pesticide *(p. 69)* ▱○
	Consult a pest control professional
Scorpions	Keep area clean and free of firewood, lumber and debris
	Pestproof house *(p. 14)*
	Control scorpions using pesticide *(p. 69)* ▱○
	Consult a pest control professional
Birds	Pestproof house *(p. 14)*
	Control birds by removing nests and using anti-roost material *(p. 69)* ▱○
	Consult a pest control professional
Rats	Keep area clean; protect garbage *(p. 71)* □◖
	Pestproof house *(p. 14)*
	Control rats using snap trap *(p. 70)* ▱○
	Consult a pest control professional
Skunks, raccoons, opossums or squirrels	Keep area clean; protect garbage *(p. 71)* □◖
	Protect bird feeder *(p. 73)* □○
	Install fence *(p. 72)* ▱●
	Control animals using live trap *(p. 70)* ▱○
	Consult a pest control professional
Snakes	Consult a pest control professional

DEGREE OF DIFFICULTY: □ Easy ▱ Moderate ■ Complex
ESTIMATED TIME: ○ Less than 1 hour ◖ 1 to 3 hours ● Over 3 hours

IDENTIFYING AN OUTDOOR PEST

PEST	CHARACTERISTICS	LOCATIONS
Biting fly	**Mosquito:** Slender, long-legged, two-winged biting fly 1/8 to 1/4 inch long *(shown, top)*. Scale-covered wings lie flat on back when at rest. Long, slender mouthparts used to prick skin of victim and suck blood. May transmit disease.	Lays eggs in small, stagnant bodies of water, especially in places such as rain gutters where rainwater accumulates. Adults remain in shady, sheltered harborage areas during day and feed from dusk to dawn.
	Blackfly: Stocky, humpbacked, black, two-winged biting fly 1/25 to 1/8 inch long *(shown, bottom)*; may have white band around body. Short antennae and gray, broad-based wings with narrow tips. Mouthparts used to bite viciously.	Lays eggs in active bodies of water such as streams and rivers in wooded areas. Adults appear in late spring and early summer; most active in vicinity of breeding sites, but may fly or be blown for 10 or more miles.
	Sandfly: Variably colored, biting fly 1/16 to 1/8 inch long; also known as black gnat, biting midge, punkie or "no-see-um." Easily visible only in flight when wings in motion; usually bites before detected.	Lays eggs in any wet location. Larvae live in moist soil around marshes, streams, tree holes and decaying plants. Adults active in vicinity of breeding sites.
Wasp	**Paper wasp:** Flying, stinging insect 3/4 inch long with distinct head featuring chewing mouthparts *(shown)*. Thorax and abdomen brightly marked yellow, brown or red on black. Wings clear or smoky brown. Spindle-shaped abdomen has stinger that gives painful sting when insect defends itself or its nest.	Builds open, flat, papery, layered nest with no protective envelope under eaves and in other protected locations. Adults scavenge for food such as nectar, fruit juices, soft drinks and meat, especially in mid-summer.
	Yellow jacket: Flying, stinging insect 1/2 inch long shaped like paper wasp. Thorax and abdomen brightly striped yellow and black. Wings clear or smoky brown. Spindle-shaped abdomen has stinger that gives painful sting when insect defends itself or its nest.	Builds flat, papery nest with outer, protective envelope below ground and in other protected locations. Adults scavenge for food such as fruit juices, soft drinks and meat, especially in mid-summer.
	Bald-faced hornet: Flying, stinging insect 3/4 inch long shaped like paper wasp. Thorax and abdomen brightly marked white and black. Wings clear or smoky brown. Spindle-shaped abdomen has stinger that gives painful sting when insect defends itself or its nest.	Builds flat, papery nest with outer, protective envelope on sides of buildings and in trees. Adults scavenge for food such as nectar, fruit juices, soft drinks and meat, especially in mid-summer.
Honey bee	Stocky, four-winged, flying, stinging insect 7/16 to 5/8 inch long with distinct head featuring two short antennae and large eyes. Abdomen fuzzy, yellow-brown to black; some types have barbed stinger that gives painful sting when insect defends itself or its nest.	Nests in trees, wall voids and holes in ground. Adults often seen flying between flowering plants where they feed on nectar and transport pollen that assists in plant fertilization.
Fly	**Housefly:** Two-winged, flying insect 3/16 to 5/16 inch long *(shown)*. Light gray with four dark stripes on thorax and head with large, red, compound eyes ringed by gold stripe. May transmit disease.	Lays eggs in moist, fermenting, organic matter such as animal manure, grass clippings and garbage. Adults feed on various materials from excrement to food waste.
	Blowfly: Two-winged, flying insect 5/16 to 1/2 inch long shaped like housefly. Dark metallic green; greenbottle fly metallic blue-green, bluebottle fly metallic blue. May transmit disease.	Lays eggs in animal manure, garbage and rotting vegetable matter. Larvae leave breeding site and pupate in decaying animal matter. Adults commonly seen buzzing at windows.
Ant	**Common ant:** Crawling insect 1/16 to 1/4 inch long *(shown)*. Segmented body varies in color from yellow to black. Legged thorax and large, distinct head featuring elbowed antennae, large eyes and chewing mouthparts. May transmit disease.	Forms colonies in soil and rotting wood, especially in protected locations such as under stones, concrete or asphalt and in wall or floor voids. Adults feed on wide range of human foods.
	Fire ant: Crawling insect 1/8 to 1/4 inch long shaped like common ant. Yellow to red-brown in color. More aggressive than common ant and administers painful, fiery sting with stinger on tip of abdomen.	Builds large, underground nests that form mounds often reaching 1 to 2 feet in height if left undisturbed. Adults feed on wide range of human foods; can chew through fabric and wire mesh. Common in southern United States.

IDENTIFYING AN OUTDOOR PEST (continued)

PEST	CHARACTERISTICS	LOCATIONS
Tick	**Dog tick:** Adult 1/8 to 3/16 inch long *(shown)* and red-brown in color; back of some types has white markings. Larva 1/32 inch long. Enlarges and may change color when feeding on blood of victim. May transmit Rocky Mountain Spotted Fever.	Found in long grass, cracks and crevices. Lays eggs and feeds on skin of animals such as pets, usually attaching to face, ear, neck, shoulder or toe; some types may also feed on humans.
	Deer tick: Adult 3/16 inch long shaped like dog tick and ranging in color from orange to brown or black; back of Lone Star Tick has silver spot. Larva size of grain of sand. Enlarges and may change color when feeding on blood of victim. May transmit Lyme disease.	Found in grassy areas and woodland habitats in spring and fall, and in winter on warm days. Common in northeastern and north-central United States; Lone Star Tick common in southern United States.
Chigger	Minute, red-colored mite that attaches itself to and feeds on animals and humans. Bite causes itchy, red blotch and tiny blister.	Breeds and active in lawns and in shaded areas of vegetation around house. Quickly lights on passing animals or humans. Common in southern United States.
Brown recluse spider	Bare-legged spider 1/3 to 1/2 inch long ranging in color from light to dark brown; also known as violin spider or fiddleback. Distinctive, dark, violin-shaped mark on back. Adminsters painful bite that turns into slow-healing ulcer.	Nests in hidden locations under rocks or in wood; builds irregular web for retreating to when disturbed. Active at night, feeding on insects. Common in midwestern United States; other less venomous species found in southern and eastern United States.
Black widow spider	Glossy, black spider 1/2 inch long with globe-like abdomen. Underside of abdomen has two red, triangular spots that form hourglass-shaped mark. Administers painful bite similar to wasp sting; serious, but rarely fatal.	Nests in dry, protected locations near ground level such as in wood piles and under rocks; builds irregular, tangled webs of thick strands. Feeds on insects.
Scorpion	Eight-legged, pincered relative of spider with long, flat body and stinger-tipped, curved tail. Varies in color from mustard yellow or tan to black. Administers painful, poisonous bite; bite of Sculptured Scorpion can be deadly.	Nests in stacks of lumber and firewood, in compost piles and under rocks; Sculptured Scorpion lives in trees. Feeds on insects. Many species common in southern and southwestern United States.
House sparrow	Brown bird 6 inches long. Male has black throat and upper breast, ash-gray crown, and chestnut-colored cape that runs from eyes along sides and back of neck. Female has gray-brown head and posterior, and black and red-brown streaked back. Droppings may transmit disease.	Nests in rain gutters and on rafters and ledges of buildings in elevated, protected locations. Builds nest of twigs, grass, paper and string; lays 3 to 7 eggs. Usually not found in high-altitude, heavily wooded or desert regions.
Pigeon	Bird 12 inches long that varies in color from white to tan, purple or black and emits distinct cooing sound. May carry fleas, ticks and mites that attack humans; droppings may transmit disease and mar surfaces.	Nests in any sheltered area of building, including drainpipes, vents and ledges. Builds nest of sticks, twigs, and grasses; lays 1 or 2 eggs.
Starling	Dark, humpbacked adult 8 1/2 inches long with white-speckled feathers; chick gray-colored. Droppings may transmit disease.	Nests in cavities in trees and buildings, and in bird houses. Feeds on fruit, seeds and sometimes garbage. Builds nest of various fibrous materials lined with fine grass or other soft materials; lays 4 to 7 eggs.
Cliff swallow	Dark bird 5 to 6 inches long with rust-colored throat, steel-blue crown and back, white forehead, pale orange-brown posterior and distinctive, square tail. May carry fleas and ticks that attack humans; droppings may transmit disease and mar surfaces.	Nests in eaves of buildings. Builds nest of mud typically measuring 6 inches in diameter; lays 2 to 6 eggs. Tirelessly rebuilds damaged nest.

CHOOSING A PEST CONTROL PRODUCT

PEST	PESTICIDE	REPELLENT OR BAIT
Biting fly (includes mosquito, blackfly and sandfly)	Treat harborage area using product containing allethrin, bioallethrin, malathion, phenothrin, pyrethrins or resmethrin. Treat infested area before using it with product containing pyrethrins. Treat windless infested area while using it with smoke coil containing allethrin.	Use liquid or spray repellent containing DEET. **Caution:** Do not use product containing more than 15% DEET for child less than 7 years old.
Wasp (includes paper wasp, yellow jacket and hornet)	Treat ground, wall-void or aerial nest using aerosol product containing resmethrin or using liquid or powder product containing bendiocarb, carbaryl, chlorpyrifos, diazinon, malathion, propoxur or pyrethrins.	To bait outdoor wasp trap, follow manufacturer's instructions to use lure supplied, changing it as often as specified; or, use fish, fish-flavored cat food or chicken, changing it daily.
Fly (includes housefly and blowfly)	Treat infested area using product containing carbaryl, chlorpyrifos, diazinon, propoxur or pyrethrins. Kill fly directly using aerosol product containing pyrethrins.	To bait outdoor fly trap, follow manufacturer's instructions to use lure supplied, changing it as often as specified; or, use milk, fruit or mixture of 1 part blackstrap molasses and 3 parts water, changing it daily.
Common ant	Treat infested area before using it with aerosol product containing pyrethrins.	None
Fire ant	Poison-bait mound using product containing fenoxy-carb or hydramethylnon. Drench mound using product containing acephate, bendiocarb, carbaryl, chlorpyrifos, diazinon, fenvalerate, malathion, propoxur, pyrethrins or resmethrin. Inject mound using product containing chlorpyrifos.	None
Tick or chigger	Treat infested area using product containing carbaryl, chlorpyrifos, diazinon, fenvalerate, propoxur or tetra-chlorvinphos.	Use liquid or spray containing DEET; or, for clothing only, use spray containing permethrin. **Caution:** Do not use product containing more than 15% DEET for child less than 7 years old.
Spider (includes brown recluse spider and black widow spider)	Treat infested area using product containing bendio-carb, chlorpyrifos, diazinon, fenvalerate, malathion or propoxur. Kill spider directly using aerosol product containing pyrethrins or resmethrin.	None
Scorpion	Treat infested area using product containing bendio-carb, diazinon, malathion, propoxur, pyrethrins or pyrethrins with silica gel. Kill scorpion directly using aerosol product containing pyrethrins.	None
Rat	Consult pest control professional	To bait snap trap, use lure such as peanut butter, hot dog, bacon, marshmallow or fruit.
Skunk	Consult pest control professional	To bait live trap, use lure such as sardine, fish-flavored cat food, cooked bacon, peanut butter or any food leftovers.
Raccoon	Consult pest control professional	To bait live trap, use lure such as bread coated with fruit jam, fish-flavored cat food, sweet corn or cooked bacon.
Opossum	Consult pest control professional	To bait live trap, use lure such as apple, cheese, sardine, fish-flavored cat food or cooked bacon.
Squirrel	Consult pest control professional	To bait live trap, use lure such as peanut butter, cereal, sunflower seeds or popcorn.

Choosing a pesticide, repellent or bait. To choose a type of pest control product appropriate for a pest, use the chart above for examples of the active ingredient required; a range of products is usually available at a pest control center, garden center or home center. Carefully check the label of a pest control product before buying it to ensure that it is recommended for outdoor use on the pest you are trying to control. Always start by choosing the least toxic pesticide available, changing to a more toxic pesticide only if necessary. When choosing a form of pesticide—aerosol, liquid, wettable powder or dust—ensure that you have on hand and know how to set up and use any application tool needed *(page 116)*. Prepare to work safely with the pesticide *(page 98)*, following the manufacturer's instructions to mix it, prepare the work area and choose the safety gear necessary for the job. After a pest control job, safely store or dispose of any leftover pesticide.

CONTROLLING BITING FLIES

Using a repellent. To prevent bites, cover as much of the body as possible with clothing and use a repellent *(page 63)*. Before applying the repellent, test it on a small area of the skin; if there is any irritation, use another type. Apply the repellent following the manufacturer's instructions; for a child, apply it sparingly. For a liquid repellent, pour a small amount into one hand, then rub it on the skin *(above)*, avoiding the eyes and lips. For a spray repellent, spray it directly onto the skin and clothing; for the face, spray repellent onto one hand and rub it on the skin, avoiding the eyes and lips. Reapply the repellent as needed.

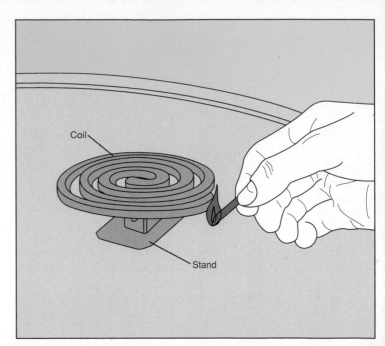

Using a smoke coil. To control a minor infestation in a windless area, buy smoke coils *(page 63)* and follow the manufacturer's instructions to use them. For the product shown, set up several smoke coils and position them 10 feet apart around the area. To set up a smoke coil, fit it onto the stand supplied. Position the smoke coil where its smoke cannot be inhaled directly, placing it on a sturdy surface away from children, pets, food and flammable material. Use a match to light the end of the smoke coil *(above)*. Set up more smoke coils as needed. Extinguish each burning smoke coil before leaving the area by cutting off the burning end of it.

Using a pesticide. To control a heavy infestation, use a pesticide to treat harborage areas such as bushes and grounds edges during the day, then use a pesticide to treat any infested area 1 hour before you use it. Choose appropriate pesticides *(page 63)*; if necessary, also application tools *(page 116)*. Prepare to work safely with the pesticides *(page 98)*, following the manufacturer's instructions to apply them. To

use a fogger on a harborage area, as shown, work when it is windless. Position the fogger up to 10 feet from the harborage area, depressing the trigger to spray it thoroughly *(above, left)*; if the fog disperses before coating the harborage area, move closer to it. To apply an aerosol product on an infested area before using it, as shown, spray the ground along each edge of it from a distance of 10 feet *(above, right)*.

CONTROLLING WASPS

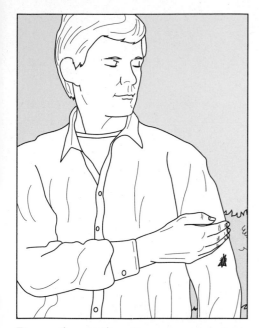

Preventing a sting. Keep wasps from lighting by staying away from any infested area. Otherwise, wear closed shoes and a hat, and cover as much of your body as possible with light-colored, unpatterned clothing; avoid using floral-scented soaps and cosmetics. If a stinging insect lights on you, do not swat it; remaining calm and still, quickly and lightly brush away the insect using the back of your hand *(above)*.

Using a trap. To control wasps outdoors, buy an outdoor wasp trap *(page 63)* and follow the manufacturer's instructions to use it. To set up the trap shown, remove the base. Wearing rubber gloves, prepare the lure by wetting a cotton ball with the attractant supplied. Place the cotton ball in the cone of the trap, then reinstall the base. To control wasps in an area, hang up the trap *(above)* beyond the reach of children and pets in a dry location at least 20 feet downwind from the area and 20 feet from any wasp nest. When wasps accumulate around the cone, ensure that they are dead, then remove the base of the trap and empty the dead wasps into a heavy-duty plastic garbage bag. Seal the bag and dispose of it in an outdoor trash can. Follow the manufacturer's instructions to replace the lure—usually every 4 to 6 weeks in the spring and every 2 weeks in the summer.

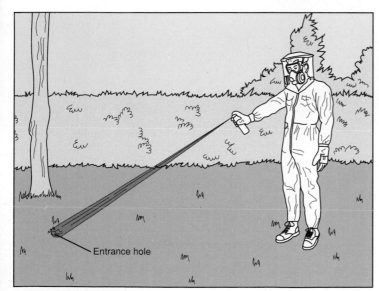

Using a pesticide to destroy a ground nest. Work at dusk when the wasps are inactive and the air is calm. Choose a pesticide *(page 63)*; if necessary, also an application tool *(page 116)*. Prepare to work safely with the pesticide *(page 98)*, wearing a bee veil and following the manufacturer's instructions to apply it. For the aerosol product shown, stand at least 6 feet from the entrance hole of the nest to spray pesticide into it *(above)*. If the wasps become active, stop spraying; remain calm and still until the activity subsides. Watch the nest for several days; if it remains active, repeat the treatment daily until it is inactive. Then, fill the entrance hole with soil.

Using a pesticide to destroy a wall-void nest. Work at dusk when the wasps are inactive and the air is calm. Choose a pesticide *(page 63)*; if necessary, also an application tool *(page 116)*. Prepare to work safely with the pesticide *(page 98)*, wearing a bee veil and following the manufacturer's instructions to apply it. For the aerosol product shown, spray pesticide directly into the entrance hole of the wall-void nest *(above)*. If the wasps become active, stop spraying; remain calm and still until the activity subsides. Watch the nest for several days; if it remains active, repeat the treatment daily until it is inactive. Then, seal the entrance hole.

CONTROLLING WASPS (continued)

Using a pesticide to destroy an aerial nest. Work at dusk when the wasps are inactive and the air is calm. Choose a pesticide *(page 63)*; if necessary, also an application tool *(page 116)*. Prepare to work safely with the pesticide *(page 98)*, wearing a bee veil and following the manufacturer's instructions to apply it. For the aerosol product shown, position yourself at least 6 feet from the nest, then spray pesticide onto it *(above, left)*. If the wasps become active, stop spraying; remain calm and still until the activity subsides. Continue spraying the nest until it is completely dampened. Watch the nest for several days; if it remains active, repeat the treatment each day until it is no longer active. When the nest is inactive, knock it down using a broom *(above, right)*. Seal the nest in a heavy-duty plastic garbage bag, then dispose of the bag in an outdoor trash can.

CONTROLLING FLIES

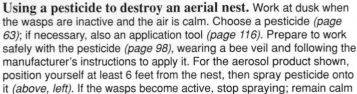

Using a trap. To control flies outdoors, buy an outdoor fly trap *(page 63)* and follow the manufacturer's instructions to use it. To set up the trap shown, fit the collection bag onto the base of it, then open the top. Mix the lure and place it in the top of the trap, then close the top. To control flies in an area, hang up the trap beyond the reach of children and pets in a shady location slightly away from it—from a soffit *(left)*, a tree or a fence post, for example. When the collection bag fills with flies, remove the bag and knot it, then fit a new collection bag onto the trap base. Leave the filled collection bag in direct sunlight to kill any active flies in it, then dispose of it in an outdoor trash can. Follow the manufacturer's instructions to replace the lure—usually every 2 to 3 weeks. Wash your hands well using soap and water after handling the trap.

CONTROLLING FIRE ANTS

Using boiling water. Before resorting to a pesticide, try using boiling water to destroy the mound of the fire ants. Work on a warm, dry morning. Wearing safety goggles, rubber gloves and rubber boots, fill a metal bucket with 1 gallon of boiling water, then carefully pour the water on the mound *(above)*. Watch the mound for several days; if it remains active, repeat the treatment each day until it is no longer active. If you cannot control the fire ants using boiling water, use a posion-bait pesticide *(step right)*, a drench pesticide *(step below, left)* or an injectable pesticide *(step below, right)*.

Using a poison-bait pesticide. Before resorting to a pesticide, try using boiling water *(step left)*. Otherwise, choose a pesticide *(page 63)* and prepare to work safely with it *(page 98)*, then follow the manufacturer's instructions to apply it. Work on a warm, dry morning in midspring. For the product shown, sprinkle a band of it 2 feet wide around the mound of the fire ants by hand *(above)* or using a drop spreader *(page 116)*. Allow the pesticide to work for the time specified—usually at least 4 weeks. If the mound remains active, repeat the treatment; if it still remains active, use another pesticide.

Activator button

Probe

Using a drench pesticide. Before resorting to a pesticide, try using boiling water *(step above, left)*. Otherwise, choose a pesticide *(page 63)* and prepare to work safely with it *(page 98)*, then follow the manufacturer's instructions to apply it. Work on a warm, dry morning. For the product shown, sprinkle 1/2 cup of it onto the mound of the fire ants *(above, left)*, then pour 1 gallon of water over it *(above, right)*. Allow the pesticide to work for the time specified—usually a few days. If the mound remains active, repeat the treatment; if it still remains active, use another pesticide.

Using an injectable pesticide. Before resorting to a pesticide, try using boiling water *(step above, left)*. Otherwise, choose a pesticide *(page 63)* and prepare to work safely with it *(page 98)*, then follow the manufacturer's instructions to apply it. Work at dawn or at dusk. For the product shown, hold the probe 18 inches from the mound of the fire ants, then depress the activator button and use a steady side-to-side motion to thoroughly dampen it. To inject the mound at points recommended by the manufacturer, depress the activator button and push the probe into the mound *(above)*, withdrawing it again to spray fleeing ants. If necessary, repeat the treatment.

CONTROLLING TICKS AND CHIGGERS

Using a repellent. To prevent bites when you are outdoors in an infested area, cover as much of the body as possible with clothing and use a tick and chigger repellent *(page 63)*. Test the repellent on a small area of the skin; if there is any irritation, use another type. Apply the repellent following the manufacturer's instructions; for a child, apply it sparingly. For a spray repellent, spray a light, even coat of it directly onto the clothing *(left)*; if the repellent contains permethrin, spray the clothing before putting it on. Also spray a light, even coat of the repellent directly onto the skin; for the face, spray repellent onto one hand, then rub it on the skin, avoiding the eyes and lips. For a liquid repellent, pour a small amount of it into one hand, then rub it on the skin, avoiding the eyes and lips. Reapply the repellent as needed. After leaving an infested area, remove your clothing and seal it in a plastic bag, then launder it as soon as possible.

Pump-up sprayer

Using a pesticide. Eradicating ticks and chiggers can be difficult, but you can use a pesticide to control a heavy infestation—such as in a lawn. Mow the lawn and trim its edges, then rake it thoroughly. Choose a pesticide *(page 63)* and an application tool *(page 116)*, then prepare to work safely with the pesticide *(page 98)*. To use a pump-up sprayer, as shown, work section by section from one end of the lawn to the other. Walking backwards, use a steady side-to-side motion to thoroughly dampen each section with pesticide *(left)*. After treating the lawn, keep off it for the length of time specified—usually 24 hours. To maximize the effectiveness of the treatment, mow and rake the lawn regularly; if necessary, repeat the pesticide treatment. After leaving an infested area, remove your clothing and seal it in a plastic bag, then launder it as soon as possible.

CONTROLLING SPIDERS AND SCORPIONS

Removing a spider web. Caution: Do not touch the nest or disturb the harborage area of a scorpion or a black widow or brown recluse spider; use a pesticide *(step right)* or call a pest control professional. Otherwise, eliminate a spider from an area by destroying its web. Wearing work gloves, use a broom covered with an old nylon stocking to sweep the web and any spider or eggs in it off the surfaces to which it is attached *(above)*. Working over a heavy-duty plastic garbage bag, carefully pull the stocking off the broom. Place the stocking in the bag, then seal it and dispose of it in an outdoor trash can.

Using a pesticide. Choose a pesticide *(page 63)*; if necessary, also an application tool *(page 116)*. Prepare to work safely with the pesticide *(page 98)*, then follow the manufacturer's instructions to apply it. To use an aerosol pesticide on an insect, stand the specified distance from it and spray the pesticide directly onto it. To use a pump-up sprayer for applying a pesticide on a harborage area, as shown, use a steady side-to-side motion to thoroughly dampen the surfaces of the area with the pesticide *(above)*, as well as any hidden locations between, behind and under them.

CONTROLLING BIRDS

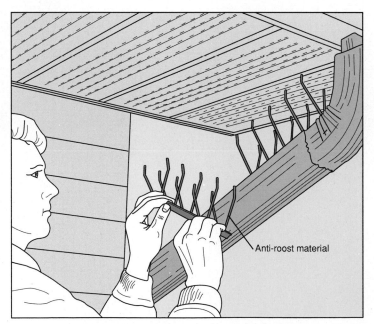

Anti-roost material

Removing a nest. Consult your local county extension service or animal control agency to identify the bird, if necessary; ensure that it is not a protected species. To remove the nest of a bird that is not a protected species, prepare to work safely on a ladder or the roof *(page 98)*. Wear rubber gloves; if there are droppings, also a respirator. If there are eggs or baby birds in the nest, leave it untouched until it is vacant. Otherwise, pull the nest off the surfaces to which it is attached *(above)*. Seal the nest in a heavy-duty plastic garbage bag, then dispose of it in an outdoor trash can.

Using anti-roost material. To prevent a bird from roosting or nesting on a surface, install anti-roost material. Buy enough anti-roost material to cover the surface at a pest control center. Prepare to work safely on a ladder or the roof *(page 98)*, then install the anti-roost material following the manufacturer's instructions. For the anti-roost material shown, cut it to fit the surface, then position it *(above)*. Fasten the anti-roost material to a wood surface using nails or screws; for another type of surface, use a glue or adhesive recommended for it.

CONTROLLING RATS USING SNAP TRAPS

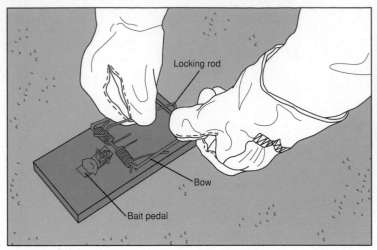

Using a snap trap. Set up a snap trap at a location where a rat or its tracks, droppings or gnawing marks are seen. Buy as many snap traps as necessary at a pest control center and choose a bait *(page 63)*. To set up the trap shown, wear work gloves to position the bait on the bait pedal. Draw the bow all the way back from the baited end of the trap and hold it down firmly against the unbaited end of the trap. Fit the locking rod over the bow *(above, left)* and hook the end of the locking rod into the bait pedal catch. Let go of the bow slowly, keeping your fingers clear of the baited end of the trap. Holding the trap carefully by the outer edges of its unbaited end, position it at the desired location. Along a wall, place one trap parallel to it *(above, right)*. Then, place another trap parallel or perpendicular to the wall next to the first trap, their unbaited ends butted together. Keep children and pets away from the traps, covering them using a cardboard box with a hole cut in each end *(inset)*. Seal any used trap and carcass in a heavy-duty plastic garbage bag, then dispose of it in an outdoor trash can.

CONTROLLING ANIMALS USING LIVE TRAPS

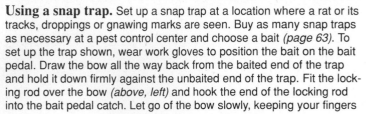

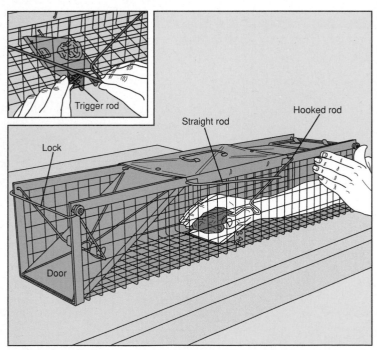

Using a live trap. Set up a live trap at a location where the pest or its tracks, droppings or gnawing marks are seen. Buy or rent a live trap of a size for the pest at a pest control center or your local animal protection agency. Choose a bait *(page 63)* and set up the trap following the manufacturer's instructions. For the trap shown, lift a door and position the bait on the bait pan *(above, left)*, then lower the door. With the door locks flipped outward, push the door rods down to raise the doors. Fit the hooked rod onto the straight rod, then fit the tip of the hooked rod around the tip of the trigger rod *(inset)*. Flip the door locks inward to rest them on top of the raised doors. Test the trap by pushing a stick through the bars to touch the bait pan and snap the doors closed; then, reset the trap. Holding the trap carefully by its handle, place it at the desired location *(above, right)*. Keep children and pets away. For a pet caught in the trap, lift a door lock and raise the door to coax it out; if it is panicky, flip both door locks outward and turn the trap upside down to let it leave on its own. For a pest caught in the trap, call your local animal protection agency or Fish and Wildlife Department for instructions.

BUILDING A TRASH CAN STAND

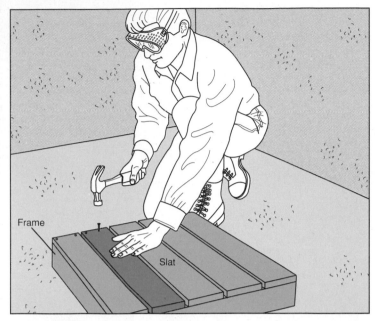

1 Building a platform. To keep a trash can out of reach of a foraging animal, build a trash can stand. Buy pressure-treated wood and weather-resistant fasteners for a stand at a building supply center; also buy a trash can with a locking lid. Measure the diameter of the trash can, then build a platform large enough to hold it. Wearing safety goggles, cut four 2-by-4s to length for the frame, then fasten the pieces together with 3-inch spiral nails. Cut 1-by-4s to length for slats, then lay them on the frame with gaps between them. Nail the slats to the frame *(above)* with 2-inch nails.

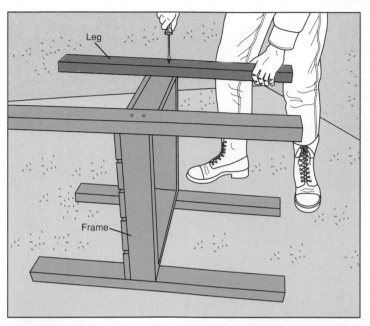

2 Installing legs. Cut four 2-by-4s to length for the legs; cut them long enough to keep the platform 18 inches off the ground and extend above the platform by 2/3 the height of the trash can. Turn the platform on its side to fasten the legs. Holding a leg against a corner of the frame, align it perpendicular to the top and extending 18 inches below the bottom of the platform. Use an electric drill to bore two pilot holes for 4-inch wood screws through the leg into the frame, then drive in the screws. Install the other legs the same way *(above)*, turning the platform as necessary.

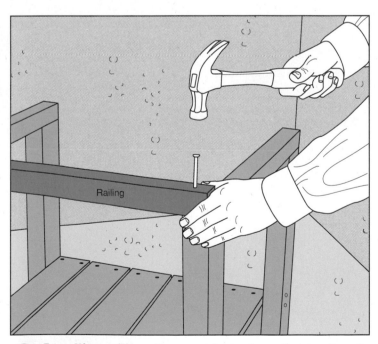

3 Installing railings. To prevent the trash can from toppling off the platform, install railings along three sides of it, attaching them in turn to pairs of the legs. Cut 2-by-2s to length for the railings. Position two railings along sides opposite each other on top of the pairs of legs, then nail them into place with 3-inch nails. To install the third railing, position it on top of the ends of the two installed railings, then nail the ends of it into place with 3-inch nails *(above)*.

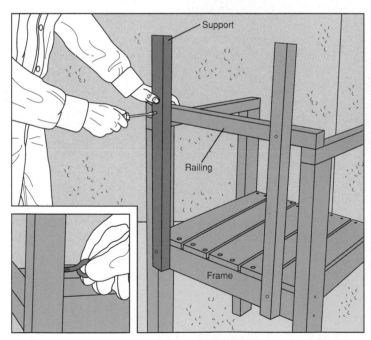

4 Installing supports. Cut two 2-by-4s to length for the supports; cut them long enough to extend above the platform by the height of the trash can. To install each support, hold it in place against the railing and frame, the bottom of it aligned with the bottom of the platform. Use an electric drill to bore pilot holes for 3-inch wood screws through the support into the frame and into the railing, then drive in the screws *(above)*. Install an eye screw in each support just above the railing *(inset)*.

BUILDING A TRASH CAN STAND (continued)

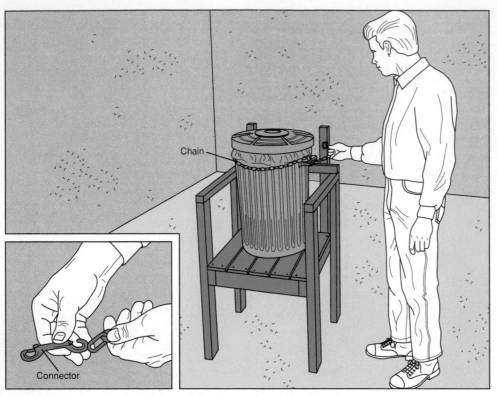

Chain

Connector

5 **Installing a chain.** Place the trash can on the stand against the back railing. To determine the length of chain needed for the stand, run a string around the trash can from one eye screw to the other eye screw, looping it through any handles on the trash can. Buy a chain and two double-ended, snap-bolt connectors for it at a building supply center. To install the chain, hook a snap-bolt connector onto each end of it *(inset)*, then hook one of the snap-bolt connectors to an eye screw on the stand. Run the chain around the trash can and through any handles on it, then hook the other snap-bolt connector to the other eye screw *(left)*. If necessary, tighten the chain by repositioning a snap-bolt connector on it. Place the trash can stand away from the house.

INSTALLING A FENCE

Post

1 **Digging a trench.** To keep an animal out of an outdoor area, build a fence around it. Consult your local county extension agent or animal control agency about specifications for a fence effective against the animal—the height, post depth and fencing material, for example. To build a fence to keep out skunks, as shown, wear work boots and work gloves. Working in turn along each edge of the area to be fenced, remove a strip of sod and vegetation, then use a spade to dig a trench 6 inches deep and 6 inches wide *(above)*.

2 **Installing fence posts.** Use non-corrosive metal pipes 4 1/2 to 5 feet long as fence posts; buy enough pipes at a building supply center to install one every 8 feet along the trench. Wearing safety goggles, work from one end of the trench to the other end to install the posts. Stand each post upright in turn on the bottom of the trench against its inside wall. Holding the post firmly, use a hand drilling hammer to drive it into the ground *(above)* until it is anchored and extending at least 30 inches above ground level.

INSTALLING A FENCE (continued)

Hardware cloth

3 **Installing fencing.** Buy 1/4-inch mesh hardware cloth for fencing at a building supply center and install it on the posts along each edge of the area. Wearing work gloves, use tin snips to cut a piece of hardware cloth equal in length to the distance between two or more posts and 6 inches wider than the height of the posts. Lay the piece on the ground and bend up a strip 6 inches wide along the bottom of it, forming a 90°-angle lip. Position the piece against the posts with its lip against the base of the trench *(above)*, then secure it to each post using mechanic's wire *(inset)*. Continue the same way.

4 **Filling in the trench.** Backfill the trench with soil and compact it, ensuring that the posts and hardware cloth are anchored in the ground. Wearing work gloves, start at one end of the trench to fill it with the soil excavated using a spade *(above)*. Then, working from one end to the other end along the refilled trench, use a 4-by-4 4 to 5 feet long to pound down on the soil, compacting it. If necessary, add more soil and compact it until the ground is level. Put back the sod or vegetation removed.

PESTPROOFING A BIRD FEEDER

Guard

Bracket

Guard

Protecting a pole-mounted bird feeder. To prevent an animal from climbing onto and raiding a pole-mounted bird feeder, ensure that the pole is at least 10 feet from any tree, fence or wall. Then, buy a guard for the feeder at a garden center and follow the manufacturer's instructions to install it. For the guard shown, remove the bird feeder from the top of the pole. Fit the guard brackets together around the pole at a point at least 5 1/2 feet above the ground and fasten them using the screws and bolts supplied, tightening the screws to hold the brackets in position. Assemble the guard and fit it onto the pole *(above, left)*, sliding it down until it rests securely on the bracket. Reinstall the bird feeder *(above, right)*.

Protecting a suspended bird feeder.
To keep an animal from climbing onto and raiding a suspended bird feeder, buy a guard at a garden center and follow the manufacturer's instructions to install it. For the guard shown, take down the bird feeder and hang it onto the hook on the bottom of the guard, then hang up the guard *(above)* away from any tree, fence or wall and at least 5 feet above the ground.

LAWN AND GARDEN PESTS

Your lawn and gardens may serve you and your family as sources of greenery and colorful blooms, luscious fruits and vegetables, as well as shade and privacy—but they can also provide homes and feeding grounds for a variety of pests. The illustration at right identifies pest troublespots typical to a lawn and gardens. Fortunately, the control of most lawn and garden pests is rarely difficult; with proper care of the lawn and gardens, a heavy infestation of a pest can usually be prevented.

Keep the lawn trimmed and dethatched. Pull weeds, clear debris, and pick fallen fruits and vegetables out of gardens. Prune diseased branches from trees and bushes. Keep the soil healthy, consulting your local county extension agent about pH and fertility tests as well as measures to correct deficiencies. Cultivate gardens during the growing season to aerate the soil and encourage water penetration; at the end of the growing season to remove plant debris. Experiment with cultural pest controls *(page 94)* and pestproof with garden blankets, guards and barriers *(page 96)*; for nuisance birds, use repelling devices *(page 91)*.

Even with the best of horticultural practices, however, no lawn or garden is ever immune to pests. Check for pests before and periodically during the growing season; in particular, for insect pests in the lawn *(page 83)* and gardens *(page 84)*. To identify an unknown insect pest, refer to the chart on page 78 for descriptions of common types and their usual locations. If you cannot identify a pest, consult your local county extension agent or a pest control professional.

If a troublesome pest problem occurs despite your efforts at prevention, use the Troubleshooting Guide *(page 76)* to help choose an appropriate pest control method, then refer to the pages indicated to undertake the pest control job. In general, first try controlling a pest using the least harsh, most environmentally safe method—for example, handpicking, cultivating or trapping insect pests *(page 86)*. For a heavy infestation of a pest or if other measures do not control it, refer to the chart on page 82 to choose a pesticide.

When buying a pesticide, choose the least harmful product available that is recommended for lawn and garden use on the pest. To use a pesticide, follow the manufacturer's instructions; only use as much as necessary to achieve the desired level of pest control. Since complete eradication of a lawn or garden pest is virtually impossible, do not overuse a pesticide and risk harming beneficial insects and animals. Test a pesticide on an inconspicuous spot of a plant, bush or tree before treating it; if there is any adverse reaction, consult a pest control or garden professional about using another product.

Some lawn and garden pest control jobs call for the use of specialized tools and materials that are readily available at a pest control or garden center. Refer to Tools & Techniques *(page 112)* for instructions on choosing, setting up and using application tools. Before starting any pest control job, read the chapter entitled Working Safely *(page 98)* for instructions on choosing the appropriate safety gear, preparing the work area, and mixing and disposing of pesticides. Read the safety information in the Emergency Guide *(page 8)*. If you doubt your ability to complete a job, do not hesitate to consult a pest control professional.

Bushes and shrubs
May be infested by insect pests such as Japanese beetles, June beetles or aphids; fruit bushes also vulnerable to insect pests such as plum curculios, scale insects or wireworms and animals such as birds or raccoons. Check for insect pests *(page 84)* and control light *(page 86)* or heavy *(page 89)* infestation. Use bird repelling devices *(page 91)* and pestproof with garden blankets, guards and barriers *(page 96)*; if necessary, control animals using poison-bait pesticide or traps.

Lawn
May be infested by insect pests such as Japanese beetles, June beetles, billbugs, chinch bugs, sod webworms, cutworms, grasshoppers or mole crickets and provide home for animal pests such as gophers, moles or voles. Check for insect pests *(page 83)* and control heavy infestation *(page 85)*. Control gophers, moles or voles using poison-bait pesticide *(page 91)*; or, control gophers with live traps *(page 70)* or gopher traps *(page 91)*, moles with mole traps *(page 91)* or voles with live or snap traps *(page 70)*.

Tree
May be infested by insect pests such as Japanese beetles, June beetles, elm leaf beetles, bark beetles, spittle bugs, leafhoppers, gypsy moths or cankerworms and vulnerable to animals such as ground squirrels, voles or rabbits; fruit trees also vulnerable to insect pests such as plum curculios, stinkbugs, aphids, mealybugs, scale insects, codling moths or peach tree borers and animals such as birds or raccoons. Check for insect pests *(page 84)* and control light or heavy infestation *(page 90)*. Use bird repelling devices *(page 91)* and pestproof with garden blankets, guards and barriers *(page 96)*; if necessary, control animals using poison-bait pesticide or traps.

Kitchen garden
May be infested by insect pests such as Japanese beetles, June beetles, flea beetles, seed weevils, squash bugs, tarnished plant bugs, leafhoppers, thrips, wireworms, leafroller caterpillars, cutworms, millipedes or slugs and vulnerable to animals such as birds, rabbits, skunks, raccoons or opossums. Check for insect pests *(page 84)* and control light *(page 86)* or heavy *(page 89)* infestation. Use bird repelling devices *(page 91)* and pestproof with garden blankets, guards and barriers *(page 96)*; if necessary, control animals using poison-bait pesticide or traps.

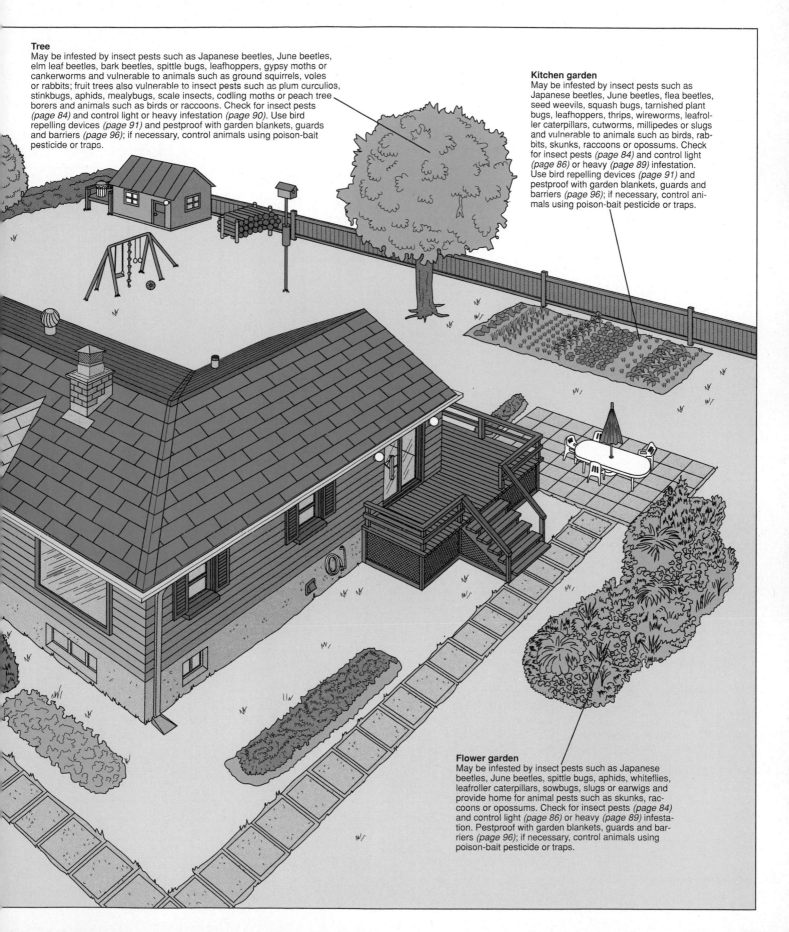

Flower garden
May be infested by insect pests such as Japanese beetles, June beetles, spittle bugs, aphids, whiteflies, leafroller caterpillars, sowbugs, slugs or earwigs and provide home for animal pests such as skunks, raccoons or opossums. Check for insect pests *(page 84)* and control light *(page 86)* or heavy *(page 89)* infestation. Pestproof with garden blankets, guards and barriers *(page 96)*; if necessary, control animals using poison-bait pesticide or traps.

TROUBLESHOOTING GUIDE

PROBLEM	PROCEDURE
Beetles: Japanese beetles, June beetles, spotted or striped cucumber beetles, flea beetles, Mexican bean beetles, Colorado potato beetles, seed weevils, elm leaf beetles, bark beetles, billbugs or plum curculios	For heavy lawn infestation of Japanese beetles, June beetles or billbugs, use pesticide *(p. 85)* ▪●
	For light garden infestation, handpick or shake pests off foliage or cultivate pests out of soil *(p. 86)* □●; clear pests from tree *(p. 90)* □○
	For heavy garden infestation, use pesticide *(p. 89)* ▪●; use pesticide for tree *(p. 90)* ▪●
	Experiment with cultural controls *(p. 94)*; if possible, control pests by treating soil, tree or bush before growing season *(p. 95)* ▪● or using garden blankets, plastic tree guards or sticky tree barriers at start of growing season *(p. 96)* □●
Bugs: squash bugs, chinch bugs, stinkbugs, tarnished plant bugs or spittle bugs	For heavy lawn infestation of chinch bugs, use pesticide *(p. 85)* ▪●
	For light garden infestation, handpick or shake pests off foliage *(p. 86)* □●; clear pests from tree *(p. 90)* □○
	For heavy garden infestation, use pesticide *(p. 89)* ▪●; use pesticide for tree *(p. 90)* ▪●
	Experiment with cultural controls *(p. 94)*; if possible, control pests by treating soil, tree or bush before growing season *(p. 95)* ▪● or using garden blankets, plastic tree guards or sticky tree barriers at start of growing season *(p. 96)* □●
Aphids	For light garden infestation, handpick or wash pests off foliage, use sticky traps or use reflective mulch *(p. 86)* □●
	For heavy garden infestation, use pesticide *(p. 89)* ▪●; use pesticide for tree *(p. 90)* ▪●
	Experiment with cultural controls *(p. 94)*; if possible, control pests by treating tree or bush before growing season *(p. 95)* ▪●
Whiteflies, thrips or psyllids	For light garden infestation, wash pests off foliage, use sticky traps or use reflective mulch *(p. 86)* □●
	For heavy garden infestation, use pesticide *(p. 89)* ▪●; use pesticide for tree *(p. 90)* ▪●
	Experiment with cultural controls *(p. 94)*; if possible, control pests by treating tree or bush before growing season *(p. 95)* ▪●
Leafhoppers or spider mites	For light garden infestation, wash pests off foliage *(p. 86)* □●
	For heavy garden infestation, use pesticide *(p. 89)* ▪●; use pesticide for tree *(p. 90)* ▪●
	Experiment with cultural controls *(p. 94)*; if possible, control pests by treating tree or bush before growing season *(p. 95)* ▪●
Mealybugs	For light garden infestation, handpick or wash pests off foliage or use reflective mulch *(p. 86)* □●
	For heavy garden infestation, use pesticide *(p. 89)* ▪●; use pesticide for tree *(p. 90)* ▪●
	Experiment with cultural controls *(p. 94)*; if possible, control pests by treating tree or bush before growing season *(p. 95)* ▪●
Scale insects	For light garden infestation, wash pests off foliage or use reflective mulch *(p. 86)* □●
	For heavy garden infestation, use pesticide *(p. 89)* ▪●; use pesticide for tree *(p. 90)* ▪●
	Experiment with cultural controls *(p. 94)*; if possible, control pests by treating tree or bush before growing season *(p. 95)* ▪●
Mediterranean fruit flies	Consult local county extension agent
Apple flies (maggots)	For light infestation of tree or bush, use red sphere sticky trap as for checking foliage *(p. 84)* □○
	For heavy infestation of tree, use pesticide *(p. 90)* ▪●; use pesticide for bush *(p. 88)* ▪●
Moths or caterpillars: Oriental fruit moths, codling moths, gypsy moths, wireworms, bagworms, cankerworms, tent caterpillars, leafroller caterpillars, sod webworms, cabbage loopers, tomato hornworms, corn ear worms, squash vine borers, cutworms or peach tree borers	For heavy lawn infestation of sod webworms or cutworms, use pesticide *(p. 85)* ▪●
	For light garden infestation, handpick or shake pests off foliage, cultivate pests out of soil or use barriers *(p. 86)* □●; clear pests from tree *(p. 90)* □○
	For heavy garden infestation, use pesticide *(p. 89)* ▪●; use pesticide for tree *(p. 90)* ▪●
	Experiment with cultural controls *(p. 94)*; if possible, control pests by treating soil, tree or bush before growing season *(p. 95)* ▪● or using sticky tree barriers at start of growing season *(p. 96)* □●
Sowbugs or pillbugs	For light garden infestation, cultivate pests out of soil *(p. 86)* □●
	For heavy garden infestation, use pesticide *(p. 89)* ▪●
Millipedes	For light garden infestation, handpick pests off foliage *(p. 86)* □●
	For heavy garden infestation, use pesticide *(p. 89)* ▪●

DEGREE OF DIFFICULTY: □ Easy ▪ Moderate ■ Complex
ESTIMATED TIME: ○ Less than 1 hour ◐ 1 to 3 hours ● Over 3 hours

PROBLEM	PROCEDURE
Slugs or snails	For light garden infestation, handpick pests off foliage, use liquid traps or use shelter traps *(p. 86)* □◒
	For heavy garden infestation, use pesticide *(p. 89)* ▭◒
	Experiment with cultural controls *(p. 94)*
Earwigs	For light garden infestation, handpick pests off foliage, use liquid traps or use shelter traps *(p. 86)* □◒; clear pests from tree *(p. 90)* □○
	For heavy garden infestation, use pesticide *(p. 89)* ▭◒; use pesticide for tree *(p. 90)* ▭◒
Grasshoppers	For heavy lawn infestation, use pesticide *(p. 85)* ▭◒
	For light garden infestation, handpick pests off foliage *(p. 86)* □◒
	For heavy garden infestation, use pesticide *(p. 89)* ▭◒
	Experiment with cultural controls *(p. 94)*; if possible, control pests by using garden blankets at start of growing season *(p. 96)* □◒
Mole crickets	For heavy lawn infestation, use pesticide *(p. 85)* ▭◒
Birds	Use repelling devices *(p. 91)* □◒; use garden blankets or plant guards at start of growing season *(p. 96)* □◒
Gophers	Use live traps *(p. 70)* ▭○ with bait of peanut butter and molasses on brown bread
	Use poison-bait pesticide or gopher traps *(p. 91)* ■◒
	Consult a pest control professional
Moles	Use poison-bait pesticide or mole traps *(p. 91)* ■◒
	Consult a pest control professional
Woodchucks	Use live traps *(p. 70)* ▭○ with bait of apple, carrot or lettuce
	Install fence around vulnerable area *(p. 72)* ▭●
	Use pesticide gas *(p. 93)* ■○
	Consult a pest control professional
Ground squirrels	Protect trees using tree guards or slippery tree barriers *(p. 96)* □◒
	Use live traps *(p. 70)* ▭○ with bait of cereal, nuts, sunflower seeds or mix of peanut butter and oatmeal
	Use pesticide gas *(p. 93)* ■○
	Consult a pest control professional
Voles (field mice)	Protect trees using tree guards *(p. 96)* □◒
	Use live traps or snap traps *(p. 70)* ▭○ with bait of peanut butter and molasses on brown bread
	Use poison-bait pesticide as for gophers or moles *(p. 91)* ■◒
	Consult a pest control professional
Chipmunks	Use live traps or snap traps *(p. 70)* ▭○ with bait of peanut butter, sunflower seeds, cereal or popcorn
	Consult a pest control professional
Rabbits	Use plant guards at start of growing season; protect trees using tree guards *(p. 96)* □◒
	Install fence *(p. 72)* ▭● or electrical-shock fence *(p. 96)* □◒ around vulnerable area
	Use live traps *(p. 70)* ▭○ with bait of apple, carrot or lettuce
	Consult a pest control professional
Skunks, raccoons or opossums	Install fence *(p. 72)* ▭● or electrical-shock fence *(p. 96)* □◒ around vulnerable area
	Use live traps *(p. 70)* ▭○
	Consult a pest control professional

DEGREE OF DIFFICULTY: □ Easy ▭ Moderate ■ Complex
ESTIMATED TIME: ○ Less than 1 hour ◒ 1 to 3 hours ● Over 3 hours

IDENTIFYING A LAWN AND GARDEN PEST

PEST	CHARACTERISTICS	LOCATION
Beetle	**Japanese beetle:** Adult 1/2 inch long *(shown, top)* metallic blue or green with coppery wing covers and patches of white hair on sides of abdomen. Larva 3/4 inch long plump and C-shaped *(shown, bottom)*; gray-white with brown head.	Found on trees, bushes and plants, and in lawn; targets include apple, bean, cherry, grape, peach, plum, quince, raspberry, rhubarb and rose. Adults skeletonize leaves, and eat flowers and fruits or vegetables. Larvae feed on roots, weakening or killing plants. Infested grass turns brown; sod feels loose underfoot. Common in eastern United States, but spreading westward.
	June beetle: Also known as June bug. Adult 1 inch long hard-shelled; red-brown or black. Larva 3/4 inch to 1 1/2 inches long plump and C-shaped; white with dark, wide head.	Found on trees, bushes and plants, and in lawn. Adults feed on leaves. Larvae feed on roots, weakening or killing plants. Infested grass turns brown; sod feels loose underfoot. Common throughout United States.
	Spotted cucumber beetle: Adult 1/4 inch long green-yellow; small black head and large spots on back. Larva 1/2 inch long beige; brown head and brown spot on last body segment.	Found on trees and plants; targets include bean, corn, cucumber, eggplant, melon, pea, potato, squash and tomato. Adults chew holes in leaves, flowers and fruits or vegetables, and transmit brown rot in fruit. Larvae eat roots and stems early in growing season, weakening or killing plants. Common in eastern United States.
	Striped cucumber beetle: Adult 1/4 inch long ranges from pale yellow to orange and brown; has three black stripes and black head. Larva 1/4 inch long white and slender.	Found on plants; targets include bean, corn, cucumber, melon, squash, pea and pumpkin. Adults chew leaves and flowers, and transmit bacterial diseases. Larvae feed on roots and underground stems, weakening or killing plants. Common in eastern United States.
	Flea beetle: Adult 1/10 inch long shiny black and may have curved, yellow or white stripes; jumps rapidly when disturbed. Larva gray with no legs.	Found on trees and plants; targets include apple, beech, broccoli, cabbage, cauliflower, eggplant, elm, plum, potato and turnip. Adults chew holes in leaves, and transmit viral and bacterial diseases. Larvae feed on roots, weakening or killing plants; may feed on foliage. Common throughout United States.
	Mexican bean beetle: Adult 1/4 inch long round in shape; yellow-brown with black spots on wing covers. Larva 1/3 inch long spined; orange in color.	Found on plants; bean chief target. Adults and larvae chew leaves from underside; may skeletonize them. Common in eastern United States and in parts of Texas, Arizona, Colorado and Utah.
	Colorado potato beetle: Adult 1/3 inch long yellow with black stripes on wing covers and dark spots behind head. Larva 1/4 inch long plump; red with black legs and black spots on each side of back.	Found on plants; targets include eggplant, pepper, potato and tomato. Adults and larvae feed on leaves. Common except in southern United States.
	Seed weevil: Adult 1/10 to 1/5 inch long flat; brown or dark green with light or dark mottling. Larva 1/6 inch long white with no legs.	Found on bean and pea plants. Adults chew holes in leaves, flowers and buds. Larvae feed within seeds and emerge from them through small holes. Common throughout United States.
	Elm leaf beetle: Adult 1/4 inch long yellow to olive green with dark stripe on each side of wing covers; may have dark spots behind head. Larva 1/2 inch long; black or black and yellow.	Found on elm trees. Adults chew holes in leaves. Larvae feed on leaves from underside, skeletonizing them. Common throughout United States.
	Bark beetle: Adult 1/16 to 1/4 inch long black, brown or dark red; cylindrical body with head usually invisible from above. Larva 1/16 to 1/4 inch long white or cream.	Found in trees. Adults of most species bore through bark and tunnel between it and wood to lay eggs; larvae hatch and bore away from parent tunnel. Presence indicated by small round holes in bark and sawdust-like deposits called frass at openings. Common throughout United States.
	Billbug: Adult 1/2 inch long with protruding snout *(shown)* brown in color. Larva 1/4 to 1/2 inch long white with brown head and no legs.	Found on plants and in lawn; targets include corn, small grain and peanut. Adults feed on leaves. Larvae feed on roots and underground stems, weakening or killing plants. Infested grass turns brown; sod feels loose underfoot. Common in wet lowlands of southeastern United States.

PEST		CHARACTERISTICS	LOCATION
		Plum curculio: Adult 1/10 to 1/4 inch long with sculptured wing covers and slightly curved, thin beak *(shown)*; dark brown with fine, white hairs on body. Larva 1/8 inch long white or gray with no legs.	Found on fruit trees and bushes; targets include apple, blueberry, cherry, peach, pear, plum and quince. Adults eat into fruits to lay eggs. Larvae mine within fruits to feed, leading to brown rot; cause fruits to deform or drop prematurely. Common in eastern United States.
Bug		**Squash bug:** Adult 1/2 inch long *(shown)* ranges from brown to black with orange or brown abdomen. Nymph smaller; green. Emits foul odor when crushed.	Found on plants; targets include cucumber, melon, pumpkin and squash. Attack leaves, causing them to wilt and blacken. Common throughout United States.
		Chinch bug: Adult 1/16 inch long black with white or brown forewings and brown legs. Nymph smaller; may be black with white spots or red with white stripe on back. Emits foul odor when crushed.	Found in lawn. Suck sap of grass and inject poison, killing it; cause irregular, sunken, yellow patches. Common in eastern United States.
		Stinkbug: Adult 1/2 inch long light green, gray, brown or black with bright orange patches. Nymph smaller and round; ranges in color from blue-gray to black with red patches. Emits foul odor when disturbed.	Found on trees and plants; targets include bean, cabbage, citrus, peach, potato, radish, tomato and turnip. Feed on young leaves and fruits or vegetables, sucking sap; cause shoots to wilt, leaves to brown and deform, and fruits or vegetables to deform. Common throughout United States.
		Tarnished plant bug: Adult 1/4 inch long brassy green to brown with yellow, brown and black markings; yellow triangular marking. Nymph smaller; yellow-green.	Found on trees and plants; targets include bean, cabbage, peach and potato. Feed on stems, buds and fruits or vegetables, sucking sap and injecting poison; cause shoots to blacken, flowers to die and fruits or vegetables to deform. Common throughout United States.
		Spittle bug: Adult 1/4 to 1/3 inch long brown with short antennae; may have stripes or bands on wings. Nymph smaller and soft-bodied; brown or green with masses of white, frothy foam.	Found on trees and plants. Suck sap from leaves and stems, leading them to wilt; cause stunting of growth or death. Common throughout United States.
Aphid		Adult 1/8 inch long *(shown)* waxy or wooly; may be green, red, brown, purple, yellow or black. May or may not have wings.	Found on trees, bushes and plants. Suck sap from leaves, stems, flowers and fruits, and secrete sticky "honeydew." Cause leaves to yellow and weakening or stunting of growth; may cause disease. Common throughout United States.
Whitefly		Adult 1/20 to 1/12 inch long moth-like *(shown)*; white in color. Gather in cluster on underside of leaves and rise up in cloud if leaves disturbed.	Found on fruit trees and bushes, and plants; targets include cucumber, lettuce and tomato. Suck sap from leaves and secrete sticky "honeydew." Cause leaves to speckle or mottle, making them susceptible to disease. Common in greenhouses throughout United States and in southern and coastal states.
Leafhopper		**Leafhopper:** Adult 1/5 to 1/3 inch long *(shown)* yellow-green to brown with large eyes on sides of head; may have white spots on head, wings and thorax. Nymph smaller; pale green in color.	Found on trees and plants; targets include bean, beet, carrot, celery, citrus, eggplant, potato, rhubarb and tomato. Suck sap from leaves, causing them to whiten and curl; may puncture or mar rinds of citrus. Common throughout United States.
		Psyllid: Also known as jumping plant lice. Adult 1/10 to 1/16 inch long brown or green and similar in shape to leafhopper with longer antennae; jumps from leaves. Nymph smaller and without wings; may be covered with sap or white, waxy threads.	Found on trees and plants; targets include pear, potato, quince and tomato. Suck sap from leaves and fruits or vegetables. Cause leaves to curl, stunting of growth and fruits or vegetables to de-form; may spread disease. Common throughout United States.
Mealybug		Adult 1/4 inch long waxy and oval-shaped *(shown)*; white.	Found on trees and woody plants; targets include avocado, citrus and potato. Suck sap from leaves and secrete sticky "honeydew." Cause leaves to yellow and curl; may kill branch or plant. Common in southern United States and California.

IDENTIFYING A LAWN AND GARDEN PEST (continued)

PEST	CHARACTERISTICS	LOCATION
Scale insect	Adult up to 1/4 inch long scaly and oval-shaped *(shown)*; white, red, brown or black with texture from hard to soft, cottony or waxy. Gather in immobile cluster on leaves and stems.	Found on trees and plants; targets include almond, apple, apricot, citrus, fig, grape, peach, pecan, pepper, potato, quince and walnut. Suck sap from leaves, stems, bark and fruits or vegetables, and secrete sticky "honeydew." Cause leaves to curl and wrinkle, making them susceptible to disease. Common throughout United States.
Spider mite	Adult up to 1/60 inch long relative of spider; red-brown in color with eight legs.	Found on trees and plants. Suck sap from leaves and fruits or vegetables; cause leaves to whiten, yellow or brown and curl; cause fruits or vegetables to dry and deform. May leave fine web on leaves or branches. Common throughout United States.
Thrips	Adult up to 1/16 inch long *(shown)* light to dark brown or black with two pairs of feathery wings. Nymph smaller; yellow in color with no wings.	Found on trees and plants; targets include bean, beet, carrot, citrus, date, grape, onion, peach and tomato. Suck sap from leaves, buds and blossoms; cause leaves to whiten and wilt, petals to streak at edges and blossoms to wither. Common throughout United States.
Fruit fly	**Mediterranean fruit fly:** Adult 1/4 inch long *(shown)* black with yellow abdomen and yellow, brown and black markings on wings. Larva 1/4 inch long white with no legs.	Found on fruit trees and bushes. Adults lay eggs in fruit rind; larvae burrow into fruit to feed, causing it to rot. Imported to Florida and California.
	Apple fly (maggot): Adult 1/4 inch long black with yellow markings on abdomen and zigzag bands on wings. Maggot 1/4 inch long white or yellow.	Found on fruit trees and bushes; targets include apple, blueberry, cherry and plum. Adults puncture fruit and lay eggs; larvae burrow into fruit to feed, causing it to rot. Common in eastern United States.
Moth or caterpillar	**Oriental fruit moth:** Adult with wingspan of 1/2 inch *(shown)* gray with brown markings. Larva 1/2 inch long gray-white to pink with brown head.	Found on fruit trees; targets include almond, apple, apricot, cherry, peach, pear and plum. Larvae bore through stem into fruit to feed on it, leaving no visible external damage. Common in eastern and northwestern United States.
	Codling moth: Adult with wingspan of 3/4 inch gray-brown with brown lines on forewings and fringed hind wings. Larva 1 inch long pink with brown head.	Found on fruit trees; targets include apple, pear, quince and walnut. Larvae enter fruit through blossom to feed; when fully grown, tunnel out of fruit, leaving brown excrement on exterior. Common throughout United States.
	Gypsy moth: Adult with wingspan of 1 1/2 to 2 inches gray or white with hairy body. Larva 2 inches long flat *(shown)*; gray in color with brown hair.	Found on trees; targets include apple, cherry and oak. Caterpillars feed on foliage at night; hide in debris on ground during day. Common in eastern United States.
	Wireworm: Adult 1/3 to 1/2 inch long cylindrical in shape *(shown)*; ranges from yellow to brown with shiny, hard skin.	Found on plants; targets include bean, beet, cabbage, carrot, corn, lettuce, onion, pea, potato, strawberry and turnip. Feed on seeds, roots and tubers, burrowing into plants; cause stunting of growth. Common throughout United States.
	Bagworm: Adult 1 inch to 2 inches long *(shown)* dark brown or black; forms brown bag of interwoven bits of dead foliage, twigs and silk attached to branch.	Found on trees; conifers chief target. Feed on foliage from within bag; may completely defoliate tree. Common in southeastern and southern United States.
	Cankerworm: Also known as inchworm or looper. Adult 1 inch long *(shown)* green or brown with legs at front and rear of body; pulls back end of body forward to form loop as it moves.	Found on trees; targets include apple, elm, hickory, maple and oak. Feed on foliage, leaving midribs and large veins. Common in northeastern, midwestern and northwestern United States.
	Tent caterpillar: Adult 2 inches long *(shown)* hairy with black and white stripes, narrow brown and yellow lines, and blue spots on sides.	Found on fruit trees; targets include apple and pear. Build net-like web tents in forks and crotches of trees; feed on foliage and may completely defoliate tree. Common throughout United States.
	Leafroller caterpillar: Adult small; green-brown in color.	Found on plants inside tightly rolled leaves. Feed on leaves and may skeletonize them; also feed on buds and fruits or vegetables. Common throughout United States.

PEST	CHARACTERISTICS	LOCATION
	Sod webworm: Adult 3/4 inch long ranges from tan to gray with black spots.	Found in web-lined burrows in soil below lawn. Chew grass at soil level, causing patches of lawn to thin, turn brown and die. Common except in midwestern United States.
	Cabbage looper: Adult 1 1/2 inches long with smooth, green body and pale stripes down back; forms body into loop as it crawls.	Found on plants; targets include bean, broccoli, cabbage, cauliflower, celery, kale, lettuce, parsley, pea, potato, radish, spinach and tomato. Chew holes in leaves; may tunnel into heads of cabbage or lettuce. Common throughout United States.
	Tomato hornworm: Adult 3 to 4 inches long with fat, bright green body; white diagonal bars on sides and small horn protruding from hind end.	Found on plants; targets include eggplant, pepper, potato and tomato. Chew leaves; may also eat vegetables. Common throughout United States.
	Corn ear worm: Also known as tomato fruitworm. Adult 1/4 inch to 2 inches long striped green, yellow, pink or brown with four pairs of legs.	Found on plants; targets include bean, corn, pea, pepper, potato, squash and tomato. Chew leaves and buds; also eat husks of corn. Common throughout United States.
	Squash vine borer: Adult up to 1 inch long fat and wrinkled; white with brown head.	Found on plants; targets include cucumber, gourd, melon, pumpkin and squash. Enter stems of vines to feed; cause vines to wilt and holes in stems to weep green frass. Common except in western United States.
	Cutworm: Adult 1 inch to 2 inches long gray-brown in color; curls up when disturbed.	Found in soil below or around plants and in lawn; targets include most vegetable plants, especially seedlings and transplants. Chew plants or grass at soil level, causing plants to die and patches of lawn to thin, turn brown and die. Common throughout United States.
	Peach tree borer: Adult 1 inch long light yellow or white with brown head; lesser peach tree borer similar.	Found in fruit trees; targets include apricot, cherry, nectarine, peach and plum. Bore into bark of trunk or at junctions of trunk and branches; leave sticky sawdust-like deposits called frass at holes. Cause foliage to wither and branches to die. Common throughout United States.
Sowbug	Adult 1/2 inch long humpbacked with armor-like segments *(shown)*; dark gray in color. Pillbug relative similar; pulls in appendages and rolls up when disturbed.	Found in moist soil or sand, in moss, under bark and under objects on ground; presence in great numbers may damage roots of young trees, oats, clover, vegetables and lilies. Common throughout United States.
Millipede	Adult 1/2 inch to 4 inches long cylindrical in shape with at least two legs per body segment *(shown)*; ranges in color from pink-brown to gray and brown. May coil up if disturbed.	Found on plants; targets include bean, cabbage, carrot, corn, potato, strawberry, tomato and turnip. Feed on decayed plant material; may damage roots and seedlings. Some types eat insects found in soil. May spread fungal diseases. Common throughout United States.
Slug	Adult 1/2 inch to 3 inches long with soft body, usually with hump in middle *(shown)*; ranges in color from gray to black and brown. Eyes located at tips of small tentacles; two other tentacles used to smell. Snail relative similar; has single shell.	Found on plants. Feed on foliage at night, scraping holes in it; hide in debris or under boards on ground during day. Common throughout United States.
Earwig	European type up to 3/4 inch long with short, leathery forewings and pincers at end of abdomen *(shown)*; red-brown.	Found on fruit trees and plants. Feed on shoots and chew holes in foliage and flowers; may infest ripening fruit, but damage usually not severe. Common in eastern United States; other species common throughout United States.
Grasshopper	**Grasshopper:** Adult 2 inches long with powerful hind legs *(shown)*; ranges in color from red-yellow to brown and green.	Found on plants and in lawn. Feed on leaves and stems of plants; may defoliate them. Infested grass discolors and dies; sod feels loose underfoot. Common throughout United States.
	Mole cricket: Adult 1 1/2 inches long similar in shape to grasshopper; green-gray to brown with short front legs and long antennae.	Found in lawn, especially bahia and Bermuda grass. Feed on roots of grass at night, tunneling into soil and leaving small piles of soil at openings. Infested grass discolors and dies; sod feels loose underfoot. Common in southeastern and southern United States.

CHOOSING A PEST CONTROL PRODUCT

PEST	RECOMMENDED PESTICIDE	ALTERNATIVE PESTICIDE OR POISON BAIT
Beetle (includes Japanese beetle, June beetle, spotted or striped cucumber beetle, flea beetle, Mexican bean beetle, Colorado potato beetle, seed weevil, elm leaf beetle, bark beetle, billbug and plum curculio)	Use product containing diatomaceous earth only in dry conditions; otherwise, use solution of 2 1/2 ounces of dishwashing liquid per gallon of water or insecticidal soap containing potassium salts of fatty acids. For control of only larvae of Japanese beetle, use product containing *Bacillus popilliae* (Bp).	Use product containing acephate, carbaryl, chlorpyrifos, diazinon, malathion, methoxychlor, pyrethrins, rotenone, ryania or sabadilla.
Bug (includes squash bug, chinch bug, stinkbug, tarnished plant bug and spittle bug)	Use product containing diatomaceous earth only in dry conditions; otherwise, use solution of 2 1/2 ounces of dishwashing liquid per gallon of water or insecticidal soap containing potassium salts of fatty acids.	Use product containing carbaryl, chlorpyrifos, diazinon, malathion, methoxychlor, pyrethrins, rotenone, ryania or sabadilla.
Aphid, whitefly, leafhopper, psyllid, mealybug, scale insect, spider mite or thrips	Use product containing diatomaceous earth only in dry conditions; otherwise, use solution of 2 1/2 ounces of dishwashing liquid per gallon of water or insecticidal soap containing potassium salts of fatty acids.	Use product containing acephate, carbaryl, chlorpyrifos, dimethoate, malathion, methoxychlor, pyrethrins, resmethrin, rotenone or ryania.
Apple fly (maggot)	None	Use product containing carbaryl, diazinon or malathion.
Moth or caterpillar (includes Oriental fruit moth, codling moth, gypsy moth, wireworm, bagworm, cankerworm, tent caterpillar, leafroller caterpillar, sod webworm, cabbage looper, tomato hornworm, corn ear worm, squash vine borer, cutworm and peach tree borer)	Use solution of 2 1/2 ounces of dishwashing liquid per gallon of water, insecticidal soap containing potassium salts of fatty acids or product containing *Bacillus thuringiensis* (Bt). For control of only cutworm, use product containing diatomaceous earth only in dry conditions.	Use product containing acephate, carbaryl, chlorpyrifos, diazinon or rotenone. For control of only cutworm, use bait containing cabaryl.
Sowbug, pillbug, millipede or earwig	Use product containing diatomaceous earth only in dry conditions.	Use product containing chlorpyrifos or diazinon. Use bait containing carbaryl or propoxur.
Slug or snail	Use product containing diatomaceous earth only in dry conditions.	Use bait containing metaldehyde or methiocarb.
Grasshopper or mole cricket	Use product containing *Nosema locustae*.	Use product containing carbaryl, chlorpyrifos or diazinon.
Gopher, mole or vole	None	Use bait containing zinc phosphide.
Woodchuck or ground squirrel	None	Use gas cartridge containing sodium nitrate, sulfur and charcoal.

Choosing a pesticide or bait. To choose a type of pest control product appropriate for a pest, refer to the chart above for examples of the active ingredient required; a range of products is usually available at a garden center, pest control center or home center. Carefully check the label of a pest control product before buying it to ensure that it is recommended for outdoor use on the pest you are trying to control. Always start by choosing the least toxic pesticide available, changing to a more toxic pesticide only if necessary. When choosing a form of pesticide—aerosol, liquid, wettable powder or dust—ensure that you have on hand and know how to set up and use any application tool needed *(page 116)*. Prepare to work safely with the pesticide *(page 98)*, following the manufacturer's instructions to mix it, prepare the work area and choose the safety gear necessary for the job. After a pest control job, safely store or dispose of any leftover pesticide.

CHECKING FOR LAWN INSECT PESTS

Flooding the sod. Check the lawn for insect pests *(page 78)* at different times for at least several days; if necessary, consult your local county extension agent for advice on what to look for and when to start control measures. For a suspected infestation of Japanese beetles, June beetles, sod webworms or cutworms, for example, work when the sun is not shining. Fill a bucket with 1 gallon of water and add 2 tablespoons of dishwashing liquid, then pour the solution onto a section of sod 12 to 24 inches square *(above, left)* and watch for rising insect pests. Repeat the procedure at several spots on the lawn, then water the sections of sod thoroughly to prevent the solution from damaging them. For a suspected infestation of chinch bugs, for example, remove the top and bottom from a can, then pound it about 4 inches into the ground with a hand drilling hammer. Fill the can with water *(above, right)* and watch for rising insect pests. Repeat the procedure at several spots on the lawn.

Cutting back the sod. Check the lawn for insect pests *(page 78)* at different times for at least several days; if necessary, consult your local county extension agent for advice on what to look for and when to start control measures. For a suspected infestation of Japanese beetles, June beetles, billbugs, sod webworms, cutworms or mole crickets, for example, locate areas of sod that feel loose underfoot. At each area, cut along three edges of a section of sod 12 to 18 inches square using a spade, then fold the section of sod along its uncut edge *(above)*; if necessary, use the spade to sever any roots. Check the soil for insect pests, then fold the section of sod back into place.

Setting traps in the sod. Check the lawn for insect pests *(page 78)* at different times for at least several days; if necessary, consult your local county extension agent for advice on what to look for and when to start control measures. For a suspected infestation of billbugs or grasshoppers, for example, set traps every 10 feet along the perimeter of the area. For a trap, use a shallow, plastic or glass container, removing a plug of sod and digging a hole deep enough for the top of it to sit at ground level. Fill the container with a mixture of 1 part molasses to 3 parts water, then sit it in the hole *(above)*. Check the traps for insect pests daily, replacing the mixture as necessary.

CHECKING FOR GARDEN INSECT PESTS

Checking the foliage. Check the garden for insect pests *(page 78)* at different times for at least several days; if necessary, consult your local county extension agent for advice on what to look for and when to start control measures. For a suspected infestation of tiny leaf eaters such as aphids, whiteflies or leafhoppers, for example, use a 10-power magnifying glass. Look closely for adult insect pests and their larvae on plants, examining the top and underside of leaves, the stems and stalks, and the joints between leaves and stems *(above, left)*, in particu- lar. On bushes and trees, examine the leaves and branches the same way; also check the bark for small bored holes or slits indicating the presence of insect pests behind it. For a suspected infestation of apple flies or Oriental fruit moths in a tree, for example, buy traps and follow the manufacturer's instructions to use them; the type shown is a red sphere that is coated with a sticky adhesive. Hang the traps from the branches of the tree at the intervals specified *(above, right)* and check them daily for insect pests, replacing the adhesive as necessary.

Checking the soil. Check the garden for insect pests *(page 78)* at different times for at least several days; if necessary, consult your local county extension agent for advice on what to look for and when to start control measures. For a suspected infestation of beetles or root eaters such as wireworms, cutworms or millipedes, for example, use a spade to cultivate the soil. Working in rows about 18 inches away from plants, dig 4 to 6 inches into the soil and turn it over *(above, left)*, then examine it closely for adult insect pests and their larvae; if necessary, use a 10- power magnifying glass. Or, for a suspected infestation of slugs, snails or root eaters such as sowbugs or pillbugs, for example, use shelter traps. For a shelter trap, use a 1-inch board at least 1 foot wide and 3 feet long. At dusk, soak the board with water and place it on the ground at the perimeter of the garden, propping up one end of it on a 2-by-4. At dawn, turn the board over and check for insect pests sheltering on it, brushing them into a jar *(above, right)*; to kill them, fill the jar with water and add a squirt of dishwashing liquid.

CONTROLLING LAWN INSECT PESTS

Pump-up sprayer

Using a liquid pesticide. For a heavy infestation of insect pests *(page 83)*, apply pesticide granules *(step below)* or a liquid pesticide. Choose an appropriate liquid pesticide *(page 82)*; if necessary, also an application tool *(page 116)*. Prepare to work safely with the pesticide *(page 98)*, following the manufacturer's instructions to apply it. Work on a calm day, marking the perimeter 2 feet beyond the infested area. To use a pump-up sprayer, as shown, adjust the nozzle to a fine spray setting. Walking backwards from one end to the other end of the infested area, use a steady side-to-side motion to thoroughly dampen it with pesticide *(left)*. After treating the infested area, keep people and pets off it for the time specified—usually 24 hours.

Drop spreader

Using pesticide granules. For a heavy infestation of insect pests *(page 83)*, apply a liquid pesticide *(step above)* or pesticide granules. Choose an appropriate type of pesticide granules *(page 82)*; if necessary, also an application tool *(page 116)*. Prepare to work safely with the pesticide *(page 98)*, following the manufacturer's instructions to apply it. Work on a calm day, marking the perimeter 2 feet beyond the infested area. To use a drop spreader, as shown, adjust its opening to the setting specified for the pesticide. Pushing the spreader at a steady pace, make overlapping passes back and forth from end to end across the infested area, spreading an even layer of pesticide on it *(left)*. Water the treated area thoroughly, then keep people and pets off it for the time specified—usually 24 hours.

CONTROLLING GARDEN INSECT PESTS (LIGHT INFESTATION)

Handpicking insect pests off the foliage. For a light infestation of insect pests on the foliage *(page 84)*, pick them off by hand, if possible. To kill the insect pests, fill a small jar or container with water and add a squirt of dishwashing liquid. Wearing rubber gloves, pick any insect pest off the foliage *(above, left)*, then crush it between your fingers and drop it into the soapy water. For a slug, snail or other insect pest adhered to the foliage, try to remove it by gently rolling it from side to side *(above, right)*; if necessary, sprinkle a little table salt onto it to help loosen its grip. Repeat the procedure at different times for at least several days; at dawn or dusk, work with a flashlight, if necessary.

Plastic sheet

Shaking insect pests off the foliage. For a light infestation of insect pests on the foliage *(page 84)*, shake them off, if possible. To kill the insect pests, fill a bucket with water and add a few squirts of dishwashing liquid. Place a plastic sheet on the ground to catch the insect pests, then wear work gloves and shake the foliage vigorously to dislodge them *(above)*. Brush the insect pests off the plastic sheet and into the soapy water. Repeat the procedure at different times for at least several days.

Washing insect pests off the foliage. For a light infestation of insect pests on the foliage *(page 84)*, wash them off, if possible. Use a garden hose fitted with a trigger nozzle, adjusting it to a forceful jet setting; turn the water on fully. Holding the nozzle close to the foliage, spray it thoroughly to dislodge the insect pests *(above)*; if necessary, support it with your hand. Soak the ground under the foliage to help drown the insect pests washed off it. Repeat the procedure at different times for at least several days.

Cultivating insect pests out of the soil. For a light infestation of insect pests in the soil *(page 84)*, cultivate to help control them. To kill insect pests sighted, fill a bucket with water and add a few squirts of dishwashing liquid. Use a spade for the soil up to 18 inches away from plants, digging 4 to 6 inches into it and turning it over. Use a hand cultivator for the soil within 18 inches of plants, digging into and dragging through it *(above, left)* as well as breaking up compacted clods. Wear rubber gloves to check the soil for adult insect pests and their larvae *(above, right)*. Pick any insect pest out of the soil, then crush it between your fingers and drop it into the soapy water. Repeat the procedure at different times of day once every week.

Sticky trap

Reflective mulch

Using sticky traps. For a light infestation of insect pests such as aphids, whiteflies or thrips on the foliage *(page 84)*, buy sticky traps and follow the manufacturer's instructions to use them; the type shown is a strip with a removable cover on each side of it. Drive stakes into the ground near the infested foliage and run string tautly between them. Then, tie the sticky traps to the string at the intervals specified without having them touch the foliage *(above)* and peel the covers off them. Keep children and pets away from the sticky traps. Check the sticky traps daily for insect pests, replacing them as necessary.

Using reflective mulch. For a light infestation of insect pests such as aphids, whiteflies or thrips on the foliage *(page 84)*, disorient and discourage them with a reflective mulch. Buy a reflective mulch and follow the manufacturer's instructions to use it. Or, make a reflective mulch by cutting plastic sheets into strips 8 to 10 inches wide and up to 6 feet long, then taping aluminum foil to them. Dig a shallow trench for the reflective mulch in the ground under the infested foliage, then unroll it in the trench and cover its edges with soil *(above)*. Check the reflective mulch every few days and recover any exposed edge.

CONTROLLING GARDEN INSECT PESTS (LIGHT INFESTATION) (continued)

Using liquid traps. For a light infestation of insect pests such as slugs, snails or earwigs in the soil *(page 84)*, attract and drown them using liquid traps. Position a liquid trap every 10 feet along the perimeter of the infested soil. For a liquid trap, use a container such as a pie plate, digging a hole deep enough for the top of it to sit at ground level. Sit the container in the hole, then fill it with stale beer *(above)*. Check the traps for insect pests daily, replacing the stale beer as necessary.

Using shelter traps. For a light infestation of insect pests such as slugs, snails or earwigs in the soil *(page 84)*, attract them using shelter traps. Position a shelter trap every 10 feet along the perimeter of the infested soil. For a shelter trap, use a 1-inch board at least 1 foot wide and 3 feet long, propping up one end of it on a 2-by-4. Or, for slugs, use plastic pipe; for earwigs, use rolled up newspapers *(inset)*. At dusk, soak the shelter traps with water. At dawn, check the shelter traps for insect pests, brushing *(above)* or washing them into a bucket; to kill them, fill the bucket with water and add a few squirts of dishwashing liquid.

Using barriers. For a light infestation of insect pests such as cutworms in the soil *(page 84)*, protect the plants from them using barriers. Position a barrier 2 to 3 inches into the soil around each plant. For a barrier, use a can or waxed beverage carton 4 to 6 inches larger in diameter than the base of the plant, removing both ends of it. To kill insect pests sighted while positioning each barrier, fill a bucket with water and add a few squirts of dishwashing liquid. Wearing rubber gloves, use a garden trowel to dig a trench 2 to 3 inches deep around the plant 2 to 3

inches away from it, checking the soil for adult insect pests and their larvae *(above, left)*. Pick any insect pest out of the soil, then crush it between your fingers and drop it into the soapy water. Carefully slide the barrier over the plant and sit it in the trench. Pack soil around the outside of the barrier *(above, right)*, tamping it down with your fingers. Check the barriers daily, repositioning them as necessary and replacing them with larger ones as the plants grow. Remove the barriers when the plants are strong enough to withstand cutworms—usually after about 6 weeks.

CONTROLLING GARDEN INSECT PESTS (HEAVY INFESTATION)

Treating the foliage with a pesticide. For a heavy infestation of insect pests on the foliage *(page 84)*, work on a calm day to apply a pesticide; to prevent harm to beneficial pollinating insects, avoid applying pesticide to the foliage of a flowering plant in bloom. Choose an appropriate pesticide *(page 82)*; if necessary, also an application tool *(page 116)*. Prepare to work safely with the pesticide *(page 98)*, following the manufacturer's instructions to use it. To apply a liquid pesticide using a pump-up sprayer, as shown, adjust the nozzle to a fine spray setting. Keeping the nozzle 6 to 8 inches away from the foliage, use a steady side-to-side motion to thoroughly dampen it with pesticide. Spray the top and underside *(above, left)* of the leaves, the stems and the stalks until they are wet but not dripping. To apply a pesticide dust using a crank duster, as shown, work the same way to coat the top and underside of the leaves, the stems and the stalks with a fine layer of it *(above, right)*. After treating the infested foliage, keep people and pets away from it for the time specified—usually 24 hours.

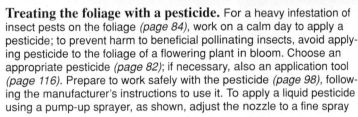

Treating the soil with a pesticide. For a heavy infestation of insect pests in the soil *(page 84)*, work on a calm day to apply a pesticide; to prevent harm to beneficial pollinating insects, avoid applying pesticide to the foliage of a flowering plant in bloom. Choose an appropriate pesticide *(page 82)*; if necessary, also an application tool *(page 116)*. Prepare to work safely with the pesticide *(page 98)*, following the manufacturer's instructions to use it. To apply a liquid pesticide using a pump-up sprayer, as shown, adjust the nozzle to a fine spray setting. Keeping the nozzle 6 to 8 inches away from the ground, use a steady side-to-side motion to thoroughly soak the soil with pesticide *(above, left)*. To apply a pesticide dust using a squeeze container, as shown, work the same way to coat the soil with a fine layer of it *(above, right)*. Cultivate the pesticide into the top few inches of soil, working carefully with a hand cultivator around the base of plants After treating the infested soil, keep people and pets off it for the time specified—usually 24 hours.

CONTROLLING TREE INSECT PESTS (LIGHT INFESTATION)

Clearing insect pests from the foliage. For a light infestation of insect pests on the foliage *(page 84)*, try handpicking, shaking or washing them off, if possible *(page 86)*. For a nest of insect pests such as tent caterpillars, position a plastic sheet on the ground under the nest to catch it and the insect pests. To kill the insect pests, fill a bucket with water and add a few squirts of dishwashing liquid. Wearing work gloves and safety goggles, prune off the branches supporting the insect pests and their nest, if possible. Otherwise, wrap a nylon stocking around a broom and use it to knock the insect pests and their nest off the branches *(above)*. Place the insect pests and their nest in the soapy water.

Clearing insect pests from the bark. For a light infestation of insect pests on the bark *(page 84)*, try handpicking or washing them off, if possible *(page 86)*. For insect pests such as peach tree borers under the bark, follow the trail of their tiny, round holes and sawdust-like frass. Using a stiff wire such as a straightened hanger, poke as far as possible into each hole to kill the insect pests; if frass reappears later, they are still alive. For stubborn insect pests, wear work gloves and dig them out using a fine-pointed surgical or art knife with a narrow blade. Making tiny cuts no deeper than 1/4 inch into the bark, enlarge a hole only enough to follow the trail of the insect pests *(above)*; if they cannot be located, consult a pest control professional.

CONTROLLING TREE INSECT PESTS (HEAVY INFESTATION)

Slide-action sprayer

Using a pesticide. For a heavy infestation of insect pests on the foliage *(page 84)*, work on a calm day to apply a pesticide; to prevent harm to beneficial pollinating insects, avoid applying pesticide to the foliage of a tree in blossom. Choose an appropriate pesticide *(page 82)*; if necessary, also an application tool *(page 116)*. Prepare to work safely with the pesticide *(page 98)*, following the manufacturer's instructions to use it. To apply a liquid pesticide using a slide-action sprayer, as shown, adjust the nozzle to a long-distance spray setting and spray the top of the tree. Moving in a circle around the tree, aim the nozzle a little higher than the foliage and allow the pesticide to settle on it, thoroughly dampening it; also spray the underside of the leaves. Working downward from the top of the tree, continue spraying the same way *(left)*, adjusting the nozzle to shorter-distance spray settings. Spray infested bark until it is wet but not dripping. After treating the infested foliage, keep people and pets away from the tree for the time specified—usually 24 hours.

CONTROLLING BIRDS

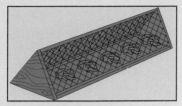

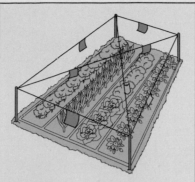

Seed and shoot protector
Frame of 2-by-2s with 1-inch wire mesh stapled to it protects seeds and shoots from birds while allowing sunlight and water to enter.

Twine and foil barrier
Strips of aluminum foil hung from twine tied in crisscross pattern to stakes in vulnerable location; birds deterred by pattern of twine and startled by light reflected off foil.

Repellent tape
Stretched between posts in open location; vibration of tape in wind causes noise to frighten birds.

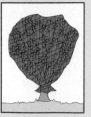

Bird netting
Protects fruit from birds. Netting of 1-inch to 1 1/4-inches mesh draped over tree and tied around base of trunk; netting of 1/4- to 1/2-inch mesh draped over bush, vine or plant and tied to stakes driven into ground.

Imitation predator
Owl or snake effigy or other scarecrow positioned in highly visible location to frighten birds; change location periodically for best results.

Scare balloon
Brightly colored and patterned balloon hung from branch of tree or on tall pole to frighten birds; alternate periodically between balloons of different colors and patterns for best results.

Repelling nuisance birds. Control birds by scaring them away or by protecting vulnerable plants, vines, bushes and trees. In general, start measures to control birds early in the growing season to help prevent them from settling in; or, if possible, undertake measures to control them only as the harvesting season approaches. Observe the behavior patterns of the birds at different times for at least several days to identify the chief feeding areas, then decide on appropriate measures of control at locations within or nearby them. For guidance in developing a strategy to control the birds, refer to the inventory of typical control measures shown above; a range of products is usually available at a garden center or through a garden supply catalogue and many devices are easy to construct. A successful strategy of control may call for experimentation—with various combinations of different types of measures in various locations at different times of the growing season.

CONTROLLING GOPHERS AND MOLES

1 Locating tunnels. Locate tunnels used by gophers by looking for mounds of raised ground—usually fan-shaped, with a steep slope on one side and a gradual slope with a plug of soil at the center on the other side. For a probe, use a 3/4-inch hardwood dowel about 4 feet long, whittling one end of it into a point. Starting about 12 inches from a mound on the side with the gradual slope, push the probe into the ground *(left)* until there is a sudden decrease in resistance, indicating it has reached a tunnel; if necessary, drive it in using a hand drilling hammer. If the probe does not reach a tunnel by a depth of 12 inches into the ground, remove it to repeat the procedure, continuing as necessary every 12 inches around the mound. Locate tunnels used by moles by looking for ridges of raised ground and flattening sections of them with your feet; a ridge reappearing within 24 hours indicates an active tunnel. After locating a tunnel, treat it with a poison-bait pesticide *(step 2)* or set traps for the gophers *(step 3)* or moles *(step 4)* using it.

CONTROLLING GOPHERS AND MOLES (continued)

2 **Using a poison-bait pesticide.** Set traps for the gophers *(step 3)* or moles *(step 4)* in a tunnel near plants used for food or around a dog that may hunt for the pests. Otherwise, gain access to as many sections of the tunnel as possible by making holes into it with a probe; for a probe, use a 3/4-inch hardwood dowel about 4 feet long, whittling one end of it into a point. Choose an appropriate poison-bait pesticide *(page 82)* and prepare to work safely with it *(page 98)*, then carefully follow the manufacturer's instructions to use it. For the type of poison-bait pesticide shown, pour 1 teaspoon of it through each hole *(left)* into the tunnel; work carefully to avoid spilling any of it on the ground around the hole. Cover the hole with a plug of sod or a stone. Check each tunnel treated with the poison-bait pesticide and the ground around it for several days. Wear work gloves to handle any carcass found, sealing it in a heavy-duty plastic garbage bag for disposal in an outdoor trash can. If a tunnel appears to remain in use, repeat the treatment.

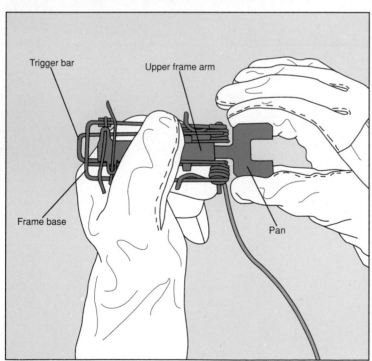

Trigger bar

Upper frame arm

Frame base

Pan

3 **Using gopher traps.** Buy two gopher traps for each tunnel located and follow the manufacturer's instructions to use them. Dig an access hole into the tunnel using a spade, then drive a stake into the ground near it for anchoring the traps. For the type of trap shown, tie a string to its spring end for anchoring to the stake. Wearing work gloves, hold the trap in one hand to carefully set it. Pressing down on the upper frame arm, fit the closed end of the trigger bar under the frame base. Then, swivel the pan up and press down on the open ends

of the trigger bar, fitting them under the pan *(above, left)*. Carefully place each trap in the tunnel on opposite sides of the access hole *(above, right)*, then tie its string to the stake *(inset)* to keep it from being dragged out of reach inside the tunnel. Cover the access hole with a board. Check the traps daily and wear work gloves to remove any carcass, sealing it in a heavy-duty plastic garbage bag for disposal in an outdoor trash can. Relocate any trap that is not triggered within two days.

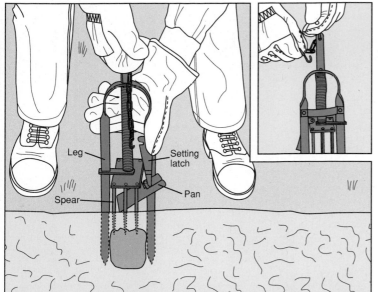

4 **Using mole traps.** Buy a mole trap for each active tunnel located and follow the manufacturer's instructions to use it. For the type of trap shown, set it up at a straight section of the tunnel, flattening the ridge with your feet. Wearing work gloves, position the legs on each side of the tunnel and push them into the ground until the pan rests on the flattened ridge. Clear a path into the tunnel for the spears by working them into the ground, pulling up and letting go of the handle *(above, left)*. Then, place the setting latch on the outside edge of the pan and pull up the handle until the platform of the spears

catches in its notch, the other end of it catching on the lip at the outside edge of the pan. Fit the safety pin into the arm of the handle *(inset)* to keep the trap from triggering accidentally. Check that the trap is set correctly *(above, right)* and remove its safety pin, then cover it with a cardboard box to help protect children and pets from it. Check the traps daily; wear work gloves and dig a hole with a spade to remove any carcass, sealing it in a heavy-duty plastic garbage bag for disposal in an outdoor trash can. Relocate any trap that is not triggered within two days.

CONTROLLNG WOODCHUCKS AND GROUND SQUIRRELS

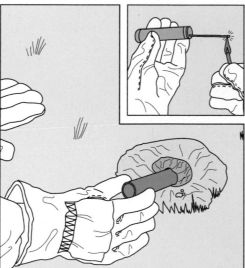

Using a pesticide gas. For woodchucks or ground squirrels with a tunnel system near the house or in sandy, porous soil, consult a pest control professional. Otherwise, buy an appropriate gas cartridge *(page 82)* and prepare to work safely with it *(page 98)*, following the manufacturer's instructions to use it; work when the soil is moist to help prevent gas from dissipating into it. If necessary, observe the behavior patterns of the woodchucks or ground squirrels to locate the entrance holes to the tunnel system. Use a plug of sod to seal each entrance hole but one—preferably the main one. Clear loose soil from this entrance

hole *(above, left)* and prepare a plug of sod to cover it. For the type of gas cartridge shown, fit the fuse into the end of it and light the fuse *(inset)*, then immediately push it fuse-end first as far as possible into the entrance hole *(above, center)*. Cover the entrance hole with the plug of sod, placing it grass-side down *(above, right)* to keep soil from smothering the flame. Check the ground above the tunnel system for escaping gas, sealing any hole with a plug of sod. If necessary, repeat the treatment following the manufacturer's instructions at a different entrance hole.

CONTROLLING PESTS CULTURALLY

PEST	PLANT DETERRENT
Japanese beetles	Garlic, geranium, rue, tansy
June beetles	Alfalfa, clover
Spotted or striped cucumber beetles	Marigold, nasturtium, radish, tansy
Flea beetles	Catnip, mint, wormwood
Mexican bean beetles	Garlic, marigold, petunia, potato, rosemary, summer savory
Colorado potato beetles	Catnip, coriander, dead nettle, flax, green beans, horseradish, nasturtium, tansy
Plum curculios	Garlic
Squash bugs	Catnip, marigold, nasturtium, tansy
Chinch bugs	Soy bean
Stinkbugs, corn ear worms or cutworms	Tansy

PEST	PLANT DETERRENT
Aphids	Chives, coriander, garlic, nasturtium, pennyroyal, petunia, southernwood spearmint, tansy
Whiteflies	Marigold, nasturtium, nicandra
Leafhoppers	Geranium, petunia
Wireworms	Buckwheat, white mustard, woad
Cabbage loopers	Mint, nasturtium, rosemary, sage
Tomato hornworms	Asparagus, borage, marigold, opal basil
Slugs or snails	Prostrate rosemary, wormwood
Gophers	Castor bean
Moles	Castor bean, mole plant, spurge, squill
Mice	Mint
Rabbits	Chive, garlic, leek, onion, shallot

Using horticultural controls. Whenever possible, try controlling pests naturally by adopting horticultural control measures. Consult your local county extension agent for suggestions on pest-resistant plants under development in your region; also ask about the best timing of plantings to avoid the most damaging life stages of pests common to your region. For a minor problem with a particular type of pest, try experimenting with companion planting—planting within a vulnerable area a type of plant that helps serves as a deterrent to the pest. Refer to the chart above for guidance in choosing a type of plant that may help to deter a specific type of pest. A successful strategy of horticultural control measures usually calls for experimentation with various combinations of different types of plants in various locations at different times of the growing season.

Using biological controls. Most insect pests, in particular, can be controlled naturally by introducing their biological predators. Consult your local county extension agent to determine if a problem with a particular type of insect pest warrants the introduction of beneficial predatory insects; also ask about the best timing for their introduction. A range of beneficial predatory insects such as lacewings, ladybugs or antlions can usually be ordered through a garden supply catalogue; consult your local county extension agency for a list of suppliers. Follow the instructions of the supplier to introduce the beneficial predatory insects; in the instance shown, spilling lacewings from the foam-cup container supplied with them onto the ground of the area *(left)*.

CONTROLLING INSECT PESTS BEFORE THE GROWING SEASON

Treating the soil. Treat the soil with a pesticide in the spring following a growing season plagued by an infestation of insect pests or if an infestation of insect pests is found prior to planting *(page 84)*. Wearing work gloves, clear the area of debris and rocks, then cultivate the soil to a depth of 3 to 6 inches. Rent a garden tiller at a tool rental center and follow the manufacturer's instructions to use it, adjusting the tines to the tilling depth desired. Work back and forth in overlapping passes across the area from one end to the other end of it to till the soil *(above, left)*. Or, till the soil using a long-handled cultivator *(inset)*. Choose an appropriate pesticide *(page 82)*; if necessary, also an application tool *(page 116)*. Prepare to work safely with the pesticide *(page 98)*, following the manufacturer's instructions to use it. To use a drop spreader for applying pesticide granules, as shown, adjust its opening to the setting specified for the pesticide. Pushing the spreader at a steady pace, make overlapping passes back and forth across the area from one end to the other end of it, spreading the pesticide evenly *(above, right)*. Recultivate the soil to mix the pesticide into it. At the end of the growing season, cultivate the soil again to clean up crop residue that may serve as a feeding source for insect pests.

Treating trees and bushes. Treat a tree or bush with a horticultural oil in the spring following a growing season plagued by an infestation of insect pests or if an infestation of insect pests is found prior to the growing season *(page 84)*. Buy a horticultural oil at a garden center; if necessary, choose an application tool *(page 116)*. Prepare to work safely with the horticultural oil *(page 98)*, following the manufacturer's instructions to use it; work on a calm day. To use a pump-up sprayer for applying an oil, as shown, adjust the nozzle to a fine spray setting. Moving in a circle around the tree or bush, work downward from the top of it, aiming the nozzle a little high and allowing the oil to settle on it *(left)*, thoroughly dampening it; spray until it is wet but not dripping. After treating the tree or bush, keep people and pets away from it for the time specified—usually 24 hours.

PESTPROOFING WITH GARDEN BLANKETS, GUARDS AND BARRIERS

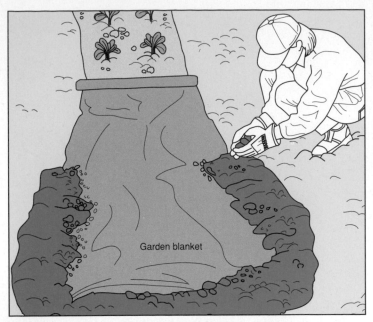

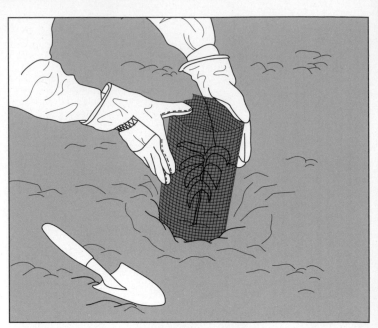

Protecting plants with a garden blanket. Protect an area of seeds or young plants from birds and animals by covering it with a garden blanket. Buy a light-weight garden blanket at a garden center and follow the manufacturer's instructions to install it. For the type of garden blanket shown, wear work gloves and use a hand trowel to dig a shallow trench along the perimeter of the area. Place the garden blanket in the trench at one end and partially along each side of the area, then secure each edge of it by covering it with soil *(above)*. Continue to the other end of the area the same way, unrolling the garden blanket and covering its edges with soil to secure it.

Protecting plants with guards. Protect a young plant from birds and animals using 1/4-inch mesh hardware cloth as a barrier. Wearing work gloves, cut a piece of hardware cloth 6 to 8 inches higher and longer than the height and diameter of the plant. Rolling the hardware cloth into a cylinder, overlap the ends by 2 to 3 inches and tie them together with mechanic's wire. Use a hand trowel to dig a trench 2 to 3 inches deep around the plant 2 to 3 inches from it. Slide the barrier over the plant and sit it in the trench *(above)*, then pack soil around it. For protection from birds, cut a piece of hardware cloth to fit the top of the cylinder and tie it in place.

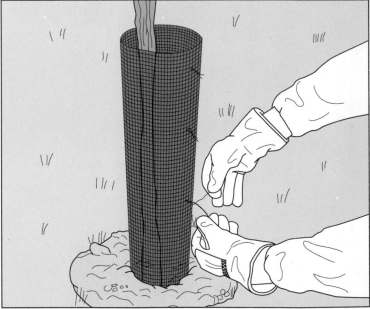

Protecting young trees with guards. Protect a young tree from animals using a guard. Buy a guard at a garden center and follow the manufacturer's instructions to install it. For the plastic type of guard shown, dig a trench a few inches deep around the base of the tree with a hand trowel. Starting about 2 1/2 feet from the ground, work down the trunk of the tree to wrap the guard around it, overlapping the edges slightly *(above, left)*. Continue to the bottom of the trench the same way, then cut off any excess guard and fill in the trench with soil. Alter-

natively, make a guard of 1/4-inch mesh hardware cloth, wearing work gloves to cut a piece of it 3 feet high and 8 to 10 inches longer than the diameter of the tree. Dig a trench 6 inches deep around the tree 3 to 4 inches from it using a spade. Roll the hardware cloth into a cylinder in the trench around the tree and overlap the ends of it by 2 to 3 inches, then fill in the trench with soil. Pull the overlapping ends of the hardware cloth together and tie them with mechanic's wire *(above, right)*.

Protecting mature trees with slippery barriers. To keep animals from climbing a mature tree, use a slippery barrier of metal flashing. Wearing work gloves, cut a piece of rust-resistant metal flashing 2 1/2 feet wide and long enough to fit around the tree. Wrap the flashing snugly around the trunk of the tree with the bottom edge of it at least 1 1/2 feet from the ground, then secure it in place near the top of it with a large hose clamp *(above)*. Remove the slippery barrier at the end of the growing season.

Protecting mature trees with sticky barriers. To keep insect pests from crawling up a mature tree, use a sticky barrier of insect trap adhesive. Cut a piece of sturdy construction paper 4 inches wide and long enough to fit around the tree. Wrap the paper around the trunk of the tree a few feet from the ground and secure its ends with waterproof tape, then fill any gap between it and the tree with cotton batten. Using a putty knife, apply a light, even coat of insect trap adhesive about 2 to 3 inches wide on the paper *(above)*. Check the barrier daily, replacing it as necessary.

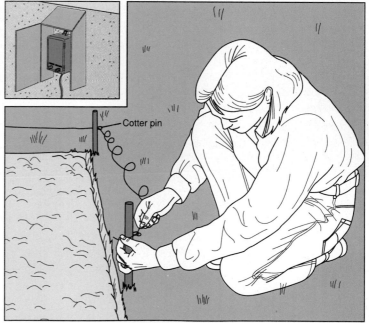

Installing an electrical-shock fence. To keep animals out of an area, install a fence that emits an irritating electrical shock; check first with your municipal authorities to ensure that its use is permitted in your community. Buy an electrical-shock fence kit and follow the manufacturer's instructions to set it up. For the type of fence kit shown, position a stake every 8 to 12 feet along the perimeter of the area. Wearing work gloves and safety goggles, use a hand drilling hammer to drive each stake 4 to 6 inches into the ground *(above, left)*. Fit a cotter pin through the hole in each stake at the height of the target animal's chest, bending back the tines to secure it. Place the controller *(inset)* in a protected enclosure, shielding it from the elements. Connect one end of the wire to the terminal of the controller marked FENCE, then run the wire tautly in turn to each stake, threading it through the cotter pin *(above, right)*. At the last stake, thread the wire through the cotter pin and loop it back, twisting it around the taut wire to secure the end of it. Cut back vegetation and install warning signs near the wire. Call an electrician to install the grounding rod and make the electrical hookups; have him check the set up of the fence before plugging it in. Keep people and pets away from the fence when it is in operation.

WORKING SAFELY

A pest control job need not be hazardous to you, your family and pets, or the natural environment if you take the time to work methodically and carefully. However, a pest control job that involves working in a location high overhead or the using of a chemical pesticide requires special precautions; use the information in this chapter to help you set up properly and safely. Before beginning a pest control job that requires working at heights, ensure that you know how to work safely on a ladder *(page 110)* or on the roof *(page 111)*. Before beginning a pest control job that involves the use of a potentially dangerous pesticide, ensure that you take the time necessary to choose the most appropriate product and that you are prepared to work safely with it *(page 100)*.

A pesticide is a powerful chemical tool that can provide fast, effective control of a troublesome pest—but it can be a health and environmental hazard if it is used excessively or carelessly. When choosing a pesticide, carefully read its product label *(page 101)* to ensure that it is recommended for control of the particular pest and can be applied on the surfaces and in the area you plan to treat—indoors or outdoors. Always select the pesticide that contains the least toxic active ingredients *(page 102)* to minimize the risk of harming the natural environment.

Before using a pesticide, prepare yourself to respond quickly to any emergency that might arise while you are using it. Carefully review the safety precautions and first-aid instructions on the product label of the pesticide. Read the Emergency Guide *(page 8)* to familiarize yourself with basic procedures for handling a pesticide spill or pesticide contamination. Then, take the time to set up properly for the job in a clean, well-ventilated work area well away from any living area of your home; a functional work area for preparing and storing pesticides is shown at right.

To use a pesticide, gather together the required tools and materials and wear the necessary personal safety gear *(page 104)*. Strictly follow the manufacturer's instructions to measure and mix the pesticide *(page 106)*, consulting Tools & Techniques *(page 112)* to set up any application tool needed. Prepare the area to be treated with the pesticide *(page 107)*, setting up barriers around it and protecting surfaces not to be treated; in an outdoor area, also test the wind direction and force to ensure that the pesticide can be applied safely. Test the pesticide on an inconspicuous spot of any surface you plan to treat with it; if there is an adverse reaction, use another pesticide. After using a pesticide, clean up thoroughly *(page 108)*, safely discarding or storing any leftover as well as properly cleaning and storing tools and personal safety gear. If you doubt your ability to work safely with a pesticide or on a ladder or the roof, do not hesitate to consult a professional.

Safety cabinet
Store pesticides as well as measuring, mixing and application tools separately, locked safely away from children, pets and other products in a locked metal cabinet that is situated in a dry, well-ventilated area away from sources of heat or ignition. Post a DANGER sign on the cabinet and install a smoke detector on the ceiling above it; in the event of a fire involving pesticides, evacuate the house and call the fire department; provide information on the nature of the fire.

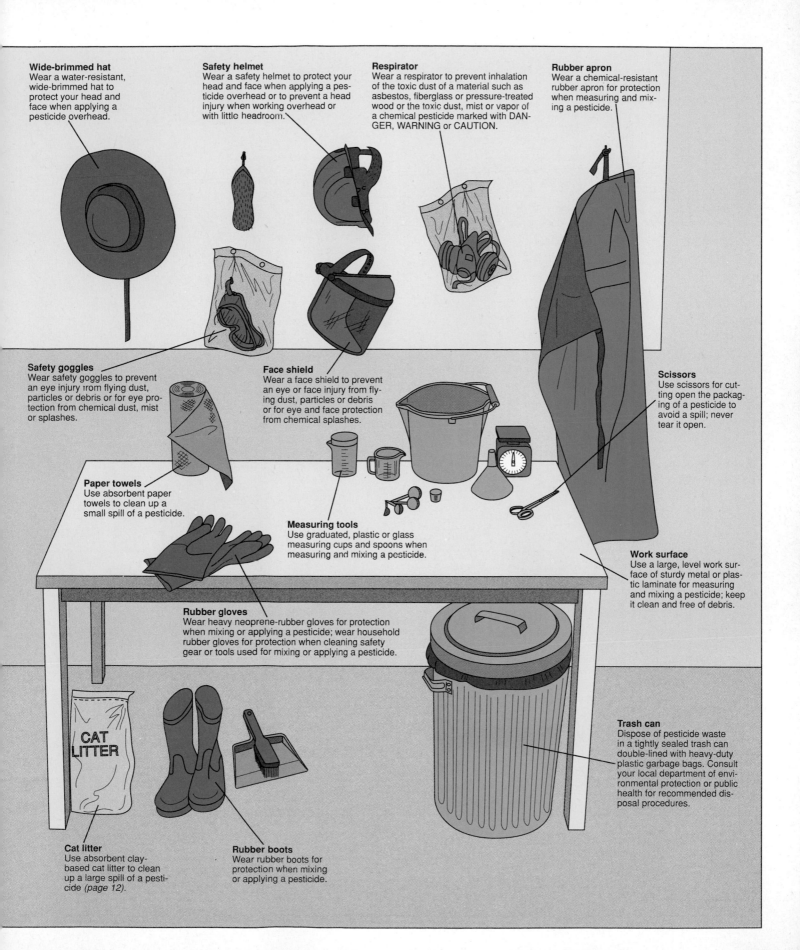

Wide-brimmed hat
Wear a water-resistant, wide-brimmed hat to protect your head and face when applying a pesticide overhead.

Safety helmet
Wear a safety helmet to protect your head and face when applying a pesticide overhead or to prevent a head injury when working overhead or with little headroom.

Respirator
Wear a respirator to prevent inhalation of the toxic dust of a material such as asbestos, fiberglass or pressure-treated wood or the toxic dust, mist or vapor of a chemical pesticide marked with DANGER, WARNING or CAUTION.

Rubber apron
Wear a chemical-resistant rubber apron for protection when measuring and mixing a pesticide.

Safety goggles
Wear safety goggles to prevent an eye injury from flying dust, particles or debris or for eye protection from chemical dust, mist or splashes.

Face shield
Wear a face shield to prevent an eye or face injury from flying dust, particles or debris or for eye and face protection from chemical splashes.

Scissors
Use scissors for cutting open the packaging of a pesticide to avoid a spill; never tear it open.

Paper towels
Use absorbent paper towels to clean up a small spill of a pesticide.

Measuring tools
Use graduated, plastic or glass measuring cups and spoons when measuring and mixing a pesticide.

Work surface
Use a large, level work surface of sturdy metal or plastic laminate for measuring and mixing a pesticide; keep it clean and free of debris.

Rubber gloves
Wear heavy neoprene-rubber gloves for protection when mixing or applying a pesticide; wear household rubber gloves for protection when cleaning safety gear or tools used for mixing or applying a pesticide.

Trash can
Dispose of pesticide waste in a tightly sealed trash can double-lined with heavy-duty plastic garbage bags. Consult your local department of environmental protection or public health for recommended disposal procedures.

Cat litter
Use absorbent clay-based cat litter to clean up a large spill of a pesticide *(page 12)*.

Rubber boots
Wear rubber boots for protection when mixing or applying a pesticide.

CAT LITTER

99

WORKING SAFELY WITH A PESTICIDE

Using a pesticide safely. A pesticide used cautiously and correctly need not be hazardous to you, your family and pets, or the natural environment. However, a pesticide typically contains substances that can harm health and accumulate in the natural environment—especially if it is used carelessly or excessively. Follow the guidelines below when working with a pesticide to minimize the risk of an accident and protect the natural environment:

- When working with a pesticide, wear the safety gear recommended to minimize any health or safety risk listed on its label; do not smoke, eat or drink.

- Before using a pesticide in an indoor area, remove food, medication and toiletries from it. Cover dishes, utensils, appliances and food preparation surfaces with plastic.

- Buy and prepare only as much of a pesticide as needed for a job, avoiding the need to store or dispose of any leftover.

- Open a container of pesticide slowly and carefully to avoid spilling it. Do not tear open a bag of pesticide; use scissors to cut it open.

- Have absorbent materials such as paper towels and clay-based cat litter on hand when working with a pesticide, prepared to clean up any spill immediately *(page 12)*.

- In the event of a spill of a pesticide onto your clothing, immediately brush off a dry product; remove clothing splashed with a liquid product.

- Before putting away or reusing clothing that is contaminated by a pesticide, launder it separately from other clothing using hot water and a strong detergent.

- After using a pesticide in an indoor area, wash dishes, utensils, appliances and food preparation surfaces in it.

- Store safety gear used for a job in a clean, dry location; check it before storing it and replace any damaged piece.

- Store a pesticide in a labeled container locked in a cabinet. Never store a pesticide in a container that might lead a child to mistake the contents for food or drink; never store a caustic pesticide in a container that might be corroded by it.

- Never use a pesticide container or tool for a purpose other than the storage or application of a pesticide.

- To dispose of a pesticide safely, consult your local department of environmental protection or public health for procedures recommended in your community. Never pour a pesticide down a drain, into a sewer or onto the ground.

- After working with a pesticide, shower thoroughly; wash your skin using soap and your hair with shampoo.

- Before eating a fruit or vegetable treated with a pesticide, wash it thoroughly using a brush and water; add a little mild dishwashing liquid to the water and rinse well or peel off and discard the skin or outer leaves.

CHOOSING A PESTICIDE

Choosing a pesticide formulation. A pesticide may be available in a variety of liquid or dry formulations. While one product may come pre-mixed in the correct proportions in a self-contained, ready-to-use applicator, another product may require careful measuring and mixing, as well as a special application tool. Refer to the information below in deciding on the formulation of a pesticide to use, ensuring that an appropriate application tool is available and that you know how to use it properly.

- **Liquid.** Contains active ingredients dissolved in a petroleum-based solvent. Liquid concentrate requires mixing with water *(page 106)* following the manufacturer's instructions; apply using a sprayer. Apply a pre-mixed liquid using a fogger *(page 116)*.

- **Aerosol.** Contains active and inert ingredients and a propellant dissolved in a petroleum-based solvent. Requires no mixing; available as a controlled-release spray or a total-release fog in a ready-to-use container. Use a product spray or fog container following the manufacturer's instructions.

- **Dust.** Contains active ingredients mixed with an inert carrier such as clay. Requires no mixing; available in a ready-to-use shaker container or in bulk. Use a product shaker container following the manufacturer's instructions; a bulk product can be applied using a squeeze applicator or a duster *(page 116)*.

- **Wettable powder.** A dry powder formulation resembling a dust formulation. Requires mixing of the wettable powder with water *(page 106)* into a liquid following the manufacturer's instructions; apply using a sprayer *(page 116)*.

- **Granules.** Contains active ingredients mixed with an inert carrier such as clay. Requires no mixing; available in a ready-to-use shaker container or in bulk. Use a product shaker container following the manufacturer's instructions; a bulk product can be applied using a spreader *(page 116)*.

- **Poison bait.** Contains active ingredients mixed with an edible, inert carrier. No mixing required; available in a ready-to-use bait-station format or in bulk. Use a bait station following the manufacturer's instructions; a bulk product can be applied using a spreader *(page 116)*.

CHOOSING A PESTICIDE (continued)

Reading a pesticide label. When choosing a pesticide, read the label carefully to ensure that it is the right product for the job. Study the sample label of a pesticide product shown below to know what to look for. In general, treat any pesticide product as if it is more dangerous than its label indicates. Check the list of active ingredients on the product to ensure that the one you require is listed, then read the list of controls to ensure that the product is recommended for the particular pest you are trying to control. Look at the toxicity rating of the product and compare it with the toxicity ratings of other similar products to choose a pesticide of the lowest toxicity possible *(page 102)*.

To double-check that a product is appropriate for the job, read the directions for use; ensure that you have the necessary tools on hand and that the pesticide can be safely applied on the surfaces or in the area to be treated. Refer to the precautions on the product to help you choose the correct safety gear for the job. Familiarize yourself with the first-aid instructions for the product in the event that you are required to use them. Prepare the surfaces or area to be treated and mix the pesticide carefully following the manufacturer's instructions. After treating the surfaces or area with the pesticide, refer to the information on storage and disposal of the product to safely handle any leftover.

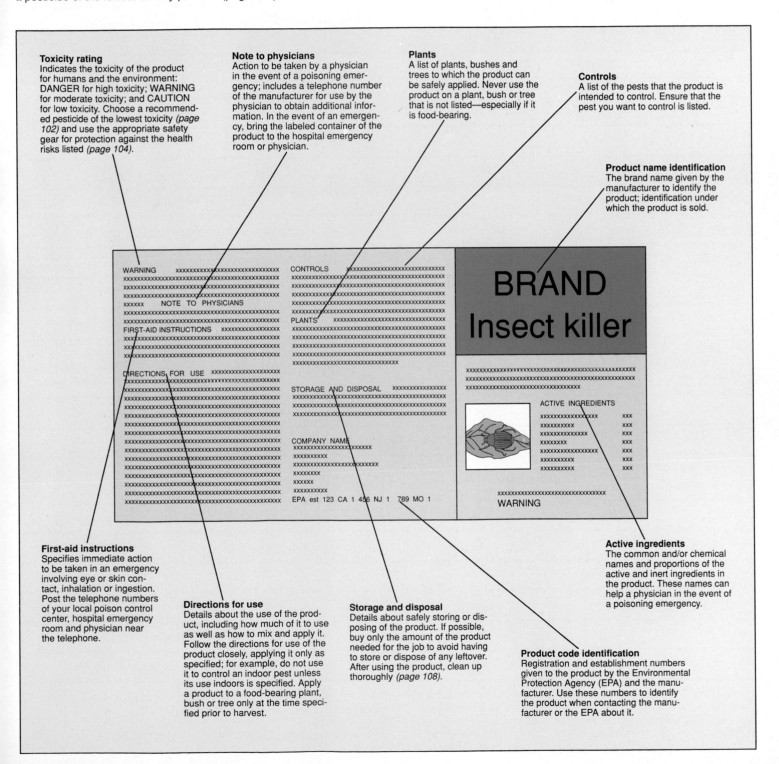

Toxicity rating
Indicates the toxicity of the product for humans and the environment: DANGER for high toxicity; WARNING for moderate toxicity; and CAUTION for low toxicity. Choose a recommended pesticide of the lowest toxicity *(page 102)* and use the appropriate safety gear for protection against the health risks listed *(page 104)*.

Note to physicians
Action to be taken by a physician in the event of a poisoning emergency; includes a telephone number of the manufacturer for use by the physician to obtain additional information. In the event of an emergency, bring the labeled container of the product to the hospital emergency room or physician.

Plants
A list of plants, bushes and trees to which the product can be safely applied. Never use the product on a plant, bush or tree that is not listed—especially if it is food-bearing.

Controls
A list of the pests that the product is intended to control. Ensure that the pest you want to control is listed.

Product name identification
The brand name given by the manufacturer to identify the product; identification under which the product is sold.

First-aid instructions
Specifies immediate action to be taken in an emergency involving eye or skin contact, inhalation or ingestion. Post the telephone numbers of your local poison control center, hospital emergency room and physician near the telephone.

Directions for use
Details about the use of the product, including how much of it to use as well as how to mix and apply it. Follow the directions for use of the product closely, applying it only as specified; for example, do not use it to control an indoor pest unless its use indoors is specified. Apply a product to a food-bearing plant, bush or tree only at the time specified prior to harvest.

Storage and disposal
Details about safely storing or disposing of the product. If possible, buy only the amount of the product needed for the job to avoid having to store or dispose of any leftover. After using the product, clean up thoroughly *(page 108)*.

Product code identification
Registration and establishment numbers given to the product by the Environmental Protection Agency (EPA) and the manufacturer. Use these numbers to identify the product when contacting the manufacturer or the EPA about it.

Active ingredients
The common and/or chemical names and proportions of the active and inert ingredients in the product. These names can help a physician in the event of a poisoning emergency.

CHOOSING A PESTICIDE (continued)

PESTICIDE	TOXICITY	AVAILABLE FORMULATION	PERSONAL PRECAUTIONS
Acephate	Low	Liquid	Avoid inhalation, ingestion, and skin and eye contact
Allethrin	Low	Liquid, aerosol	Avoid inhalation, ingestion, and skin and eye contact
Avermectin	Low	Poison bait	Avoid ingestion, and skin and eye contact
Bacillus popilliae (Bp)	None	Liquid	Avoid inhalation, ingestion, and skin and eye contact
Bacillus thuringiensis (Bt)	None	Liquid	Avoid inhalation, ingestion, and skin and eye contact
Bendiocarb	Moderate	Dust, wettable powder	Avoid inhalation, ingestion, and skin and eye contact
Bioallethrin (d-trans-allethrin)	Low	Liquid, aerosol	Avoid inhalation, ingestion, and skin and eye contact
Boric acid	Low	Dust	Avoid inhalation, ingestion, and skin and eye contact
Brodifacoum	Low	Poison bait	Avoid ingestion, and skin and eye contact
Bromadiolone	Low	Poison bait	Avoid ingestion, and skin and eye contact
Bromethalin	Low	Poison bait	Avoid ingestion, and skin and eye contact
Carbaryl	Low	Dust, wettable powder, granules, poison bait	Avoid inhalation, ingestion, and skin and eye contact
Chlorophacinone	Low to moderate	Poison bait	Avoid ingestion, and skin and eye contact
Chlorpyrifos	Moderate	Liquid, dust, granules, poison bait	Avoid inhalation, ingestion, and skin and eye contact
Cholecalciferol	Low	Poison bait	Avoid ingestion, and skin and eye contact
Cyfluthrin	Moderate	Aerosol, wettable powder	Avoid inhalation, ingestion, and skin and eye contact
Cypermethrin	Moderate	Liquid, wettable powder	Avoid inhalation, ingestion, and skin and eye contact
DEET	Low	Liquid, aerosol	Avoid ingestion and eye contact
Diatomaceous earth (silicon dioxide)	None	Dust	Avoid inhalation, ingestion, and skin and eye contact
Diazinon	Low to moderate	Liquid, dust, wettable powder, granules	Avoid inhalation, ingestion, and skin and eye contact
Dichlorvos (DDVP)	High	Aerosol, pest strip	Avoid inhalation, ingestion, and skin and eye contact
Dimethoate	Moderate	Liquid	Avoid inhalation, ingestion, and skin and eye contact
Diphacinone	Low	Poison bait	Avoid ingestion, and skin and eye contact
Disulfoton	High	Granules, insecticidal stick	Avoid ingestion, and skin and eye contact
D-limonene	Low to moderate	Liquid, aerosol	Avoid inhalation, ingestion, and skin and eye contact

Evaluating the toxicity of a pesticide. To minimize any risk to the natural environment when using a pesticide product to control a pest, choose the least toxic one possible for the job, avoiding potential harm to plants or beneficial insects and animals. When choosing a pesticide product, first determine the active ingredients required for control of the pest, using the examples listed in the chart of the appropriate chapter: Indoor Pests *(page 41)*, Outdoor Pests *(page 63)* or Lawn And Garden Pests *(page 82)*. Then, refer to the chart above to help you choose a pesticide product that contains the least toxic of the active ingredients required for control of the pest.

PESTICIDE	TOXICITY	AVAILABLE FORMULATION	PERSONAL PRECAUTIONS
Fenoxycarb	Low	Liquid, aerosol	Avoid inhalation, ingestion, and skin and eye contact
Fenvalerate	Low to moderate	Liquid, aerosol	Avoid inhalation, ingestion, and skin and eye contact
Horticultural oil (dormant)	Low	Liquid	Avoid inhalation, ingestion, and skin and eye contact
Hydramethylnon	Low	Poison bait	Avoid ingestion, and skin and eye contact
Hydroprene	Low	Liquid, aerosol	Avoid inhalation, ingestion, and skin and eye contact
Insecticidal soap	None	Liquid	Avoid inhalation, ingestion, and skin and eye contact
Malathion	Low	Liquid, dust, wettable powder, poison bait	Avoid inhalation, ingestion, and skin and eye contact
Metaldehyde	Low	Poison bait	Avoid ingestion, and skin and eye contact
Methiocarb	Moderate	Poison bait	Avoid inhalation, ingestion, and skin and eye contact
Methoprene	Low	Aerosol	Avoid inhalation, ingestion, and skin and eye contact
Methoxychlor	Low	Liquid, aerosol, dust, wettable powder	Avoid inhalation, ingestion, and skin and eye contact
Nosema locustae	None	Liquid	Avoid inhalation, ingestion, and skin and eye contact
Permethrin	Low	Liquid, aerosol, wettable powder	Avoid inhalation, ingestion, and skin and eye contact
Phenothrin	Low	Aerosol	Avoid inhalation, ingestion, and skin and eye contact
Propetamphos	Low	Liquid	Avoid inhalation, ingestion, and skin and eye contact
Propoxur	Moderate	Aerosol, wettable powder, poison bait	Avoid inhalation, ingestion, and skin and eye contact
Pyrethrins	Low	Liquid, aerosol, dust	Avoid inhalation, ingestion, and skin and eye contact
Resmethrin	Low	Liquid, aerosol	Avoid inhalation, ingestion, and skin and eye contact
Rotenone	Moderate	Liquid, aerosol, dust	Avoid inhalation, ingestion, and skin and eye contact
Ryania	Low	Dust	Avoid inhalation, ingestion, and skin and eye contact
Sabadilla	Moderate	Dust	Avoid inhalation, ingestion, and skin and eye contact
Silica gel or aerogel	Low	Dust	Avoid inhalation, ingestion, and skin and eye contact
Sodium nitrate and sulfur	Moderate	Gas cartridge	Avoid inhalation, and skin and eye contact
Sulfluramid	Low	Poison bait	Avoid ingestion, and skin and eye contact
Tetrachlorvinphos	Low	Dust, wettable powder	Avoid inhalation, ingestion, and skin and eye contact
Tetramethrin	Low	Aerosol, dust	Avoid inhalation, ingestion, and skin and eye contact
Zinc phosphide	Low	Poison bait	Avoid inhalation, ingestion, and skin and eye contact

If possible, choose a pesticide product containing an active ingredient that is a natural disease of the pest you are trying to control—for example, *Bacillus popilliae* (Bp), *Bacillus thuringiensis* (Bt) or *Nosema locustae*; or, that is a plant-derived chemical—for example, pyrethrins, rotenone, ryania or sabadilla. Check the toxicity rating on the label of the pesticide product *(page 101)*: DANGER for high toxicity, WARNING for moderate toxicity and CAUTION for low toxicity. **Caution:** Even a pesticide product of low toxicity is a potential health hazard to humans and pets; observe the manufacturer's precautions and wear the appropriate safety gear *(page 104)*.

USING PERSONAL SAFETY GEAR

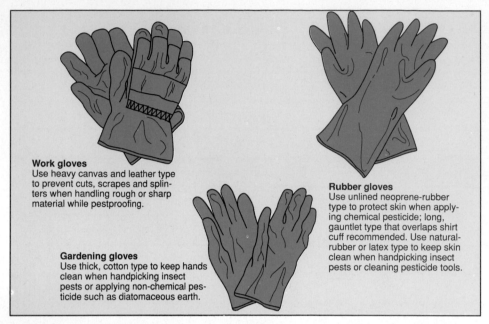

Work gloves
Use heavy canvas and leather type to prevent cuts, scrapes and splinters when handling rough or sharp material while pestproofing.

Gardening gloves
Use thick, cotton type to keep hands clean when handpicking insect pests or applying non-chemical pesticide such as diatomaceous earth.

Rubber gloves
Use unlined neoprene-rubber type to protect skin when applying chemical pesticide; long, gauntlet type that overlaps shirt cuff recommended. Use natural-rubber or latex type to keep skin clean when handpicking insect pests or cleaning pesticide tools.

Using skin and hand protection. To prevent burns, allergic reactions, cuts, scrapes and splinters when handling toxic, rough or sharp material, cover as much of your skin as possible. Protect your legs and arms by wearing long pants and a long-sleeved shirt or jacket of tightly woven cotton; ensure that the cuffs fit snugly. To protect your feet, wear rubber boots. Protect your hands by wearing an appropriate type of gloves *(above)*; ensure that the gloves fit snugly without restricting your hand movement. When working with a chemical pesticide, ensure that the rubber gloves you wear are resistant to it; check the information on the packaging of the gloves or consult the retailer or manufacturer.

Using head protection. When applying a pesticide overhead, protect your head and face by wearing a wide-brimmed, water-resistant hat *(above, top)* or a safety helmet. Otherwise, for protection of your head from injury, use a safety helmet rated by the American National Standards Institute (ANSI) or Canadian Standards Association (CSA); ensure that it fits snugly *(above, bottom)*.

Using eye and face protection. To prevent an eye injury, wear safety goggles; for eye and face protection, wear a face shield. Use a type of safety goggles or face shield that is rated by the American National Standards Institute (ANSI) or Canadian Standards Association (CSA) and recommended for the particular hazard. For work with chemicals, use safety goggles with baffled vents for protection from dust, mist and splashes. Test the fit of the safety goggles *(left)*, adjusting the headstrap as necessary until they are snug; if they are scratched, clouded or otherwise damaged, replace them. For work such as drilling, hammering or cutting, use safety goggles with perforated vent holes for protection from flying dust, particles and debris; test and check them the same way. When using a face shield, test and check it using the same procedure *(inset)*.

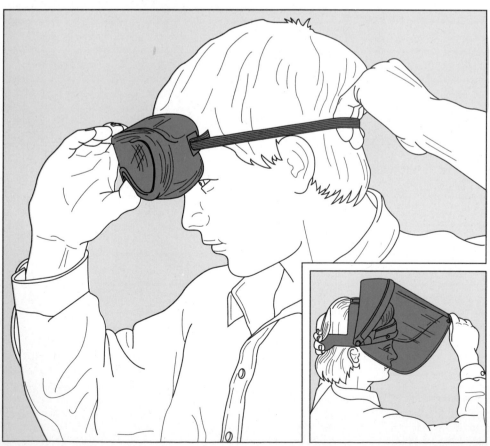

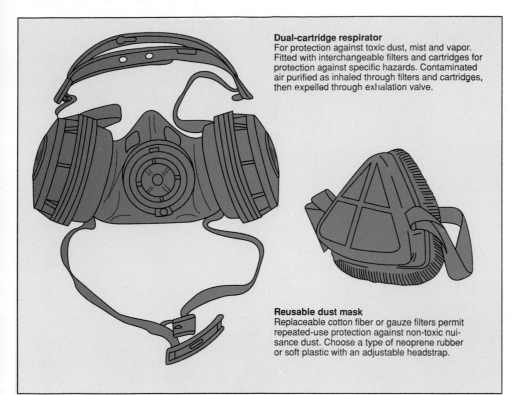

Dual-cartridge respirator
For protection against toxic dust, mist and vapor. Fitted with interchangeable filters and cartridges for protection against specific hazards. Contaminated air purified as inhaled through filters and cartridges, then expelled through exhalation valve.

Reusable dust mask
Replaceable cotton fiber or gauze filters permit repeated-use protection against non-toxic nuisance dust. Choose a type of neoprene rubber or soft plastic with an adjustable headstrap.

Using respiratory protection. For work with a chemical that emits toxic dust, mist or vapor or a tool that causes nuisance dust, ensure that the work area is well ventilated and wear an appropriate respiratory protection device *(left)*; ensure that the device is approved by the National Institute of Occupational Safety and Health (NIOSH) or the Mine Safety and Health Administration (MSHA). For protection against the toxic dust of a material such as asbestos, fiberglass or pressure-treated wood or the toxic dust, mist or vapor of a chemical pesticide marked with DANGER, WARNING or CAUTION, use a dual-cartridge respirator fitted with appropriate cartridges and filters *(step 1, below)*. For protection against the nuisance dust of wood, metal, drywall, masonry or a non-chemical pesticide such as diatomaceous earth, use a reusable dust mask with a clean filter.

PREPARING TO USE A RESPIRATOR

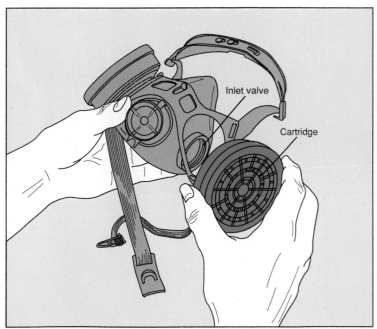

Inlet valve

Cartridge

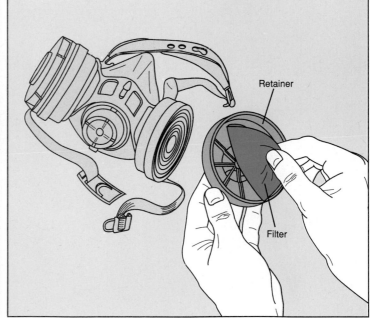

Retainer

Filter

1 Installing the cartridges and filters. Fit a respirator only with cartridges and filters designed for protection against the particular hazard, following the manufacturer's instructions; if necessary, consult the owner's manual or a safety-equipment supply company for recommended cartridges or filters suited to your model. Always buy cartridges and filters in pairs, one for each inlet valve on the respirator; check the date on each cartridge and filter to ensure that it has not expired. For the model of respirator shown, first install the cartridges, screwing each one onto an inlet valve *(above, left)*. To install the filters, fit each one into a retainer *(above, right)*, then snap the retainer onto a cartridge.

PREPARING TO USE A RESPIRATOR (continued)

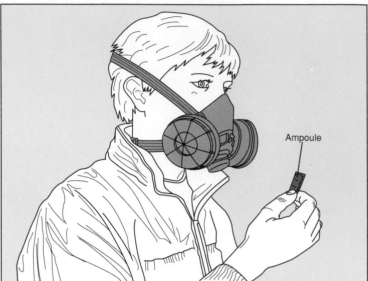

Ampoule

2 **Testing the respirator.** To put on the respirator, hold it cupped under your chin with the facepiece low on your nose, then pull the headstraps back over your head; if necessary, adjust them until the respirator fits snugly. To check the fit of the respirator, block the outlet valve with your hand *(above, left)*, then exhale gently; there should be no air leakage around the facepiece edges. If there is air leakage, adjust the headstraps and repeat the check; if there continues to be air leakage,

replace the respirator. Otherwise, test the respirator using a test ampoule of banana oil (isoamyl acetate)—available at a safety-equipment supply company. Break the ampoule and hold it near the respirator *(above, right)*, then breathe deeply several times and move it along the facepiece edges; you should detect no banana odor. If you detect a banana odor, move to another area, adjust the headstraps and repeat the test; if you continue to detect a banana odor, replace the respirator.

PREPARING A PESTICIDE

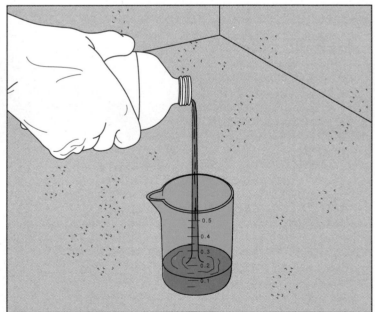

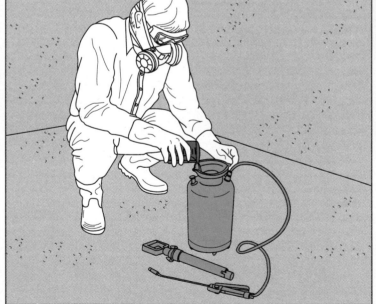

Measuring and mixing a pesticide. Read the precautions on the label of the pesticide product *(page 101)* and wear the appropriate safety gear *(page 104)*. Work in a well-ventilated area, having on hand graduated measuring cups and spoons for use only with pesticides. Mix the pesticide following the manufacturer's instructions, making any measurement conversion necessary *(page 107)*. To mix a liquid concentrate for application with a pump-up sprayer, fill the canister with the required amount of water, then measure the required amount of liquid concentrate *(above, left)* and

pour it into the canister *(above, right)*. To mix a wettable powder for application with a pump-up sprayer, measure into a bucket the required amount of wettable powder and water, then stir them together and pour the solution through a clean cloth filter into the canister. Rinse the measuring and mixing tools with water three times over the canister, collecting the used rinse water in it. Close the canister and shake it to mix the pesticide solution, then store the measuring and mixing tools safely away from children, pets and other products in a locked cabinet.

PREPARING A PESTICIDE (continued)

VOLUME	1 gallon	1 quart	1 cup	1 fluid ounce	1 tablespoon	1 teaspoon
U.S. CONVERSION	128 fluid ounces 16 cups 4 quarts	32 fluid ounces 4 cups	8 fluid ounces 16 tablespoons	1/8 cup 2 tablespoons 6 teaspoons	1/2 fluid ounce 3 teaspoons	1/6 fluid ounce
METRIC CONVERSION	3.8 liters	.95 liters 950 milliliters	.24 liters 240 milliliters	30 milliliters	15 milliliters	5 milliliters

Converting a pesticide measurement. Use the chart above to make any necessary measurement conversions when buying or preparing a pesticide. For example, if the directions for use of a pesticide product call for the treatment of an area of a given size using 4 tablespoons of the product and 1 gallon of water, you can calculate the amounts required to treat an area 1/4 of the given size: 1 tablespoon of the product (1/4 X 4 tablespoons) and 1 quart of water (1 gallon = 4 quarts; 1/4 X 4 quarts). Or, for example, to measure an amount equal to 1 fluid ounce, you can use a measuring cup to measure 1/8 cup, a tablespoon to measure 2 tablespoons or a teaspoon to measure 6 teaspoons; for an amount equal to 2 fluid ounces, you can double each measure: 1/4 cup (2 X 1/8 cup), 4 tablespoons (2 X 2 tablespoons) or 12 teaspoons (2 X 6 teaspoons).

PREPARING AN AREA FOR PESTICIDE TREATMENT

Barrier tape

Restricting access to and marking an area. Restrict access to and mark an area to be treated with a pesticide. For an indoor area, close and lock the doors to it or block it off using gates or rope. For an outdoor area, close and lock the gates to it and mark the perimeter of it using plastic barrier tape—available at a building supply center. Drive stakes into the ground every 8 to 10 feet a little beyond the perimeter of the area, then run the barrier tape between them, wrapping it one turn around each stake to secure it *(left)*. Have a helper closely monitor children and pets, keeping them well away from the area and carefully instructing them that it is not to be entered; if necessary, keep a pet tied up. After treating the area, keep it off limits for the time specified by the manufacturer of the pesticide, referring to the product label *(page 101)*.

PREPARING AN AREA FOR PESTICIDE TREATMENT (continued)

Protecting surfaces. Protect surfaces that are close to an area to be treated with a pesticide by closing nearby doors, windows and vents. Within the area, protect surfaces not to be treated with the pesticide by moving them out, if desired; for example, freestanding items such as tables or eating utensils. Otherwise, protect surfaces not to be treated with the pesticide by covering them with plastic sheets: for example, food preparation surfaces or an aquarium indoors *(above, top)*; plants, bushes or trees outdoors *(above, bottom)* that are not listed for treatment by the manufacturer of the pesticide on the product label *(page 101)*.

Testing wind direction and force. Treat an outdoor area with a pesticide in the early morning or evening, periods when the air is usually calmest. Before treating the outdoor area, test the direction and force of the wind with the application tool to be used. Fill the tool with water and make any nozzle adjustment necessary, then use the tool to apply the water to a small section of the area *(above)*; the water should settle directly onto surfaces within the section and not drift or stray onto surfaces outside it. If wind causes the water to drift or stray, wait for a calmer period to treat the area with the pesticide.

CLEANING UP AFTER USING A PESTICIDE

Disposing of leftover pesticide. Wear the appropriate safety gear *(page 104)* to dispose of a pesticide, checking the product label for special instructions *(page 101)*. **Caution:** Never pour a pesticide down a drain, into a sewer or onto the ground, or throw it out with other refuse. Return leftover pesticide that is undiluted and not contaminated to its original container and cap it, then store it safely *(page 109)*. To dispose of leftover pesticide that is a liquid product, funnel it into a glass or plastic container *(left)* and cap it; for a dry product, empty it into a heavy-duty plastic garbage bag and seal it. Label the leftover pesticide and store it safely for disposal. If your community does not have a designated Household Hazardous Waste Clean Up Day, consult your local department of environmental protection or public health for recommended disposal procedures.

CLEANING UP AFTER USING A PESTICIDE (continued)

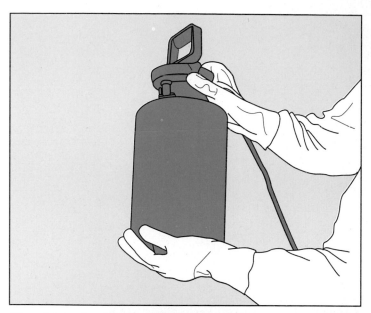

Storing a pesticide. When storing a pesticide, check the product label for special instructions *(page 101)*. Keep unused pesticide in its original container and cap it. For pesticide that is not in its original container, label it clearly. **Caution:** Never store a pesticide in a container that might lead a child to mistake the contents for food or drink; do not store a caustic pesticide in a container that might be corroded by it. Store the pesticide safely away from children, pets and other products in a locked cabinet *(above)* that is situated in a dry, well-ventilated area away from sources of heat or ignition.

Cleaning and storing an application tool. Wear the appropriate safety gear *(page 104)* to empty and clean an application tool. For a sprayer, fill the canister 1/4 full with water and close it, then shake it *(above)* and apply its contents to the area treated with pesticide. Repeat the procedure twice, then open the canister and stand it upside down to dry. For a duster, open it and shake its contents into a heavy-duty plastic garbage bag. For a spreader, move it to the area treated with pesticide, then rinse it using a garden hose and let it dry. To store the application tool, hang it up safely away from children, pets and other tools—if possible, locked in a cabinet.

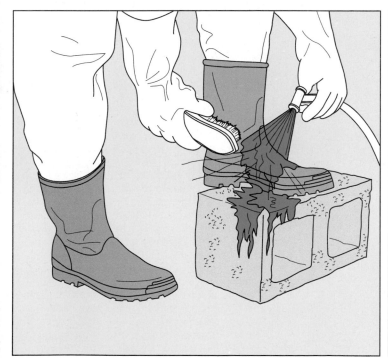

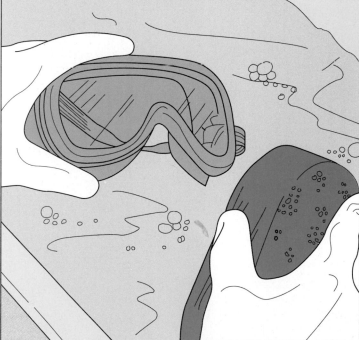

Cleaning and storing personal safety gear. Wear rubber gloves *(page 104)* to clean safety gear. Launder washable work clothing separately as soon as possible; until then, keep it sealed in a plastic bag. For waterproof work clothing, scrub it using a soft-bristled fiber brush and a solution of mild detergent and water, then rinse it with water *(above, left)* and let it dry. Store work clothing away from stored pesticides. Wash safety goggles using a sponge and a solution of mild detergent and warm water *(above, right)*, then rinse them thoroughly and let them dry. Wash a face shield the same way. For a respirator, remove its filters and cartridges for storage, then disassemble the other parts of it for cleaning following the manufacturer's instructions. Scrub the parts of the respirator using a soft-bristled fiber brush and a solution of mild detergent and water, rinse them and let them dry, then reassemble them. Store safety goggles, a face shield and a respirator separately in sealed plastic bags away from pesticides.

WORKING SAFELY ON A LADDER

Spreader brace

Bucket tray

Siderail

Using a stepladder. To work up to 10 feet off the ground, use a stepladder at least 2 feet longer than the height at which you need to stand. Do not use a stepladder if it is damaged—a worn foot, loose step or bent spreader brace, for example. Set up the stepladder on a firm, level surface, opening its legs and locking its spreader braces. Outdoors, if the ground is soft or uneven, support and level the feet with boards; indoors, if the feet slip, place a non-slip rubber mat under them. Pull down the bucket tray and set tools and materials on it before climbing the stepladder; or, carry tools in a tool belt. Climb the stepladder using both hands to grasp the steps—not the siderails. Lean into the stepladder to work from it, keeping your hips between the siderails *(left)*; do not stand higher than the third step from the top. Never overreach or straddle the space between the stepladder and another surface; instead, climb down and reposition the stepladder.

Fly section

Rung lock

Shoe

Using an extension ladder. For work more than 10 feet off the ground such as at a roof edge, use an extension ladder that can reach 3 feet above it. Do not use a ladder if it is damaged—a worn shoe, loose rung or bent rung lock, for example. Place the unextended ladder on the ground perpendicular to the wall, its fly section on the bottom and its feet out from the wall 1/4 of the height to which it will be raised. With a helper bracing the bottom of the ladder, raise the top of it above your head, then walk under it toward the bottom of it, moving your hands along the rails to push it upright. Bracing the bottom of the ladder with your foot, pull the rope to release the fly section and raise it *(left)* to the height desired, then ease pressure on the rope to lock it. Carefully rest the ladder against the roof edge; if the ground is soft or uneven, place a board under its feet. To stabilize the ladder, drive a stake into the ground between it and the wall, then tie each rail to the stake. Climb the ladder using both hands to grasp the rungs, keeping your hips between the rails. Never overreach or straddle the space between the ladder and another surface; instead, climb down and reposition the ladder.

WORKING SAFELY ON THE ROOF

Getting onto the roof. Caution: Consult a professional for work on a roof with a pitch greater than 6 in 12—a slope of 6 inches vertically every 12 inches horizontally. To work on a roof that slopes 4 to 6 inches vertically every 12 inches horizontally, use a safety harness or belt. Set up an extension ladder *(page 110)* on the side of the house opposite the work area; if you are using a safety harness or belt, fasten a 5/8-inch diameter fall-arrest rope to it and to a sturdy, fixed object on the same side of the house. Carry tools in a tool belt or load them into a bucket for raising to the roof. Climb the ladder until your feet are on the rung just below the roof edge; tie any fall-arrest rope to the left siderail. Holding onto the top of the rails with your hands, keep your left foot on the rung of the ladder and step onto the roof with your right foot *(above, left)*. Grasp the right rail with your left hand, then remove your right hand from it and step onto the roof with your left foot *(above, right)*. When both feet are on the roof, let go of the ladder; if you are using a safety harness or belt, tie the fall-arrest rope back onto it. To raise a bucket of tools, have a helper tie a rope to it and his belt loop, then climb the ladder to pass the rope to you. Sitting on the roof with your feet planted firmly, pull up the rope to raise the bucket to the roof.

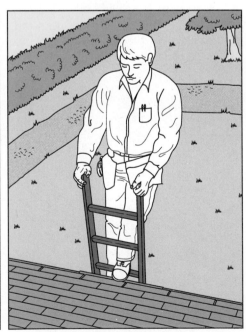

Getting off the roof. Lower tools to the ground by reversing the procedure used to raise them to the roof. If you are using a safety harness or belt, untie the fall-arrest rope and drop it to the ground. Standing to the left of the ladder and facing it, grasp the top of the rail closest to you with your right hand *(above, left)*. Then, swing your left foot onto the center of the rung just below the roof edge and grasp the top of the other rail with your left hand *(above, center)*, pivoting on your right foot. Swing your right foot onto the center of the rung below your left foot, still grasping the rails with your hands *(above, right)*. Step down one rung with your left foot and spread your legs slightly, keeping your feet against the rails. Climb down the ladder one rung at a time.

TOOLS & TECHNIQUES

This chapter presents the tools and techniques that are basic to household pestproofing and pest control. Shown below and on page 114 is an inventory of the standard tools and equipment used for pestproofing and pest control jobs; most of these items as well as a range of traps and pesticides are usually readily available at a building supply center or a hardware store. Special equipment such as a power garden tiller typically can be obtained at a tool rental agency; some traps, pesticides and pesticide application tools may be available only at a pest control supply company. The techniques presented in the chapter include how to use a caulking gun or mix a batch of mortar *(page 125)* for a pestproofing job, as well as how to use a pesticide application tool such as a duster *(page 117)*, a spreader *(page 118)* or a pump-up sprayer *(page 121)* for a pest control job.

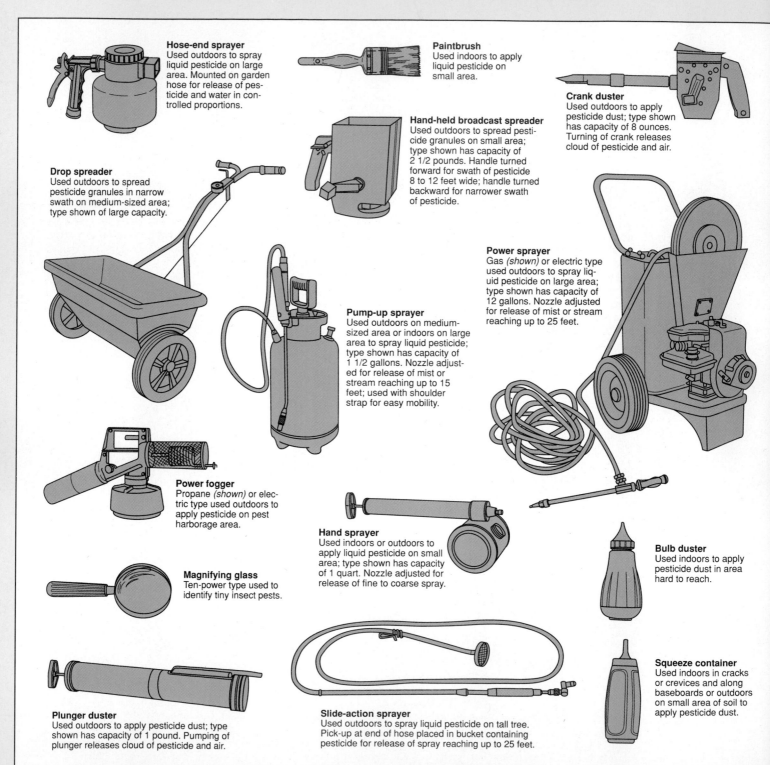

Hose-end sprayer
Used outdoors to spray liquid pesticide on large area. Mounted on garden hose for release of pesticide and water in controlled proportions.

Paintbrush
Used indoors to apply liquid pesticide on small area.

Crank duster
Used outdoors to apply pesticide dust; type shown has capacity of 8 ounces. Turning of crank releases cloud of pesticide and air.

Drop spreader
Used outdoors to spread pesticide granules in narrow swath on medium-sized area; type shown of large capacity.

Hand-held broadcast spreader
Used outdoors to spread pesticide granules on small area; type shown has capacity of 2 1/2 pounds. Handle turned forward for swath of pesticide 8 to 12 feet wide; handle turned backward for narrower swath of pesticide.

Pump-up sprayer
Used outdoors on medium-sized area or indoors on large area to spray liquid pesticide; type shown has capacity of 1 1/2 gallons. Nozzle adjusted for release of mist or stream reaching up to 15 feet; used with shoulder strap for easy mobility.

Power sprayer
Gas *(shown)* or electric type used outdoors to spray liquid pesticide on large area; type shown has capacity of 12 gallons. Nozzle adjusted for release of mist or stream reaching up to 25 feet.

Power fogger
Propane *(shown)* or electric type used outdoors to apply pesticide on pest harborage area.

Hand sprayer
Used indoors or outdoors to apply liquid pesticide on small area; type shown has capacity of 1 quart. Nozzle adjusted for release of fine to coarse spray.

Bulb duster
Used indoors to apply pesticide dust in area hard to reach.

Magnifying glass
Ten-power type used to identify tiny insect pests.

Squeeze container
Used indoors in cracks or crevices and along baseboards or outdoors on small area of soil to apply pesticide dust.

Plunger duster
Used outdoors to apply pesticide dust; type shown has capacity of 1 pound. Pumping of plunger releases cloud of pesticide and air.

Slide-action sprayer
Used outdoors to spray liquid pesticide on tall tree. Pick-up at end of hose placed in bucket containing pesticide for release of spray reaching up to 25 feet.

For the best results, always use the correct tool for the job—and be sure to use the tool correctly. For example, choose an appropriate application tool for a pesticide *(page 116)*, taking into account the formulation of the product, the size of the area to be treated, and whether the area is indoors or outdoors. When buying a tool, get the highest-quality one that you can afford. Take the time to care for your tools properly. Follow the manu-facturer's instructions to lubricate or otherwise maintain a tool. Clean a pesticide application tool thoroughly after using it *(page 108)*; when it is dry, store it in a safe place, hanging it up or locking it in a cabinet away from children and pets. Keep a tool used for applying a pesticide separate from other tools and use it only for work with a pesticide; if necessary, label it to avoid using it for another purpose.

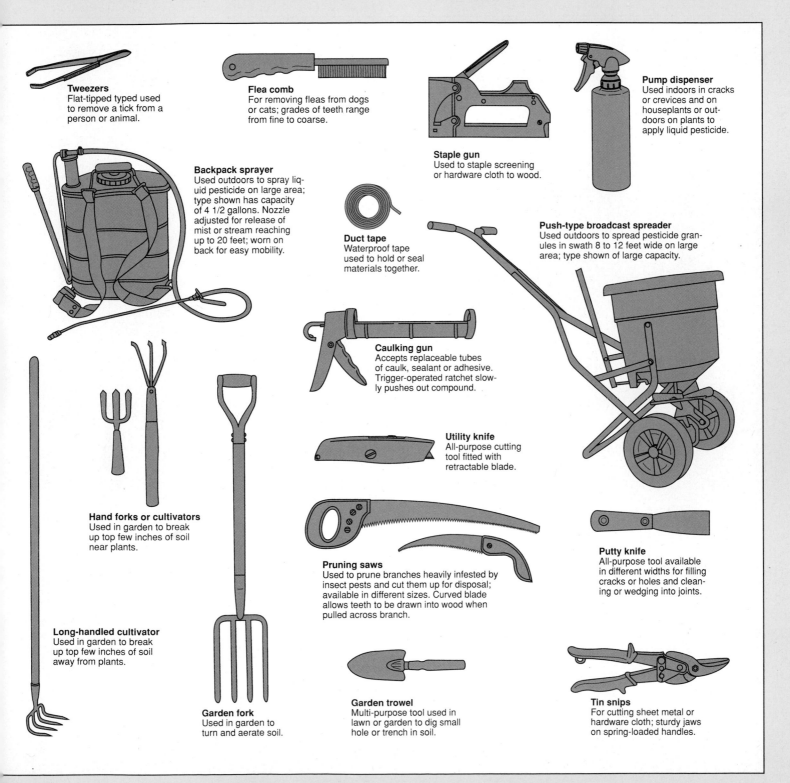

Tweezers
Flat-tipped typed used to remove a tick from a person or animal.

Flea comb
For removing fleas from dogs or cats; grades of teeth range from fine to coarse.

Staple gun
Used to staple screening or hardware cloth to wood.

Pump dispenser
Used indoors in cracks or crevices and on houseplants or out-doors on plants to apply liquid pesticide.

Backpack sprayer
Used outdoors to spray liq-uid pesticide on large area; type shown has capacity of 4 1/2 gallons. Nozzle adjusted for release of mist or stream reaching up to 20 feet; worn on back for easy mobility.

Duct tape
Waterproof tape used to hold or seal materials together.

Push-type broadcast spreader
Used outdoors to spread pesticide gran-ules in swath 8 to 12 feet wide on large area; type shown of large capacity.

Caulking gun
Accepts replaceable tubes of caulk, sealant or adhesive. Trigger-operated ratchet slow-ly pushes out compound.

Utility knife
All-purpose cutting tool fitted with retractable blade.

Hand forks or cultivators
Used in garden to break up top few inches of soil near plants.

Pruning saws
Used to prune branches heavily infested by insect pests and cut them up for disposal; available in different sizes. Curved blade allows teeth to be drawn into wood when pulled across branch.

Putty knife
All-purpose tool available in different widths for filling cracks or holes and clean-ing or wedging into joints.

Long-handled cultivator
Used in garden to break up top few inches of soil away from plants.

Garden fork
Used in garden to turn and aerate soil.

Garden trowel
Multi-purpose tool used in lawn or garden to dig small hole or trench in soil.

Tin snips
For cutting sheet metal or hardware cloth; sturdy jaws on spring-loaded handles.

Refer to the chapter entitled Working Safely *(page 98)* before starting a pestproofing or pest control job; it provides details on working safely on a ladder and on the roof, as well as on how to work safely with a pesticide. Always read the product label of a pesticide thoroughly. Follow the precautions listed for a pesticide, wearing the proper protective clothing and safety gear for each stage of handling it: the measuring and mixing, the filling of an application tool and the application, the storing or disposing, and the cleaning and storing of tools. Read and follow the safety advice in the Emergency Guide *(page 8)*; know how to deal with an emergency situation before one arises. Get qualified help when you need it; if you ever doubt your ability to undertake or complete a pestproofing or pest control job, do not hesitate to consult a professional *(page 115)*.

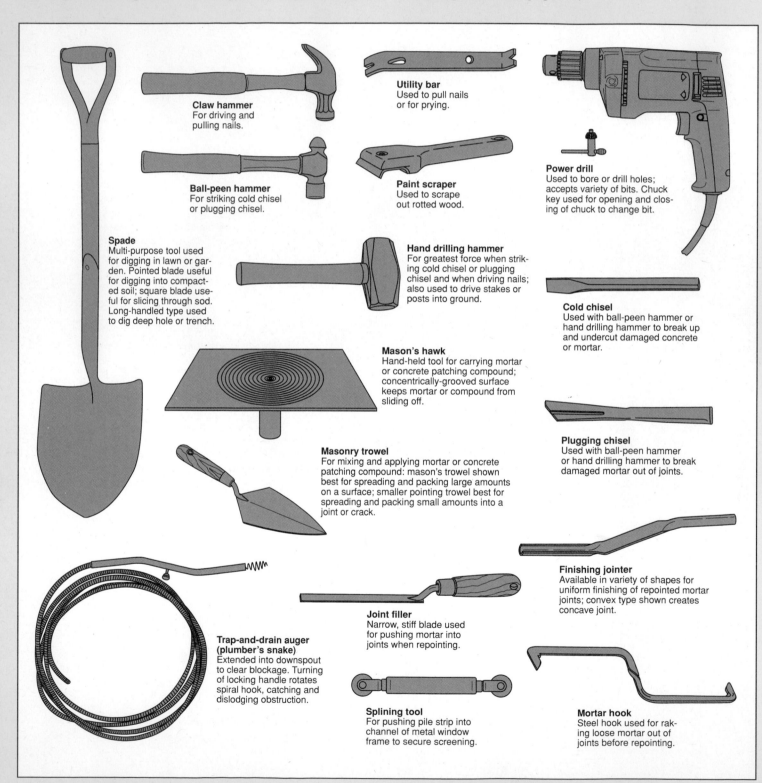

Claw hammer
For driving and pulling nails.

Ball-peen hammer
For striking cold chisel or plugging chisel.

Spade
Multi-purpose tool used for digging in lawn or garden. Pointed blade useful for digging into compacted soil; square blade useful for slicing through sod. Long-handled type used to dig deep hole or trench.

Utility bar
Used to pull nails or for prying.

Paint scraper
Used to scrape out rotted wood.

Power drill
Used to bore or drill holes; accepts variety of bits. Chuck key used for opening and closing of chuck to change bit.

Hand drilling hammer
For greatest force when striking cold chisel or plugging chisel and when driving nails; also used to drive stakes or posts into ground.

Cold chisel
Used with ball-peen hammer or hand drilling hammer to break up and undercut damaged concrete or mortar.

Mason's hawk
Hand-held tool for carrying mortar or concrete patching compound; concentrically-grooved surface keeps mortar or compound from sliding off.

Plugging chisel
Used with ball-peen hammer or hand drilling hammer to break damaged mortar out of joints.

Masonry trowel
For mixing and applying mortar or concrete patching compound: mason's trowel shown best for spreading and packing large amounts on a surface; smaller pointing trowel best for spreading and packing small amounts into a joint or crack.

Finishing jointer
Available in variety of shapes for uniform finishing of repointed mortar joints; convex type shown creates concave joint.

Trap-and-drain auger (plumber's snake)
Extended into downspout to clear blockage. Turning of locking handle rotates spiral hook, catching and dislodging obstruction.

Joint filler
Narrow, stiff blade used for pushing mortar into joints when repointing.

Splining tool
For pushing pile strip into channel of metal window frame to secure screening.

Mortar hook
Steel hook used for raking loose mortar out of joints before repointing.

IDENTIFYING PESTS

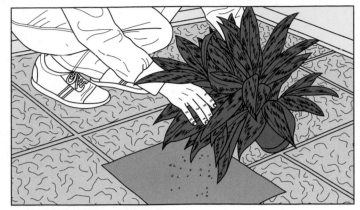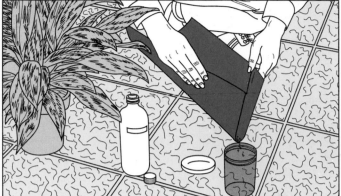

Capturing and monitoring pests for identification.

Examine an insect pest closely to note its size, shape, color and other characteristics; if necessary, use a 10-power magnifying glass. Study a bird or other animal pest and record its size, color, and feeding or foraging, sheltering and other habits. To identify an insect pest, refer to the inventory of the appropriate chapter: Indoor Pests *(page 39)*, Outdoor Pests *(page 61)* or Lawn And Garden Pests *(page 78)*. For help in identifying a pest, consult a professional *(step below)*. Often, a professional can identify a pest from a verbal description or a photograph of it; or, for a bird or other animal pest, from a photograph of its damage, shelter, tracks or trails, or feces or other deposits. For an insect pest, a sample may need to be taken following specific capturing, preserving and shipping instructions. For example, insect pests may need to be collected by snipping off an infested part of a plant and sealing it in a plastic bag; or, by shaking the insect pests onto a piece of cardboard *(above, left)* and sliding them into a jar *(above, right)*, then adding a little rubbing alcohol and sealing it. Along with the sample of insect pests, information may be needed on their location and feeding habits.

GETTING HELP FROM PROFESSIONALS

Consulting professionals. Consult a professional for help in identifying pests, developing control strategies, or choosing specific pest control devices or products—or to undertake a pestproofing or pest control job. Many different types of professionals can provide a range of information or services on household pestproofing and pest control; to find a professional in your community for assistance with a problem, check the listings of the blue and yellow pages in your local telephone book.

● **Cooperative Extension Service (CES).** The government-funded CES is staffed by county extension agents, including entomologists, and can help you coordinate the safest possible pest control program for outdoor or lawn and garden pests. Call your local office of the CES for information on pests particular to your area, their life cycles and control methods for them, as well as on choosing and safely handling pesticides. Information can also be obtained from the CES on keeping a lawn and gardens healthy, preventing a pest problem.

● **United States Department of Agriculture (USDA).** The USDA is staffed by a wide range of agricultural professionals who can provide you with information on pest control methods and products, as well as refer you to state-run agricultural research stations and other sources of information. The Animal Damage Control Office of the USDA or the Fish and Wildlife Department, for example, can be used as a source of information on handling specific bird and other animal problems.

● **Environmental Protection Agency (EPA).** The EPA is responsible for the regulation of pesticides; an office in your region can provide you with up-to-date information on the safe preparation, application and storage of pesticides.

● **Animal protection agencies and humane societies.** Your local animal protection agency or humane society can advise you on dealing with an animal pest problem.

● **Garden centers and nurseries.** An employee of your local garden center or nursery can help you choose appropriate pest control methods and products for your lawn or garden, as well as advise you on how to keep it healthy and avoid a pest problem.

● **Pest control operators and contractors.** If you doubt your ability to handle a pest control job, you may wish to hire a pest control operator; or, for a pestproofing job, a contractor. Ask friends and neighbors for recommendations; check the names of companies with your local consumer affairs office, asking for complaints registered. Obtain estimates from a few companies, getting written explanations of procedures and conditions of guarantees. For assurance that a company is abreast of developments in pest control methods and products as well as safety regulations, ask if it belongs to the National Pest Control Association and a state or local pest control association. Check that the company holds any state or local licence required and carries adequate general liability and workmen's compensation insurance.

CHOOSING A PESTICIDE APPLICATION TOOL

APPLICATION TOOL	PESTICIDE FORMULATION	INDOOR USES	OUTDOOR USES
Squeeze applicator (step below)	Dust	Cracks or crevices, along baseboards or small area hard to reach	Soil around base of plants
Plunger or crank duster (page 117)	Dust	Not recommended	Plants or soil around base of plants
Spreader (page 118)	Granules	Not recommended	Lawn or garden: drop spreader for medium-sized area; broadcast spreader for large area
Power fogger (page 119)	Liquid	Not recommended	Harborage areas of insect pests
Hand sprayer (page 120)	Liquid; wettable powder	Spot-treatment of cracks or crevices, along baseboards or small area	Spot-treatment of lawn or garden
Hose-end sprayer (page 121)	Liquid; wettable powder	Not recommended	Medium-sized or large area of lawn or garden; short tree
Pump-up sprayer (page 121)	Liquid; wettable powder	Cracks or crevices, along baseboards or large area	Medium-sized area of lawn or garden; short tree
Backpack sprayer (page 122)	Liquid; wettable powder	Not recommended	Large area of lawn or garden; small number of short trees
Slide-action sprayer (page 123)	Liquid; wettable powder	Not recommended	Tall trees
Power sprayer (page 124)	Liquid; wettable powder	Not recommended	Large area of lawn or garden; large number of trees

USING A SQUEEZE APPLICATOR

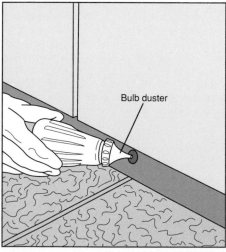

Using a squeeze container or a bulb duster. Prepare to work safely with a pesticide dust (page 98), following the manufacturer's instructions. To treat cracks or crevices or a small exposed surface, use a squeeze container. Open the squeeze container and use a spoon intended only for pesticide to carefully fill it with pesticide, then close it tightly. Hold the nozzle just above the surface to be treated and gently squeeze the container, emitting a light coat of pesticide on it. Continue along the surface using the same procedure (far left). To treat a hidden surface, gain access to it (page 56) and use a bulb duster the same way, fitting the tip of the nozzle into an opening of a void space (near left) and sharply squeezing the bulb.

USING A DUSTER

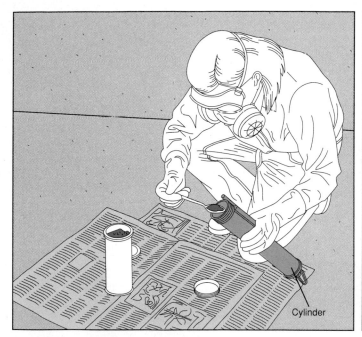

Using a plunger duster. To treat plants outdoors, prepare to work safely with a pesticide dust *(page 98)* and use a plunger duster, following the manufacturer's instructions. For the plunger duster shown, remove the cap and use a spoon intended only for pesticide to carefully fill the cylinder with pesticide *(above, left)*, then screw the cap back on tightly. To operate the plunger duster, hold the cylinder in one hand and the handle in the other hand, aiming the nozzle at the surfaces to be treated. Keeping the cylinder steady, push the handle in and out smoothly to emit a fine cloud of pesticide *(above, right)*; move only the handle and not the cylinder. Continue the same way until the surfaces are coated evenly with a thin layer of pesticide.

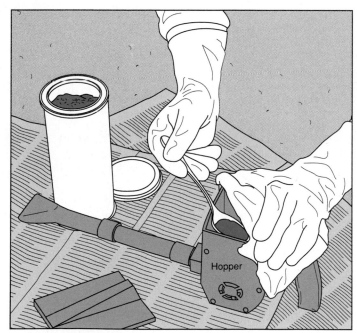

Using a crank duster. To treat plants outdoors, prepare to work safely with a pesticide dust *(page 98)* and use a crank duster, following the manufacturer's instructions. For the crank duster shown, lift off the lid and use a spoon intended only for pesticide to carefully fill the hopper with pesticide, holding a cloth over the opening to contain it *(above, left)*. Snap the lid back onto the hopper tightly. To operate the crank duster, aim the nozzle at the surfaces to be treated and turn the crank smoothly to emit a fine cloud of pesticide *(above, right)*. Continue the same way until the surfaces are coated evenly with a thin layer of pesticide. To keep the tube leading to the nozzle from clogging, tap it gently with your hand periodically.

USING A SPREADER

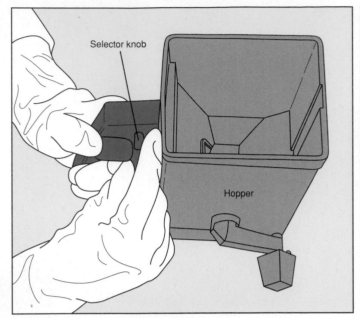

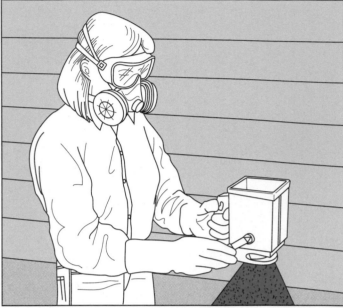

Using a hand-held broadcast spreader. To treat a small area outdoors, prepare to work safely with pesticide granules *(page 98)* and use a hand-held broadcast spreader, following the manufacturer's instructions. For the broadcast spreader shown, set the selector knob to the application rate specified for the pesticide *(above, left)*. Calculate the area to be treated, then measure the amount of pesticide required for it and carefully pour the pesticide into the hopper. Treat the area in passes that overlap each other by about 6 inches, working back and forth across it from one end to the other end of it. To operate the broadcast spreader, walk at a steady pace behind it, holding it firmly by the handle and keeping it out from you. Start walking, then press the trigger and turn the crank smoothly clockwise *(above, right)*, completing one revolution for each step with your right foot. Release the trigger just before you stop walking.

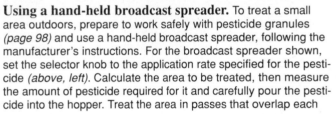

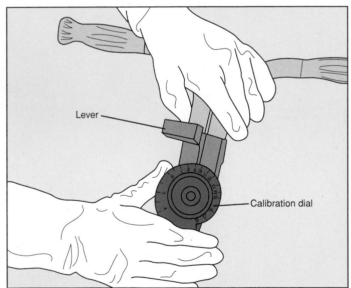

Using a drop spreader. To treat a medium-sized area outdoors, prepare to work safely with pesticide granules *(page 98)* and use a drop spreader, following the manufacturer's instructions. For the drop spreader shown, set the lever to OFF to close the hopper and set the calibration dial to the application rate specified for the pesticide *(above, left)*. Calculate the area to be treated, then measure the amount of pesticide required for it and carefully pour the pesticide into the hopper. Treat the area in slightly overlapping passes, working first across each end of it and then back and forth between the ends of it. To operate the drop spreader, walk forward at a steady pace behind it, starting to push it just before setting the lever to ON and setting the lever to OFF just before stopping it; do not pull it backward when the lever is set to ON. Continue using the drop spreader the same way *(above, right)*, overlapping each pass by an amount equal to the width of a wheel.

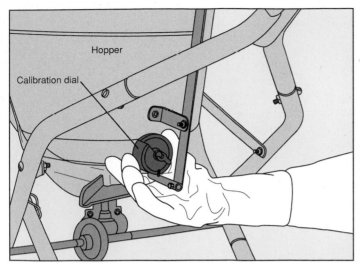

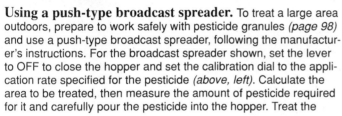

Using a push-type broadcast spreader. To treat a large area outdoors, prepare to work safely with pesticide granules *(page 98)* and use a push-type broadcast spreader, following the manufacturer's instructions. For the broadcast spreader shown, set the lever to OFF to close the hopper and set the calibration dial to the application rate specified for the pesticide *(above, left)*. Calculate the area to be treated, then measure the amount of pesticide required for it and carefully pour the pesticide into the hopper. Treat the area in passes that overlap each other by about 6 inches, working first across each end of it and then back and forth between the ends of it. To operate the broadcast spreader, walk forward at a steady pace behind it, starting to push it just before setting the lever to ON and setting the lever to OFF just before stopping it; do not pull it backward when the lever is set to ON. Continue using the broadcast spreader the same way *(above, right)*.

USING A POWER FOGGER

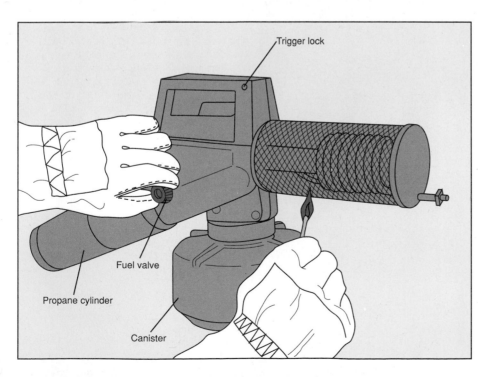

1 Preparing the power fogger. To treat a harborage area of insect pests outdoors on a calm day, prepare to work safely with a liquid pesticide *(page 98)* and use a power fogger, following the manufacturer's instructions. For the propane type of fogger shown, work outdoors away from any open flame. Engage any trigger lock and close the fuel valve, then unscrew the canister and use a rubber band to hold a clean, lint-free cloth over its opening. Carefully fill the canister up to 3/4 full with an oil-based pesticide designed for the fogger, straining it through the cloth, then remove the cloth and screw the canister back on tightly. Wearing work gloves, screw a cylinder of propane gas onto the fogger following any precautions listed on it. Hold a lit match under the coil and open the fuel valve only 1/4 turn *(left)*. If the coil does not light immediately, close the fuel valve and check that the cylinder is full and installed correctly. Wait 30 seconds, then try to light the coil again. When the coil lights, let it heat up for a few minutes; wait for any flame at the nozzle to disappear.

USING A POWER FOGGER (continued)

2 Operating the power fogger.
Hold the power fogger out from you and carry it to about 10 feet from the area to be treated. Aim the nozzle at the area, then release any trigger lock and pump the trigger every 3 to 4 seconds to emit a light, dry fog of pesticide *(left)*, allowing it drift into the area; if necessary, move closer to the area. **Caution:** If a flame appears at the nozzle, stop pumping the trigger and immediately close the fuel valve. Set the fogger down on a level surface and wait for the flame to disappear, then relight the coil *(step 1)* and continue using the fogger the same way. Do not touch the shroud around the coil during or after operation of the fogger. After treating the area, engage any trigger lock and allow excess fuel in the coil to burn off. When the nozzle stops emitting a steady fog of pesticide, close the fuel valve and allow the fogger to cool.

USING A HAND SPRAYER

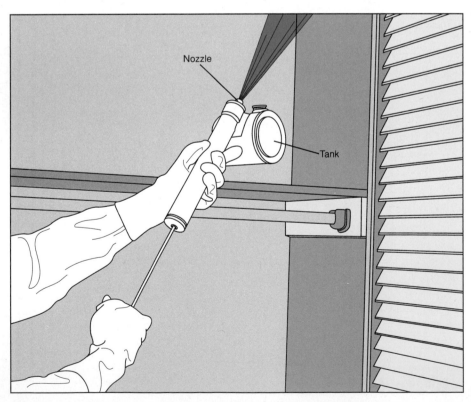

Nozzle

Tank

Preparing and operating a hand sprayer. To treat a small area, prepare to work safely with a liquid or wettable powder pesticide *(page 98)* and use a hand sprayer, following the manufacturer's instructions. For the hand sprayer shown, remove the cap and carefully fill the tank with pesticide, then screw the cap back on tightly. To treat the area, aim the nozzle away from you and set it to an appropriate spray setting: turning it clockwise for the finest spray possible indoors; turning it counterclockwise for a coarser spray at a close distance outdoors. Aim the nozzle at the area and pump the handle in and out *(left)*, testing the spray setting. **Caution:** Spray is emitted from the nozzle for a few seconds after each pump of the handle; keep the nozzle pointed away from you to adjust the spray setting. When the nozzle is adjusted, continue pumping the handle to emit a spray of pesticide, treating the area evenly until it is wet but not dripping.

USING A HOSE-END SPRAYER

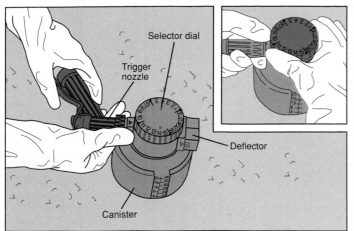

Preparing and operating a hose-end sprayer. To treat a large area outdoors, prepare to work safely with a liquid or wettable powder pesticide *(page 98)* and use a hose-end sprayer, following the manufacturer's instructions. For the hose-end sprayer shown, set the selector dial to OFF and unscrew the canister. Calculate the area to be treated, then prepare the amount of pesticide required for it and carefully pour the pesticide into the canister. Screw the canister back on tightly and adjust the deflector to a spray of an appropriate width. Connect a trigger nozzle to the sprayer *(above, left)* and a garden hose to it, then turn on the water fully and set the selector dial to the application rate specified for the pesticide *(inset)*. Treat the area in slightly overlapping passes, working back and forth across it from one end to the other end of it. Holding the sprayer away from you, squeeze the trigger to emit a spray of pesticide *(above, right)*, treating the area evenly until it is wet but not dripping.

USING A PUMP-UP SPRAYER

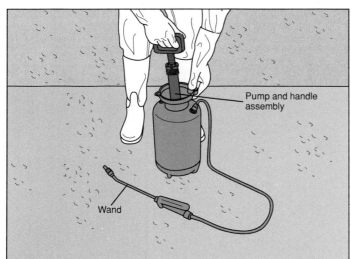

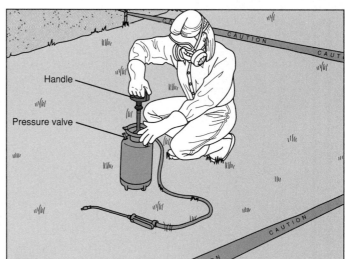

1 Preparing the pump-up sprayer. To treat a medium-sized area outdoors or a large area indoors, prepare to work safely with a liquid or wettable powder pesticide *(page 98)* and use a pump-up sprayer, following the manufacturer's instructions. For the pump-up sprayer shown, unscrew the pump and handle assembly, then lift it out of the canister *(above, left)*. Check that the hose is connected securely to the canister and to the wand, tightening any nut by hand as necessary. Calculate the area to be treated, then prepare the amount of pesticide required for it and carefully pour the pesticide into the canister. Slide the pump and handle assembly back into the canister and screw it on tightly. Carry the pump-up sprayer to the area to be treated and set it down level, then pressurize the canister. Turning the handle 1/4 turn counterclockwise to release it, pump it fully up and down *(above, right)*, continuing until it cannot be pumped further or air is released from the pressure valve.

USING A PUMP-UP SPRAYER (continued)

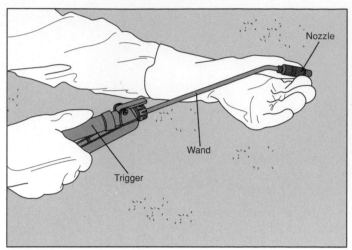

2 Operating the pump-up sprayer. Test the spray setting of the nozzle by aiming it at the area and squeezing the trigger. To adjust the nozzle, keep it pointed away from you and turn it: clockwise for a coarse spray at a distance outdoors *(above, left)*; counterclockwise for a finest spray possible indoors. Aim the nozzle and squeeze the trigger to emit a spray of pesticide, treating the area evenly until it is wet but not dripping. As the force of the spray drops, release the trigger and pump the handle

to repressurize the canister *(step 1)*. Shake the canister periodically to help keep the pesticide mixed thoroughly. To treat the underside of leaves, turn the wand upside down to aim the nozzle at them *(above, right)*. To treat a tree, adjust the nozzle to emit a stream and aim a little high, letting pesticide settle onto it. Before removing the pump and handle assembly for refilling or cleaning, pull up the pressure valve to release the pressure of air inside the canister.

USING A BACKPACK SPRAYER

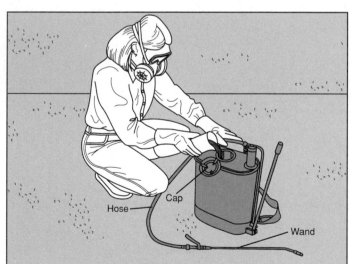

1 Preparing the backpack sprayer. To treat a large area outdoors, prepare to work safely with a liquid or wettable powder pesticide *(page 98)* and use a backpack sprayer, following the manufacturer's instructions. For the backpack sprayer shown, check that the hose is connected securely to the canister and to the wand, tightening any clamp as necessary. Calculate the area to be treated and prepare the amount of pesticide required

for it. Remove the cap and carefully pour the pesticide into the canister *(above, left)*, filtering it through the strainer, then screw the cap back on tightly. Wear the backpack sprayer on your back, adjusting the shoulder straps as necessary until it sits comfortably. Carry the backpack sprayer on your back to the area to be treated, then pressurize the canister by gripping the operating lever and pumping it up and down *(above, right)*, continuing until it cannot be pumped further.

USING A BACKPACK SPRAYER (continued)

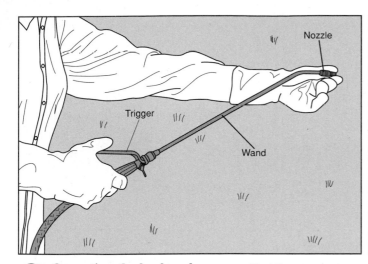

2 **Operating the backpack sprayer.** Test the spray setting of the nozzle by aiming it at the area and squeezing the trigger. To adjust the nozzle, keep it pointed away from you and turn it: counterclockwise for a fine spray at a close distance; clockwise for a coarser spray at a greater distance *(above, left)*. Aim the nozzle and squeeze the trigger to emit a spray of pesticide, treating the area evenly until it is wet but not dripping; pump the operating lever slowly to keep the canister pressurized evenly. Shake the canister periodically to help keep the pesticide mixed thoroughly. To treat the underside of leaves, turn the wand upside down to aim the nozzle at them. To treat a tree, adjust the nozzle to emit a stream and aim a little high, letting pesticide settle onto it *(above, right)*. When refilling or cleaning, remove the cap slowly to release the pressure of air inside the canister.

USING A SLIDE-ACTION SPRAYER

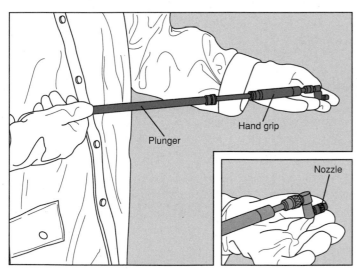

Preparing and operating a slide-action sprayer. To treat a tall tree, prepare to work safely with a liquid or wettable powder pesticide *(page 98)* and use a slide-action sprayer, following the manufacturer's instructions. For the slide-action sprayer shown, prepare the pesticide carefully in a bucket intended only for pesticide, filling it no more than half full. Carry the bucket to the tree, then set the pick-up end of the hose in the pesticide and clip the hose to the bucket. Wearing waterproof clothing, aim the nozzle at the tree, then prime the sprayer. Holding the hand grip steady, pump the plunger rapidly back and forth *(above, left)*, keeping a finger on the nozzle for each push stroke *(inset)*. When you feel pesticide come out of the nozzle, keep it aimed and turn it to adjust it: clockwise for a coarse spray at a far distance; counterclockwise for a finer spray at a closer distance. Treat the tree evenly with pesticide until it is wet but not dripping; for branches out of reach, aim a little high and let pesticide settle onto them *(above, right)*.

USING A POWER SPRAYER

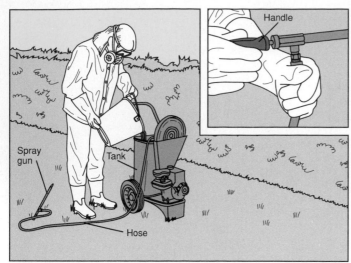

Preparing and operating a power sprayer. To treat a large area outdoors, prepare to work safely with a liquid or wettable powder pesticide *(page 98)* and use a power sprayer, following the manufacturer's instructions; practice preparing and operating it with water until you are comfortable using it. For the gas type of sprayer shown, add fuel as necessary and check that the hose is connected securely to the pump and the spray gun. Calculate the area to be treated and prepare the amount of pesticide required for it, then wear waterproof clothing to carefully pour the pesticide into the tank *(above, left)*. Start the sprayer and test the setting of the nozzle, aiming it at the area and turning the handle *(inset)* to adjust it: clockwise to open the nozzle and for a coarse spray at a far distance; counterclockwise for a finer spray at a close distance and to close the nozzle. Treat the area evenly *(above, right)* until it is wet but not dripping. Stir the pesticide periodically to keep it mixed thoroughly. To treat a tree, adjust the nozzle to emit a stream and aim a little high, letting pesticide settle onto it.

DISPOSING OF PESTS

Handling dead or trapped pests. Wear work gloves or rubber gloves to handle a dead or trapped pest. Vacuum or sweep up dead insect pests and seal them in a heavy-duty plastic garbage bag in an outdoor trash can for disposal with other refuse. Dispose of a sticky trap, a stocking used to dislodge a web or nest, a bird nest or a treated wasp nest the same way. For vegetation damaged by pests, use the same procedure; if necessary, first cut it up with a pruning saw *(left)*. Use a spade to pick up the carcass of an animal pest rather than touch it, then dispose of it the same way; dispose of a snap trap used for a rat along with the carcass. If desired, leave the carcass of a burrowing animal pest such as a mole buried underground. For an animal pest in a live trap, consult your local animal protection agency or the Fish and Wildlife Department for recommendations; for an animal pest such as a mouse, release it in an uninhabited area or submerge the trap in water to drown it, then dispose of the carcass.

APPLYING CAULK, SEALANT OR ADHESIVE

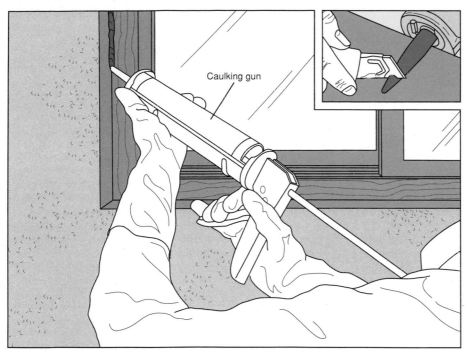

Using a caulking gun. Buy a cartridge of caulk, sealant or adhesive and follow the manufacturer's instructions to apply it, ensuring that its use is recommended for your job and surfaces. To fill a gap that may expand or contract, as shown, use a urethane type of elastomeric sealant. Scrape loose particles off the surfaces with a putty knife, then use a solution of mild detergent and water to wash them and let them dry; apply any primer recommended and let it dry. For a gap deeper than 1/2 inch, fill it to within 1/4 inch of the surface using foam backing rod. Load the caulking gun with the cartridge and use a utility knife to cut off its tip at a 45° angle, making an opening slightly narrower than the gap to be filled *(inset)*; puncture the seal with an awl or a long nail. Working from one end to the other end of the gap, hold the caulking gun at a 45° angle to it and squeeze the trigger, ejecting a continuous bead of sealant into it *(left)*. Smooth and shape the sealant using a wet finger protected with a rubber glove or the wet blade of a putty knife.

PREPARING MORTAR

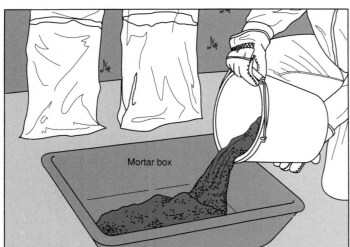

Mixing mortar. Buy a packaged mortar mix and prepare it following the manufacturer's instructions. Or, make mortar from scratch with dry ingredients; for Type N mortar used to repoint masonry joints, use 1 part portland cement, 1 part hydrated lime and 6 parts sand. Wearing work gloves, mix the mortar in a clean mortar box, filling it no more than 3/4 full. Measure the correct proportion of each dry ingredient by volume with a graduated container and add it *(above, left)*; for a large volume, use full or partial spadefuls. Mix the dry ingredients thoroughly with a mason's hoe *(above, right)*, then form a well in the center and add clean water a little at a time. Lift and turn the mix to blend it thoroughly, adding water until it achieves a thick, buttery consistency that holds its shape. To test the mix, use a mason's trowel to place a mound on a mason's hawk or plywood, then slice it in half *(inset)*; it should flow slightly and hold its shape, separating firmly without crumbling or collapsing. If the mix crumbles or is too stiff, add water a little at a time; if it collapses, add dry ingredients in the correct proportions.

INDEX

Page references in *italics* indicate an illustration of the subject mentioned, Page references in **bold** indicate a Troubleshooting Guide for the subject mentioned.

ACKNOWLEDGMENTS

The editors wish to thank the following:
Brian Archer, Safety Supply Canada Ltd., Richmond Hill, Ont.; William A. Banks, M.S., United States Department of Agriculture Research Service, Gainesville, FL; Chuck Beach, S.C. Johnson and Sons Ltd., Brantford, Ont.; Stephen Belliveau, Agriculture Canada, Ottawa, Ont.; Don Booth, PhD, Bartlett Tree Research Laboratory, Charlotte, NC; H. Leroy Brooks, PhD, Extension Entomology, Kansas State University, Manhattan, KS; Steve L. Brown, PhD, Extension Entomology, University of Georgia, Tifton, GA; Patricia F. Campbell, American Cyanamid Company, Wayne, NJ; Enrico Caprari, M.P.H., Westchester County Department of Health, White Plains, NY; Joy Carroll, Chemfree Environment Inc., Kirkland, Que.; Harold C. Chapman, PhD, American Mosquito Control Association, Lake Charles, LA; Kevin Clark, Critter Control Inc., Plymouth, MI; Patricia P. Cobb, Department of Entomology, Auburn University, Auburn, AL; Homer Collins, United States Department of Agriculture, Fire Ant Laboratory, Gulfport, MS; Robert M. Corrigan, Department of Entomology, Purdue University, West Lafayette, IN; Don Cudmore, Green Cross, Mississauga, Ont.; Mark Dockser, Safer Inc., Newton, MA; Cathy Dowdell, S.C. Johnson Wax Inc., Racine, WI; Environmental Protection Agency, Information Services Branch, Washington, DC; Richard Falco, PhD, Westchester County Department of Health, Vahalla, NY; Peter Foley, Unique Insect Control, Citrus Heights, CA; Marc-André Fortin, Canadian SPCA, Montreal, Que.; Bruce Fraedrich, PhD, Bartlett Tree Research Laboratory, Charlotte, NC; Sondra Goodman, The Household Hazardous Waste Project, Springfield, MO; Jeff Hahn, Minnesota Extension Service, University of Minnesota, St. Paul, MN; Mary Harper, S.C. Johnson and Sons Ltd., Brantford, Ont.; Jill Haukos, The National Pesticide Telecommunications Network, Texas Tech University, Lubbock, TX; John Henry, Farm Products Group, Rochester, MN; John Hepburn, H.D. Hudson Manufacturing Co., Chicago, IL; Stuart Jenkins, Necessary Trading Company, Newcastle, VA; Margaret Jones, Environmental Protection Agency, Chicago, IL; Arthur Katz, Knockout Pest Control, Uniondale, NY; Keith Kennedy, PhD, S.C. Johnson Wax Entomology Research Center, Racine, WI; Jane Kochersperger, National Coalition Against the Misuse of Pesticides, Washington, DC; James Kovach, Hollister-Stier, Etobicoke, Ont.; William MacKay, PhD, Department of Biological Sciences, University of Texas, El Paso, TX; Sandy Mays, Necessary Trading Company, Newcastle, VA; Patrick McBride, RPh, MicroMedix, Denver, CO; Environmental Protection Agency, Information Services Branch, Washington, DC; Louis McCann, Canadian SPCA, Montreal, Que.; Bill McDonnell, D.B. Smith and Burgess Products, Chadwicks, NY; McGill University, Staff of Plant Science Department, Ste. Anne-de-Bellevue, Que.; Steve McLean, Safety Supply Canada Ltd., Richmond Hill, Ont.; Kitty Miller, Woodstream Corp., Lititz, PA; Richard Miller, PhD, Extension Entomologist Emeritus, Ohio State University, Columbus, OH; Gary Mount, PhD, United States Department of Agriculture-ARS, Gainesville, FL; Weste Osbrink, PhD, S.C. Johnson Wax Entomology Research Center, Racine, WI; Bill Perlberg, Hartz Mountain Corp., Harrison, NJ; Schrade Radtke, O.M. Scott and Sons, Marysville, OH; Yvonne Randall, H.D. Hudson Canada, Mississauga, Ont.; Gary Reed, Thornell Corp., Penfield, NY; Stephen Rogers, Zoecon Canada Inc., Whitby, Ont.; Ivan Rossi, Melnor Manufacturing Ltd., Brantford, Ont.; Kate Ryffranck, Lennoxville, Que.; Rod Schneidmiller, Sterling International Inc., Liberty Lake, WA; Richard Schrader, Senoret Chemicals, St. Louis, MO; Carl E. Schreck, United States Department of Agriculture-ARS, Gainesville, FL; Hilary Skurnowitz, S.C. Johnson Wax Inc., Chicago, IL; James Stewart, Center for Disease Control, Atlanta, GA; Katrine Stewart, Plant Science Department, McGill University, Ste. Anne-de-Bellevue, Que.; Ron Stinner, PhD, Entomology Department, North Carolina State University, Raleigh, NC; Dan Suomi, Cooperative Extension Service, Washington State University, Pullman, WA; Terry Sutton, EKCO Canada, Inc., Niagara Falls, Ont.; Sylvia Szot, Safer Ltd., Scarborough, Ont.; Yvon Tardif, Benmax Inc., Montreal, Que.; Lonnie Tinfow, Randall Manufacturing, Newark, NJ; Peter L. Tovoli, Interstate Professional Applicators Association, Milton, WA; Paul Webster, Quaker Industries, Woodbridge Ont.; Jim Whitaker, Reemay Inc., Old Hickory, TN.

The following persons also assisted in the preparation of this book:
Marc Gendron, Graphor Consultation Inc., Shirley Grynspan, Linda Jarosiewicz, Ron and Louise Laberge, Solange Laberge, Francine Lemieux, Shaunie MacFarlane, Karl and Janet Marcuse, Jennifer Meltzer, Edward Renaud, Lana Romandini, Sherlock, Shirley Sylvain.

Time-Life Books Inc. offers a wide range of fine recordings, including a *Big Bands* series. For subscription information, call 1-800-621-7026, or write TIME-LIFE MUSIC, P.O. Box C-32068, Richmond, Virginia 23261-2068.